THE KING of CANE GARDEN

My Life & Times, from Teacher Boy
to the Corporate Heights and Depths

THE KING *of* CANE GARDEN

My Life & Times, from Teacher Boy
to the Corporate Heights and Depths

IRVINE WEEKES

GREAT HOUSE
Miami

A GREAT HOUSE BOOK
Published by Kingston Communications

Copyright © 2019 by Irvine Weekes

All rights reserved, including the right to reproduce this book or portions thereof in any form whatsoever. For information, address KIN 3830, 1 Aeropost Way, Miami, FL 33206 USA or email weekesirvine@gmail.com

Library of Congress Control Number: 2019918238
ISBN 978-0-578-59745-4

First Great House printing November 2019

Typeset: Bembo 12/13 point

10 9 8 7 6 5 4 3 2 1

Great House Books is a tradename of Kingston Communications
www.kingstoncom.com

Cover Illustration by Patrick Kitson
Cover Design by MG Design, LLC.

Printed in the United States of America

*Trust the Lord. Live in the moment.
Learn from the past, but do not dwell on it.
Do not try to control the future either,
for that is God's work.*

God looks after all His children.

ACKNOWLEDGMENTS

I have benefited from the goodwill of many sources and people in my life, but I have to start with the good people of my boyhood village. In recent years, intellectuals have talked about how "it takes a village", and I can attest to its value, for I felt it from my earliest days. Everyone in my village of Cane Garden loved me and looked out for me. As a boy, I couldn't and wouldn't pass any house without calling out greetings to the householder, and many of them would ask after my health and wish me a good day in return. I knew all the home-owners and their families; they knew me and most members of my earlier generations.

The goodwill of my village folks was not without obligation on my part. It came with and out of the expectation that I would uphold the tradition of respect for my elders and a sense of family honor and responsibility. My behavior was consequently shaped by equal portions of obligation and fear – obligation that I was expected to be on exemplary behavior and fear that a villager's complaint to my parents would certainly be met with punishment, usually a flogging.

My parents are due special thanks for their foresight. My mother Leslyn drilled into me the recognition that education was my way out of the trap of sub-par performance in which we found ourselves, and she groomed my sister and me for the manners and behaviors expected from properly brought-up children.

My father "Pretty's" influence on me was reactive and proactive, reactive in the sense that unlike him, I wanted to see and test the world. I would be more than just a product of my village; I wanted to play in a bigger arena. The proactive part is my father's input: "Mr. Gay and Mr. Watson may be teaching you Latin and French," he would say to me, "but no child of mine is going to grow up as a damn fool."

He then proceeded to teach me how to look after livestock, how to select and plant food crops to match the seasons, how to slaughter and dress animals, how to harness work animals like donkeys and mules, how to calculate quantities of building materials, how to square a building, how to use hand tools, the difference between linear and square feet when measuring construction work, how to measure wood, and the importance of paying workers promptly and properly.

My life has been filled with equal portions of dealings with the sophisticated and highly educated and with tradesmen, technicians and common laborers. My degreed colleagues find no amazement in my ability to hold my own, and craftsmen wonder at my basic knowledge of how things work. My parents' hands, like the hands of God, are constantly upon me, and I have never failed to meet a payroll on time in any of my endeavors.

I am forever indebted to my earliest teachers. First, there was R.A. Dottin, my first headmaster. Born around 1870, he taught my grandparents, parents, aunts and uncles, before he got to me during 1940-1943. Then there were A.L. Gay and George 'Emma' Watson until 1948. These latter two men gave me free private lessons and fought with my grandmother to convince my father to spend the money on the required fees so I could attend a top high school.

My high school headmaster Louis Lynch influenced me tremendously. He awakened my sense of self-worth and introduced me to a top level of achievers, contemporaries with whom I never had a chance to rub shoulders before.

Three Bahamian families had a great impact on my life, and I am forever thankful for knowing them: the Bellots of Gladstone Road, the Gibsons of Dean's Lane, and the Davises of Blue Hills Road and West Bay Street, all of Nassau, Bahamas.

Mr. Earnest Marshall, retired high court judge, and his dear wife Gladys, a retired medical doctor, both of Edmonton, Alberta, Canada, have been my friends and supporters since our undergraduate days in the early 1960s at the University of Alberta. Their steadfastness has been a source of inspiration.

Professor Gainer, my macroeconomics and public finance professor in college introduced me to the tools that I have mainly used to make my living, and Dr. Whata Winiata sharpened those tools in graduate school at the University of British Columbia in Vancouver, Canada.

I must also recognize my most recent graduate school, Clayton State University in Atlanta, Georgia, where I earned my Master of Health Administration degree in 2012. Here, I really re-sharpened my intellect and learned to use the computer as a constructive tool.

Rip Robinson and John Lucas of the credit union movement in Vancouver taught me compassion, and Phil and Irene Perceval of Surrey, British Columbia reminded me of the value of true friendship. Tomas Désulmé of Haiti and Jamaica had the greatest influence on me as an adult, and Oswald Simpson of Jamaica taught me an awful lot about commercial livestock rearing and meat processing.

The idea of being taught runs like a constant stream throughout my thinking for I shall forever remain a student. In this regard, my three children Leslyn, Scott and Melanie, as well as my three grandchildren Christopher, Alexandria and Taylor teach me every day.

I owe special thanks to Kingston Communications/Great House Books for helping me to bring *The King of Cane Garden* to fruition, and particularly to their principal, Mr. Michael Grant, who took the lead on this project and literally taught me what I had to do to make a written work ready to be a book.

Special thanks are due to two of my universities, the University of Alberta, Edmonton and the University of British Columbia, Vancouver, both in Canada, for their willing assistance in aiding with photographs and corroboration of my activities whilst I was under their influence as a student, particularly with names of my professors and counsellors.

I also want to thank the media libraries from places where I have lived, especially the Bahamas Historical Society, *The Gateway* at the University of Alberta, *The Vancouver Sun, Jamaica Gleaner,* and the National Archives UK for providing archival photographs and news reports that parallel some of my life and times. Michele Webster and Angela Lynch-Clare were also very helpful in supplying pictures of me or their family members in aid of the project.

The greatest person in my life, however, has been Vilma, my wife for the past fifty-four years. No-one has ever been such a constant, no-one has ever been as wise and no-one has ever been as long-suffering as "Miss Vilma", whom I call "The Closer". Baseball fans will immediately understand: when she came into the game, she shut it down, took charge and saved my life.

– Irvine Weekes

CONTENTS

1. Introduction — 1
2. American Me — 3
3. Closer To Thee? — 11
4. Cane Garden — 17
5. Louis Lynch — 31
6. My Barbados, Right Or Wrong — 41
7. Porgy's [P]Luck — 45
8. Bahamian Odyssey — 49
9. The Nassau Scene — 60
10. Wild Oats, Rum & Ginger — 69
11. Never Say Goodbye — 84
12. Back In The Books — 112
13. A Real Job — 135
14. This Changes Everything — 146
15. The Wheel Turns — 163
16. New York, New Work — 169
17. Jamaican Prosperity — 175
18. Things Fall Apart, Then Together — 193
19. After Five Acts, A Sixth — 207

1. INTRODUCTION

My story really begins in a series of twenty-eight short stories in my book *From the Inside Looking Out*, about experiences and observations I had as a youngster between the ages of four and thirteen.

Why I should be so presumptuous as to think that my memoir is worth writing, and further, that anyone would gain anything by reading it? I believe that my particular set of experiences is unique and that they speak to at least three separate and distinct audiences. First, there is the audience of my Caribbean people; second, there are the colonial peoples from all over the world, and third, there is that world-wide audience which has had little or no exposure to the struggles or concerns of the colonized. The latter group includes people from "mother countries", as former colonizers have been called.

Interestingly, most people in the mother countries were not privy to what went on in the colonies. It has been said that had the British people known what went on, their colonial system would have met a much earlier demise. As late as my early school days, when India, under the leadership of Mahatma Gandhi and Jawaharlal Nehru was pressing for independence, Winston Churchill was reported to have said that he did not become His Majesty's Chief Minister to preside at the dissolution of the empire.

This memoir slides easily into the boy's pluck in shaping his own education, and how advanced academics can lead to never-imagined corporate success, political power and of course, money. There is a wild erotic period before marriage, which should not be dwelt upon, except by those who enjoy reading of such titillations but rather treated as a mere precursor to the enlightenment that I found in the early afternoon of my life. There very well may be a kind of redemptive and motivational aspect to my life as I stumbled through hardship in my quest to understand and function in the United States while holding my family together.

Understanding the USA takes a lifetime of study, even more so for a black immigrant, but I have been accompanied and led perhaps longer than I realized it, by an unseen hand. I make no claim to be a Christian. I am a work in progress, but I believe that the Holy Spirit, that inscrutable part of the Trinity, has always been with me, guiding and protecting me, leading me towards my purpose in this life.

I will tell the story of Porgy (my childhood nickname) in his own words because I know him best. I first thought of him as a separate construct when my elementary school headmaster, Leslie Gay, started teaching me Latin in 1944 when I was eight years old. I have not reflected much on this subject, but when you think of it, it makes one wonder what Mr. Gay could have been up to, introducing me to Latin so early. But it was an immensely effective way of teaching me English grammar and the fundamentals of language.

Even though English was the *lingua franca*, however, it was as foreign in my part of Barbados as was Latin. The local folk spoke a Creole in which the verb endings did not often follow the attraction of the subject, nor was there any rigor in the handling of tenses or cases. I can truly say that I learned Latin before I correctly learned to speak the Queen's English, to the credit of Mr. Gay who selected me for private lessons at that tender age, and to the grudging appreciation of my children who have often been pricked by my suggestions of proper English usage, oral or written. I did learn by teaching my immediate offspring and have had a gentler trip exchanging proper usage of English with my grandchildren, all of whom were born in the United States. I willingly confess that I have studiously avoided explanation of the pluperfect tense, for it is better at my level of maturity and advancing years to rank fun over correctness.

2. AMERICAN ME

In no way was I prepared for living in the USA. My friend and business associate, Tom Désulmé, had warned me that the United States was not built to accommodate the black man, and that I would not be able to duplicate the standard of living that I'd enjoyed in Jamaica. Carlton Alexander of Grace Kennedy & Company commented that he would not leave Jamaica to become a second-class citizen in the USA. I was leaving with my family, and I knew I could pick up from where I had left off in Jamaica and carry on. Could I really?

I was terribly mistaken.

★★★

Three months after my family did, I arrived in Atlanta on a warm September day of 1985. I was satisfied that we had made the right choice, opting to settle in the southeastern part of the country. I started applying for jobs right away but in the interim, I enrolled in a real estate sales program.

Six weeks after my arrival in the USA, I acquired a realtor's license even before I knew my way around the metro area. I never really wanted to be a realtor, but I figured that it was a worthwhile pastime while I waited to be called for that special corporate job that matched my experience and education. That call was very slow in coming. I had never thought about it beforehand, but I had no real job-hunting skills. From the time I left my Barbados home at age eighteen through my experiences in the Bahamas, Canada, New York, and Jamaica, jobs had always found me. I was embarking on an odyssey of personality-changing proportions.

There were two large real estate companies in Stone Mountain in 1985, Coldwell Banker and Royer Realty. On receiving my license, I drove over to Royer, about ten miles from my home on the east side of the famous sculptured mountain, walked in and introduced myself to the resident broker. He hired me right away. Why not? He was an exposed individual out of California, with an education identical to mine, and I would be the only black on his staff, sales or clerical. The firm had everything to gain and nothing to lose by taking me on. They also would get fifty percent of my commissions, as well as the public relations coup of having the first black man in their Stone

Mountain office.

Royer Realty had an excellent training program and they taught me an awful lot about real estate and about what I would have to face in the USA. I spent two years working with them and never saw another black in any of their offices (they did, however, hire a Korean woman during my second year). In the meantime, I kept looking for permanent employment more in line with my professional experience but got no replies, not even an acknowledgment of my applications.

I must have responded to over a hundred advertisements over those first two years without receiving a response. During staff meetings at Royer, I noted that no one paid any attention to any contributions I tried to make, even on topics where they knew I had managerial experience. It was as if I did not exist as a person. I was Ralph Ellison's *Invisible Man*. I may be a slow learner, but the reality of America was coming through to me. In the meanwhile, my household was costing us fifty thousand dollars per year, and my wife and I were only bringing in about half that amount in revenue. We would soon be broke.

In 1987 our firstborn, Leslyn, graduated from high school and received a partial scholarship to Washington & Lee University in Virginia. She was proud to be among the first classes of women to attend that excellent liberal arts college, which was designed to give General Robert E. Lee something to do after the Civil War. I was tickled to have my daughter going to an institution originally dedicated to the preparation of Southern white gentlemen for roles among the higher echelons of society. It was at this juncture that I started doing substitute teaching in Dekalb High Schools. I needed the extra money and needed the intellectual stimulation, but I also loved teaching and had done some version of it at all stages of my life. I was wholly untrained as a teacher, but I have usually been able to explain knotty mysteries to the struggling.

I recall a ten-week assignment when the Grade 12 English teacher was overtaken by cancer and I had to take over her class. The assigned texts were *Twelfth Night* and *The Catcher in the Rye*, and we had great fun with them. I had done the Shakespeare comedy for my high school GCE matriculation back in 1953 and I remembered many of the by-heart pieces that we had to prepare in those far-off days. The class had a lot of fun with my non-American English. The Principal offered to show me how to qualify as a teacher, but I could not support the lifestyle that I wanted on a teacher's pay. Unfortunately, I had no awareness of the various career paths that existed for educators and the excellent remuneration achievable by administrators.

When 1988 came around, with still no prospect of a job, I became increasingly despondent. Here I was, a man accustomed to the clubby company of other men, out of a society where I had derricks for my support and constancy, where people spoke to me wherever I went, mostly with respect and goodwill, where neighbors came to borrow a tool, or just walked into our yard to say hello as they passed our way, where folks came for a letter of recommendation, or a support document to a foreign embassy for obtaining emigration papers, where my bank manager would never even consider returning a check that would overdraw my account, and where the local police would escort me home on a late night coming out of Spanish Town and heading up into my hill country, especially if I appeared a little tipsy. And where I, a first-class citizen, offered willing service in return, at all the levels and in whatever capacity I was needed. But now, here I was, a stranger in a land upon which I was forcing myself, an unforgiving land, built on open exploitation, ready to take advantage of the unaware until he learned the road of awareness, a land that will chew you up and spit you out and start on the next generation, until you figure out the way forward.

It was almost impossible to live with me. The toll on my wife and children was nigh unbearable. It was particularly hard on my eldest daughter, who by nature enjoyed the trappings of our former "good life" – at least more than the younger ones did. A particular incident is noteworthy. One Saturday morning when Leslyn came home from college, she accompanied me around the shops on Memorial Drive, which was at that time the main shopping area in Stone Mountain.

When it came time to pay for our purchase, the white store manager would not accept my check but offered to accept my daughter's instead. I was mortified, and Leslyn shook her head, saying "Let us go, daddy, we don't need to be in this store." I was reminded of an incident of similar ilk when I was pulled over up in Virginia by a policeman while taking Leslyn back to college, and given a ticket for no apparent reason. I was a black man with a valid driver's license, driving an insured BMW in Virginia within the speed limit, on the way to a prestigious university. Good enough reasons to be given a ticket, I suppose.

It had never struck me before that the poorer and hungrier you are as an immigrant, the easier it is to adapt to the conditions faced by one. My education and exposure must have contributed to my slowness in assimilating to my new circumstances. All around me were people from our islands who were working at whatever jobs they could find, buying homes, or living in small apartments – sometimes overcrowded – yet sending their children to school and getting on with it. But there I was, so proud and unbending, unwilling to accept simply what I was being offered.

I think I must have been going a bit daft, too. My long-suffering wife Vilma suggested that I go see this psychologist she knew, and she also wanted me to go with her to church. The psychologist, with whom I visited twice, was a disaster for both of us. She had no empathy whatsoever with me. She had never had a client from outside her culture and had no understanding of problems faced by immigrants, or indeed the challenges faced by ambitious black Americans.

After much persuasion, I agreed to accompany Vilma to the Episcopal Church of the Holy Cross in Decatur, Georgia. She had been raised Methodist but chose to attend the Episcopalian church in hopes of getting me to come back to the church. Luckily, the priest was a savvy Jamaican man around my age. We found immediate identifications. I was raised in the Anglican Church as were my great grandparents, and as far as I am aware no one in my family had ever been anything but Anglican, except for one grandfather who got so pissed with the colonial church that he formed his own. This was short-lived however, for Aunt Dru, the grandmother with whom I was close, put an end to it when poor Alfred started illicit relationships with some of the prettier young female members. Grandfather Alfred knew the side on which his bread was buttered.

Throughout my conscious boyhood, I harbored misgivings about the nature of the Anglican Church, which was a part of the State during that time, and most members of my family were on the non-favored side of the social equation.

I've always struggled with the promotion of God and Equal God Jesus as white men with beards, one old and one young, and these constructed anomalies in a society where white Europeans owned pretty much everything and black Africans owned very little. It never seemed right in a Christian society, and that was the nature of my naivety.

There was also significant personal conflict over my relationship with my priest when I was a boy. Father Fielder was an Englishman who came to our parish in the early 1920s after service in World War I. He had buried our great-grandparents, married our parents, baptized and prepared my generation for confirmation. He had taught us as Scouts and Church Lads Brigade members. He schooled us in the rudiments of self-defense and showed us how to box. As the only white man in our village, he would sometimes have a drink in the local rum shop with the fellows, but he never allowed his children to have any interplay with us. His oldest daughter Betty was about eight years older than the kids in my group, and she sometimes taught Sunday School, but the two children our age were kept cloistered. They were homeschooled and stayed indoors all day and night. They were as pale-skinned as sheets, and if you ran into any of them on the pathway from the vicarage to the church, they seemed as startled as birds. What an assignment to have – what a life!

One Sunday school day, the question of nationality came up. This was shortly after World War II while England was still the supreme motherland. Father Fielder asked the class if we knew what nationality we were. Up shot my hand in a flash. "English, sir!" I shouted.

"And what part of England were you born, bright boy?" came his rejoinder.

I was mortified. I have never forgotten the put-down, for I was reawakened to the reality of the brainwashing and psychological scars of colonialism.

My high school headmaster encouraged the intellectual inquisitiveness that eventually led me on a path away from the church. The attractions of the world during my early adult years provided the pleasure that dulled my sensitivities to religious concerns and my professors, especially in graduate school, introduced me to philosophy that developed a kind of questioning thought process that left no room for faith. Corporate success and the heady wine of money or association with power so consumed me that I left the church when I was thirteen, and never returned until I was past fifty years of age.

By 1988, I had spent over one hundred thousand dollars of my earlier savings on the transition to America, some of which went back to savings that I had left in the USA and Canada before I emigrated to Jamaica in 1969. After being ripped off by Ponzi schemes, and a crooked employment agency to the tune of five thousand dollars in 1989, I took a job as a taxi driver in the hotel district that included Sandy Springs and Dunwoody. On the one hand, I felt that the upscale nature of the area would offer better earnings, but equally motivating was the fact that the area was far enough away from my home area of Stone Mountain that I would be unlikely to run into folks who knew me, and therefore I would be sparing myself the embarrassment of having them see me driving a cab.

Also by this time, we had two children in college, Leslyn at Washington & Lee in Lexington, Virginia, and Scott at Georgia State in Atlanta. To supplement my income and conserve whatever savings I had left, I waited on tables at an upscale restaurant at Gwinnett Mall. I received excellent tips, and on one occasion, I got the compliments of a customer's young son who asked me if I were some sort of prince. I guess I treated my guests in the restaurant as I would have welcomed them in my own home. Service to my Past Masters at the Festive Board in Lodge had given me an assurance that was noticeable, but this gig was short-lived. I took the hint and got out of there when I found a bullet hole in the driver's side window of my BMW which I'd parked in the alley behind the restaurant.

By the end of 1989, I had formed my own taxicab company and was running three cabs operating out of Chamblee, Georgia. On weekends my teenaged children and I drove the routes. I received the calls by transferring our company landline to my cell phone and dispatching the calls by digital radio to Scott and Leslyn in their cabs. My cell phone was a big old thing in a bag in those days, but in spite of the clunky communication, the three of us had a grand time running calls from Perimeter Mall Hotels to the airport, and all over Dunwoody, Sandy Springs, Roswell, Alpharetta, and East Cobb. We treated the exercise like motor rallies, with no GPS to help us in those days; we all used maps. My teenagers were by far the most intelligent and efficient drivers I have ever worked with. We eventually had six cabs when I closed the business in 1991.

I explored professional financial services in the early 1990s with modest success, and by the end of 1993, I was ready for new ventures. I still had never found a proper job in the USA and had followed the advice of an old white man who told me that I did not need a job, for I was educated like a rich white boy and what I needed was capital. By this time, two of our three children had graduated from college, and our son had his business going, repairing cars out of our garage at home. Scott had shown an aptitude for vehicle maintenance since he was a child on our farms back in Jamaica, and I had exposed him to machine shops in both the plastics and citrus industries when he started high school. He became an early graduate of Dekalb Technical College and has had his own business from the day he graduated. Our youngest child, Melanie, had by this time graduated with a master's degree in city and economic planning from Georgia State University. Soon thereafter, Leslyn gained her MBA.

My children were all aware of my limited cash flow and my tireless efforts to maintain a standard of living that I considered a minimum for my family. This led my son Scott to ask me one day in early 1994, "Daddy, why don't you buy a tow truck?" I had seen trucks towing cars, but had never considered this a worthwhile enterprise. My son explained to me the need for the tow-truck business and the possibilities for daily cash generation. I took fifteen thousand dollars out of my last twenty thousand dollars of savings and bought a secondhand Ford F350 flatbed tow truck for cash. I put away my tailored suits and sports coats, bought well-fitted khakis and good work boots and started towing cars. I went around to all the mechanic shops and body shops that I knew and asked them for business. No-one turned me away. Americans need their cars as much as they need their homes and in many cases more than they needed shelter.

In the first week, I netted $750. It was not all smooth sailing, however, for in the first month I broke the sub-frame of the tow bed and bent several stabilizing bars of clients' vehicles. A second-hand tow bed cost me $4,000 and I had to replace the stabilizing bars on the damaged cars. Luckily, an understanding and experienced operator showed me the rudiments of hooking up vehicles, how to always look for the towing points under the frame and the way to connect hooks to unbendable sections. He showed me to take the bed as far up the run as you can, just lowering it a few inches before sliding it under the bottom latch. In this way, pressure on the frame is severely reduced and breaking the frame is almost impossible. In the sixteen years that we operated tow trucks I never had another broken frame, for I trained every new driver personally. We had a few bent control arms and stabilizers, but once the driver realized that we were not joking about our rules and that they had to pay for careless and sloppy procedures, that problem was solved. I've had to lie down in snow, mud, and water to hook up cars and trucks in ditches, and can proudly state that I received bigger tips from customers than any hired hand, and produced more per week when I had to operate a truck myself, than anyone – except my son when he drove.

One year after entering the business, we leased a tow yard in Stone Mountain and acquired a AAA contract to cover three adjoining cities. We got an impound license and entered into contracts to impound vehicles for many apartment complexes and commercial operations in Stone Mountain and environs. We ran as many as six trucks and trained dozens of drivers over the sixteen years that we were in full operation. Many of the men that I hired and trained – and some others who came to the yard to hang out and observe – have built highly successful tow businesses of their own, some of them much larger than our enterprise. I take great pleasure in seeing their trucks on the road, and in the deference that they show me on the few occasions that we meet.

After sixteen years in the towing business, I bought a small commercial lot across the street from our tow yard, gave up the leased property (I thought the landlord wanted too much for it) and just ran a storage yard, mostly for cars that I or my son was trading. I had grown too old and slow to keep up with the nimble young drivers, so it was time to wind things down.

3. CLOSER TO THEE?

Every Sunday morning, I sat in quiet contemplation at the Episcopal Church of the Holy Cross, as the ritual and the hymns that I readily recalled from my youth washed over me. I began to look forward to the sincere greetings from the congregation and particularly the ad hoc preaching of the Reverend Don Taylor. The Catholic/Episcopalian Lectionary is so constructed that over a three-year period, a worshipper is taken through the Bible by a series of readings from the Old Testament, the Epistles, and the Gospels, and the preacher takes his text from the particular Sunday's Gospel reading. The congregation has a preconception of what it will get every Sunday and Don Taylor delivered every time without note or pause, succinctly and to the point.

In the exit greetings line one Sunday, Reverend Taylor reminded me that I was needed in the church. My response was that I was a bad man and not worthy. Don's reply was that I did not really know what bad was, for I could in no way be as bad as David, and God had work for him. He also had plenty of tough jobs for tough men.

I took note, but I did not act. My family developed an increasingly close relationship with Don, his wife Rosalie and daughter Tara, and gradually started to read lessons, and to sing out from my pew, but I still distrusted organized religion in general. My life was still about me and not about my relationship with the Almighty. Gradually, I was getting the idea that if I thought more of what I could add to the life of others and less about what I was doing for me, I might find more comfort in my existence. I started teaching Sunday School, and began to relive all the wonderful instances that had accompanied my earliest years at St. Savior's Church in the wild woods of St. Andrew back in Barbados from the late 1930s until the late 1940s.

Life is never idyllic, at least not for long. My priest Don Taylor ran for the Bishop of Atlanta seat in 1989. He was doing well in the voting despite being in a highly competitive field. There were several candidates who would have competently filled the new office of Bishop of the Atlanta Diocese, and up to the tea break Taylor was ahead.

Those of us from a cricketing culture are well aware of the drastic change that can overtake a wicket after tea. The home team usually has an advantage, for the groundskeepers know what they have to do to change the way the wicket is playing, whether to use the heavy roller or the light roller. And so, it might be cynically construed in

Don's case, for the wicket played totally differently in the late afternoon, and Don faded into oblivion, but only in that particular match. He went on to greatness elsewhere.

★★★

The Episcopal church and the Anglican church have the same original roots, but they are not the same. I could not do justice to either by definitively explaining their roots and present-day modus operandi, but suffice it to say that they both come out of the Catholic tradition. The Anglican Church is the successor to the Roman Catholic Church in England and came out of King Henry VIII's firing of the Pope and taking over the Church and its lands. Henry's successors became head of the new Church of England. His reasons have been the subject of debate for centuries, but envy of the church's power, wealth, and lands was as motivating a reason for Henry's actions as his need to divorce Catharine of Aragon. The Anglican Church still considers the British monarch as its head, administered by the Archbishop of Canterbury.

After some of the Founding Fathers of the United States of America got through forming the Constitution of the United States of America, they went across the street and formulated the rules and regulations of the Episcopal Church of the USA. They could not very well have the King of England as their church's head, so they designated a Primate that would be elected by the bishops of the dioceses themselves. The Episcopal Church remains in union with the Anglican Church, basically follows the same ritual practices, is not subject to the rulings or dictates of the Archbishop of Canterbury, does not have archbishops, and is not beholden to edicts from a central universal head. Of course, there is a sharing of ideas and an exchange of information, common recruitment of clergy, and common access to due process apparatus, but the bishop is not supreme, since each church is expected to maintain its autonomy under an agreed set of rules and tenets.

Don Taylor was succeeded at the Episcopal Church of the Holy Cross in Decatur by Buck Belmore, a young priest from North Carolina, and he encouraged me out of the comfort of the pews into taking an active interest in church affairs. I found new life, new energy, and a satisfaction not previously attained on my American odyssey. Buck Belmore prepared me for confirmation in the Episcopalian

Church. I had been the only member of my group of twelve year-old boys not confirmed in my village church. I simply had not liked the set-up. As a Sunday School teacher, I thoroughly enjoyed assuming the teacher role by literally reliving my pleasant boyhood experiences. In short order, I occupied every position on the vestry except senior warden, serving two stints as junior warden, and co-chair of a million-dollar capital campaign to build a new wing and narthex onto the sanctuary. My eldest daughter did become senior warden, serving two terms before she was thirty-five. I have had the honor of being selected as a delegate to the committee for the election of a Bishop of Atlanta, but my most satisfying ministry has been the joy of singing in the church choirs.

For years I had sung out from the congregation, but never thought I could afford the time to commit to choir practices. And then with the advent of a new administration in the church, a contemporary choir was formed. The members were all women, and I simply could not refuse their call. A new organist came on board and she persuaded me that she needed my voice in the chancel choir, and so I found myself singing in two choirs along with my other church activities. I was now so busy serving, and my week was so full that I had no time or patience for non-productive activity. My wife Vilma continued her accustomed role as family manager, and whether we had little or plenty, good or lean cash flow, we managed to share and to keep our home open and friendly.

I still cannot say that I am a man of God. I love the Lord as I understand Him to be, but I do not trust organized religion. I have learned that too close an alignment with the administration of church affairs reduces one's quality of worship experience. I often opine that to the extent that one's faith approaches that of a child's, is to approach the godly ideal. I have not yet let go of the questions. Christianity is not an easy thing.

My close involvement with church administration led me to an indelible and highly educational exercise with Episcopal church politics. There was a considerable body of opinion in our church that the management style of our new rector would eventually redound to the detriment of the church. A feeling had grown that he was not prepared to listen to or share opinions with experienced leaders in the church, or indeed with anyone, that his management style was dictatorial, only his ideas were operable, that he was not sufficiently mindful of the sensibilities of many members of the congregation, to the extent that we were losing the most generous members, that his wife had developed a disruptive group of followers in the choir, and that very few members wanted to serve on the vestry. Some of the seniors felt that their observations and concerns were being summarily dismissed.

I was selected along with a legal practitioner in the church to try to help the rector reassess his way of doing things and to arrange a meeting for us with the vestry. We knew that church doctrine directed that matters of this sort had to be dealt with eventually through the vestry, but we wanted to give the rector the benefit of our thoughts before the matter ever had to go to the vestry.

We submitted our request in writing. The rector dismissed us abruptly and told us that he did not have to speak with us, that he was employed by the bishop and was advised not to speak with us as a group. He would, however, speak singly with any member who sought an appointment. He sent our letter to the bishop of the diocese.

What followed was a political battle that I knew we could not win. Any victory would have been pyrrhic. Some may want to argue that the rector's attitude would be indefensible, but scholars can mount a plausible defense for any position. For starters, the fact that a bishop has to protect his priests, for if it should ever be the consensus that a bishop was not protecting his priests, he would have difficulty attracting to his diocese the kinds of priests that he would prefer. I could probably cite more supporting evidence for the institution's side if pressed. The matter was thrown into the Episcopalian Diocesan cooler, a centuries-old process of doing nothing in a hurry. In the interim, several families left the church, including ours, and others reduced their annual pledges. Many were prepared to see how long, if at all, the diocese would pay the rector's salary. It wasn't long before we learned that the rector had found a position as a canon to a bishop in a northern state, out of a line position and into a staff position. Thus, the ability to do damage was reduced or ended. Apparently, the system has some panache and unquestionable effectiveness.

Ten years ago, the wife of one of the brothers who introduced me to freemasonry called me and asked me to visit a more elderly brother whose wife had recently died. She stated that he was not doing well health-wise and would appreciate my visit. I called on Alvin and found that we had much to share. Alvin eventually invited me to accompany him to Rotary. After several visits he said to me, "You are a Rotarian." I asked him to explain himself, and his answer was that

I displayed all the attributes of a good Rotarian, and he wanted to introduce me to become a member of the Rotary Club of Stone Mountain, Georgia. I reminded Alvin that Rotary was a rich man's club, and I was not in that league. Alvin's rejoinder was that the organization was not a men's club – for there were many women in Rotary, and hardly a rich man's club, even though there were many successful men in the organization. For ten years now I have been a Rotarian and find its motto "Service Above Self" a worthy call.

Through Rotary, I have had the opportunity to discover many of the needs of my community and have seized the opportunity to work with others in helping to satisfy those needs. Much of my interest has centered around school programs in our Stone Mountain area, but I have also volunteered for a couple of years with the neighborhood Club House, an organization that provides therapy for individuals who have been brain injured. Individuals can acquire these injuries through a variety of circumstances, and the therapy centers around helping the members adjust to their new levels of capability as they progress to a new normal. I found working with them to be most beneficial to the members and myself as I truly learned the meaning of empathy. Brain injury will reduce one from his former position of leadership of home, corporation, supervisory position, athletic prowess or regular competence, to a position of dependency on others for daily decision-making, protection and motivation. I trust that they enjoyed having me around.

As I muse over my life, on my good fortune in institutions of higher education, from travel, from exposure to business leadership, political leaders, personal business success and failures, and my awakening to the satisfying enlightenment that comes from service beyond self, I sometimes think of what could have been.

Would I have better paid my debt to life had I returned to my native land and joined in the political effort to improve its prospects? Could I have fit in? Would I have had the temperament to cope with the challenges that would come? One must plow the land on which he stands.

As much as I may have wanted to reward or even thank those who have helped me on my way, I have had little opportunity to do so. In this regard I am not unique, I'm sure. The guiding principle in life is to pay it forward, and so I serve my country as my God has given me to serve others.

A SONG FOR MY VILLAGE
Sons and daughters have I given up
To the Carolinas in the mid-nineteenth
To sister islands and mainlands in the late-
To Colon and Cuba in the early twentieth
To Britain and America in the mid-
But don't mourn for me my children
My topsoil may have moved to the streams
Washed away by Afrique storms
My fruit trees have ceased to bear
My peasant farms go untended
And my Blackbellied rams are neutered
But do not mourn for me
My sires are in the world
Where they belong.

4. CANE GARDEN

Cane Garden, nestled in a very fertile valley with excellent rainfall, was the prettiest little Barbadian village one could hope to be from. To the east, there were Chalky Mount and Bissex and Parks; in the southeast were Fruitful Hill and Sugar Hill. In the south were Sturges and Welchman Hall – all hills – and west of us were Mount Hillaby and White Hill. We were in a saddle between these high points, with plains in the north running down to Belleplaine and the Atlantic Ocean. From my grandmother's backyard arrowroot patch, we looked east to Chalky Mount and Bissex and confirmed the time of day by noting the ball on the flagpole at District F Police Station, which they posted at 8.45 a.m. and took down at 9.00 a.m. From Aunt Dru's front door, we looked across the valley from Sturges to Mount Hillaby and White Hill, idyllic and inspiring.

I liked to retreat to my favorite breadfruit tree at the far end of our land and compose ditties as they came into my head. Once I got to be about eight and Mr. Watson had taught me the rudiments of music, my tools were 'do' and 're' below the first line, 'mi' was on the first line, 'fa' was in the first space, and 'so' was on the second line. I knew the scale and just took it from there. I drew my lines and put in my notes as they came to me. I always drew the staff neatly as if I were paying respect to the discipline. I spent hours dreaming undisturbed. To this day, so long as I hear and see that first note on a page, I can sing the tune.

Four rivers ran through my village. In the dry season, they dwindled to streams, but when the rains came, these streams became treacherous watercourses as they thundered down from the surrounding hillsides, often taking livestock into the nearby Atlantic Ocean. Many were the times when we had to run to the riverside to gather our animals and pen them safely under our cellars to protect them from thundering streams and tropical downpours. Sometimes, the rain would fall unbroken like a tap was left open, and we would cut plantain leaves to shield our bodies from the torrent as we got our livestock together.

Village life was very simple. It was a place where most men cultivated their small acreages and hired their labor out to the plantations as the seasons dictated, or to their fellow villagers as needed. All the skills required to keep things going could be found at arm's length. There were carpenters, seamstresses, two tailors, a shoemaker, a joiner, two shopkeepers, a bus service operator, two motor mechanics, a dynamiter, a schoolmaster, a schoolmistress, someone who kept the public hedges and gutters weed-free, and the priest. There was one doctor for the entire parish and one chief sanitary inspector. There was one almshouse and one police station, both located in Belleplaine, the parish center.

I lived for the outdoors; one could say I practically lived outside. I remember that distinctly because I could often be found racing behind my first significant toy, an iron hoop from the old nave of a discarded buggy wheel. I ran everywhere with that wheel, steering it just ahead with a fustic stick from our backyard heap of firewood. It was as if I never walked, running on every errand, to the point that Deighton Roach – our local village sophisticate who had visited his mother in New York, and seen Gershwin's *Porgy and Bess* – gave me the name Porgy. Just like Porgy, I never walked. While he was disabled and had a goat cart to drag him around, I had my hoop that magically pulled me all around as I ran.

The name stuck as I graduated to larger and larger hoops. Even today, one of my cousins, Wilton, still calls me Porgy. No one else seems to remember the name, but then there are very few of my early childhood friends left.

When we all weren't in school, the children in my village were mostly out combing the surrounding woods and river courses, feasting on mangoes, cashew bobbas (the 'apple' part above the external seed that is removed and roasted), cherries, guavas, star apples, mammy apples, Indian jujube or 'coolie plums', sweet sops, soursops, golden apples, guineps, plums, sugar cane and all the other delicacies I can't recall. We never peeled the sugar cane before eating it; we tore into the stem with our teeth, which is perhaps why we all had perfect teeth and no need for the dentist. We ate so much fruit and cane that we often had no space in our stomachs for a hot meal.

We kids made all our own toys. There were always older boys to help us, like my cousin Harold, who was extremely adept at making cars and trucks, and our neighbor Aden Carrington, the expert at making tops. We used empty tins to make cars and trucks; corned beef cans made excellent truck bonnets, and the empties from sardines and salmon made car fenders and bodies. We liked the Fray Bentos corned beef can the best, and during the long holidays from elementary school, we would place our orders with neighbors, asking them to save those tins for us. There weren't that many available, but there were numerous condensed milk cans we could use. Every house used that product, since it was inexpensive and double-purpose, providing milk and sweetener at the same time.

There was one summer when I went through a series of tops, all of which were scramblers. When spun, they would wander all over the road like they were picking rice, like the grains we got during World War II, filled with stony debris. We heard that this variety came from Burma. Sometimes villagers had to wash that rice two or three times to clean it up after picking out the gravel so they could cook it. We just couldn't make a top that was capable of staying in one place and 'sleeping'.

To get a good one made, my father decided to help me scout the woods for a likely guava root stump. We found one and Aden, our gifted craftsman, helped me make a top from the raw material. When we thought we had it right, I searched for the appropriate ten-penny nail, cut it to the appropriate length with a file from my late grandfather's old toolbox and helped Aden affix and sharpen the point. I got some marlin twine, wrapped the top and sent it spinning. It hummed and slept in place like a baby. My playmates gathered around to watch me spin it and beg for a turn, but I would not grant that favor to anyone. This was mine alone.

Not so for Aden, though. He felt that the top was too sweet for a little boy like me, and he took it away. I don't know what made him think that he could get away with a move like that, knowing my mother's fabled fearlessness. Momma went after him without asking him to give it back, instead putting a licking on him until he begged her to let him return it.

A serious problem ensued in our village.

Aden's mother, Winnie Carrington, sued my mother for assault and battery of her son and would not 'draw out' (withdraw) the complaint until my father paid her ten shillings. Winnie was the local sore-foot healer, and everyone would eventually need her. She knew the value of every healing bush and where to find it. No matter how far gone a lame foot was, Winnie could cure it. We didn't go to the parish doctor; we went to Winnie. The suit was quashed, and there was peace in the village. I had my top, Winnie Carrington could buy a lot of tinned delights for her family, and we could call on her to wash and dress our sore feet and legs. I would need her a lot during my early years.

Marbles was another indispensable pastime for us. I have fond memories of my 'steelie' (a ball from a discarded motor car engine bearing), which I kept well into my high school years. We played marbles for cashew seeds and enjoyed roasting them at the end of the cashew season. I was particularly good at marbles and could provide hundreds of cashew seeds for our annual roasts. There is no sweeter smell than that of a freshly roasted cashew seed.

Cricket was our favorite game of all. As children, we played "marble cricket", where the bat and ball are miniaturized to match the size convenient for children. The batsman, bowler and wicketkeeper play from a kneeling position and all fielders play standing. I have never heard of anyone going to a store and buying bats and balls or knee pads for marble cricket, since we made our own gear. We made our bats out of coconut bough, and sometimes out of clammy cherry wood. We made our kneepads out of banana leaves and old fabric.

Our cricket balls were by far the most interesting kind. There was this spring at the foot of Spa Hill, where we would skim the globules of tar off the water, soak old cloth in the tar, wrap and build the contents patiently with twine until we had fashioned a ball of the appropriate size. When this ball dried, we had the perfect marble cricket ball. Stumps also called 'sticks', and bails were easiest to make. Just three pieces of wood with sharpened points were stuck into the ground. From our knees, we learned to bowl any type of ball called for, whether leg breaks, off-breaks or fast balls. No bouncers were possible with the tar ball, but we could try googlies (leg-breaks with an off-break action). In my time, our area of the island produced two outstanding test cricketers and many good local competitors, all of whom had started at the marble-cricket level.

★★★

Mr. Seale was a most interesting man. He was of my grandparents' generation, and like so many of the male elders in my village had gone to work on the Panama Canal in the early 1900's. Unlike my grandfathers who came straight back home, Seale had spent a few years in Cuba and Haiti before returning to Barbados. He lived on the southern boundary of the village and did not engage in normal village life. He seemed to grow everything that he needed in the isolation of his small acreage.

Folks noticed that Seale's only visitors were single women and the vicar of our church. Rumors tend to fill vacuums, and the villagers convinced themselves that he was an obeah man. The fact that he had sojourned to Cuba – and Haiti in particular – gave stronger support to this conclusion, for these two largest Caribbean islands supposedly were harbingers of the African cults far more developed than anything our small island had to offer.

Given that the assumptions of the villagers were true, why would Seale's visitors only be single women and the local priest? The conclusion was that the three parties had a common bond. The island in general had a low marriage rate. Villages like mine that were close to the sugar estates in particular, and therefore closer to the slave tradition of couples either not getting married, or only establishing primitive marriage ceremonies, fueled a low propensity to marry. The more successful that Mr. Seale's obeah practice was in bringing reluctant men into official state marriage, the more successful the vicar, and perhaps the spinsters, would be. Thus, there was an unholy alliance of demon obeah and the official church, working for God, the devil and themselves altogether.

Regardless, the Anglican church was a great training ground for the boys and girls in Cane Garden, with boys having many more activities than girls. I became a Cub Scout at a very early age because my cousins Wilton and Vernon were two years older than I was – and I had to be involved in whatever they were doing. I don't remember them going on to the 51st Barbados Scout Troop with me since my troop centered around my elementary school and my cousins went to Mr. Dean's Elementary School in Sugar Hill on the St. Joseph side of the St. Andrew-St. Joseph boundary.

It was at Scout camps that I learned to pitch a tent, to fraternize with boys who were not my village mates, to sleep on groundsheets, to be independent, resourceful, and engage in teamwork. I had great fun at camps and still remember my camp leaders to this day. I loved my uniform, especially my scout belt, so much so that I kept my scout belt until many years later when I moved to the Bahamas.

★★★

One of my special responsibilities as a growing lad was to ring the church bell for the Wednesday morning six o'clock service. Most people who went to this service depended on hearing that bell to get to church since clocks were not a household fixture at this time. Our vicar and the sexton must have had great confidence in me to assign me that job. I was probably about nine or ten when I first took on the bell, a real old-fashioned church type sitting up in the belfry with a long rope hanging down the front of the church. Calling the faithful to service was relatively easy, but tolling the bell for funerals was tricky, as was ringing the angelus prayer during communion.

On an unusually dark Wednesday morning, I faced a severe challenge when I got to the church for my regular duty. Neither the sexton nor the priest was present. The graveyard that started right outside the front door of the church only had a low wall separating me from all the duppies waiting to scare me, and all the living late sleepers waiting at home to hear the bell. I had to ring it, for the living late folks could do me more harm than the late dead folks, so ghosts be dammed. There would be no more whistling or running when I passed a graveyard, so I rang the bell and cleared that hurdle.

Towards the end of World War II, my entire scout troop was converted into a Boys' Brigade. I do not know why, but we started to drill more seriously and to march with unarmed rifles. Our uniforms were no longer khaki but white shirts and black short dress pants, with black shoes and white socks. We now used marshal ranks like corporal, lance sergeant and sergeant. Our headdress was an English cap like those worn by the local policemen, with the crest in the front. I guess we were being readied to defend the Empire against the onslaught of the Hun in Europe.

In typical Barbadian fashion, there was a group comprised mainly of females referred to as the "third class" who earned their living picking grass and weeds from the estate crops. By the process of deduction, if there existed a third class, there must have been a first and a second. I fear getting into the weeds myself to explain this class structure, but at minimum, I know my village was too insignificant to have created it. The system must have come out of the wider cultural experience of the plantation model. I don't remember this causing any open discriminatory problem among the villagers, nor do I remember any identification of it as our voluntary apartheid system. I do remember the vitriolic use of "third class" referring to particular persons and particular behaviors.

As I'd said, Mr. Gay, my headmaster, continued to give me private lessons from age eight, and at ten years of age, Mr. Watson took over. These two men were preparing me for the Senior First Grade Exhibition. The top performer winner would go to Harrison College on scholarship, since that was the leading high school in the island

and the institution from which most present and future Barbadian leaders emerged. My teachers felt that I, too, should be there. The fight was with my grandmother, who wanted me to run her errands rather than devote my time to the higher pursuits.

Every Saturday morning, I went up to Mr. Watson's home at Mount Hillaby for lessons which he designed, and in 1948 at age twelve, I wrote the scholarship exam. My results placed me second overall, but there was only one scholarship.

My father could have paid for me to attend Harrison College, but he refused to do so. I did not want to go to the Alleyne School, the government high school in my parish, nor was I keen on Combermere in Bridgetown, the capital. I had now exhausted the elementary school's educational program. Both my headmaster Mr. Gay and his brother Lawrence, who was an Inspector of Schools, felt that I should have been awarded a scholarship to Harrison College, and arranged for me to be a pupil-teacher at St. Savior's Boys School instead. Fortune would have to lead me where I should go. I spent four terms there teaching and learning from my young peers before entering Modern High School in January 1950 at the start of the second term. I was in my fourteenth year. Why, one may ask, was I two years behind my peers in entering high school, and why was I entering Modern High, a private school, rather than the more prestigious Harrison College or Combermere High?

Many contributing factors led to my delay in entering high school – but I'll come back to that. I must first tell you about the social and family dynamics of my village.

My mother came from a family group whose members were derisively in some instances, and enviously, in others, called Boar Rats. According to village lore, just like the rodent, the Boar Rats were very smart and adaptable people who constantly displayed an uncanny ability to survive and thrive in the face of every challenge. This is the generous definition. The less charitable explanation is that the Boar Rats were smart traders who came out best in every deal and taught their offspring survival skills and family cooperation. They were not the village elite.

My father's family did consider themselves the village elite – at least the women did. It all started with Old Missie, the clan mother. She was born around 1840, in the first generation of free Blacks after the abolition of slavery in the English-speaking Caribbean. She was the product of a Scottish plantation manager and a slave woman, inheriting the physique and strength of her African ancestors and the business acumen of her Scottish forbears. She amassed several acres of land and became a highly respected farmer and village leader. Much of her property is still in place but has been devoured by bush.

Missie raised five daughters and three sons. Two of her daughters emigrated to the United States in the 1890s; two sons went to live in the United States in 1919 after helping to build the Panama Canal. One son was killed fighting for the British during the Boer War in South Africa in the early years of the twentieth century.

My paternal grandmother was one of the daughters who stayed home in Barbados, one of those who were considered the village belles. On the weekdays they wore their stiff aprons and white turbans that had to be starched, ironed, and tied. My grandmother's turban was never dismantled between washings but served sentry duty on her dressing table every night, with that ubiquitous hatpin a sword beside it. On Sundays, the uniform became corsets, high-topped laced boots and store-bought hats.

These ladies were the pillars of the Anglican Church, serving on the Altar Guild, the Mother's Union, fundraising committees, floral committee, and every other area except for the vestry since women didn't have that privilege. The vestry essentially ran the entire parish, a political geographic area, and not the typical church-delineated area. It was at the homes of these women that officials stopped for cool drinks and refreshment when passing through our village on personal or official business. All of them had their "drawing-room wagon", a kind of tea trolley decorated with English bone china and white-handled Sheffield cutlery, with cups and saucers that only the priest could use. Maybe God would have been allowed if He sat for a while.

My great aunts, like Old Missie, raised large families, but my grandmother raised only a son and a daughter. It is worth noting that all these ladies had hardworking, successful husbands, but as I now can assess, these men were all gentle types. They were not at all like the local men of that era, domineering and intimidating. Perhaps they were just smart.

My paternal grandmother did not like my mother, nor her breed. To be blunt, she felt that no woman was good enough for her son, who was so handsome he was nicknamed "Pretty" as a boy and bore that moniker all his adult life. My father loved my mother nonetheless and won her as his future partner in her late teens before the local plantation bosses got a chance to deflower her, as was the usual practice in those days.

I like to describe my mother as fully grown. She was a reasonably tall woman for that time, full-sized, with a smile that warmed the cockles of your heart and invited instant conversation. She was the second-to-last child of a family of two girls and five boys, and for her to look after the whole brood was as natural to her as drinking water. She was like an amateur psychiatrist or psychologist whose counsel people sought.

In those early days after the war, when most women had to depend on a man for sustenance and definition of themselves, mother managed quite nicely without a husband. My sister Thelma and I were her pride, joy, and *raison d'être*. She constantly reminded me that I had to do well in school because education was my way towards upward mobility. She had a way of using epigrams without knowing what they were. She would remind me that "There is no one looking like you, selling cloth in no store on Broad Street. But lots of people looking like you are lawyers, magistrates, doctors, schoolmasters, sergeants, and master tradesmen." The message was clear to me. If I hoped to function at a reasonably successful level in my society, I would have to be educated.

No contemporary woman dressed better than my mother did. In those days, the stores in Bridgetown did not carry ready-made clothing. Every man had a tailor, and every woman had a dressmaker. My mother retained two. Dressmakers were unreliable, she insisted, and she could not place her wellbeing in the hands of just one seamstress. The same thing could be said of the local tailors, for I distinctly remember a time when my tailor Stephen, a close relative, took one full year to make what turned out to be my last pair of short pants, fashioned from a dark-grey English pinstripe. We had bought the fabric from the itinerant Syrian trader by paying him a shilling a week. I concluded then at age fourteen that no tailor would ever reduce me to such agony again.

Quite often, Sunday-morning people would look out for mother as she arrived by hired car at St. Leonard's Anglican Church, just to see what she was wearing. But before she left home, she would accommodate the one or two neighbors who would stop by to see what interesting fragrances "Miss Leslyn had to share" with them.

As far as possible, my mother avoided dealing with subordinates. She would wait if necessary, to talk with the head man. Her motto was "you go to the head of the spring to get clear water". That advice was not lost on me, and it has constantly shone as a light in my mind and on my behavior.

My mother died of a massive stroke at sixty-seven in 1985. She had found marital bliss late in life when she and Louis combined their properties near District A Police Station in Bridgetown. People in the area will remind you that Mrs. Hollinsworth, as mother became, had a yard full of chickens, ducks, pigeons, turkeys and rabbits, none of them as pets. Additionally, or was it mainly, she and Louis also kept a home dairy, maintaining twelve high-producing dairy cows in stalls, and delivering fresh milk to homes in Station Hill, Bush Hall, and Bank Hall, surrounding suburbs of Bridgetown, every day. It's nothing short of amazing how clean her small yard was, considering the numbers of live animals they had in that small space.

On one of my trips to Barbados from Jamaica, I took a client and his family with me, and as we sat in the dining room at the back of the house eating mom's cou-cou and harslet,* the children could reach out and touch the tail of a cow. We were all farmers, marveling at the sight of what could be done in small spaces with some determination and good sanitation management.

Mom had died two months after I left Jamaica for Atlanta; I went home to Barbados for her funeral. She was buried beside a mahogany tree in the driveway of St. Leonard's Anglican church on Westbury Road in Bridgetown. Many women from the area flocked the churchyard, probably hoping to see what Ms. Leslyn would be wearing this time. Mr. Watson, my elementary school teacher who gave me private lessons back in the 1940s was there, as well as Mrs. Lynch, wife of my late high school headmaster, along with former classmates and students whom I had taught and were now distinguished men and women in medicine, the civil service, education and other fields.

My stepfather Louis thought life unlivable without my mother. He quit taking his medication and stopped observing his dietary disciplines, passing away just three months after she did.

★★★

During World War II most of the able-bodied young men in our

---

*Harslet is pig's liver prepared in a deep brown gravy, a Barbados delicacy served with turned cornmeal and boiled okras.

village were going off somewhere, to other jobs and opportunities for self-improvement and to create better opportunities for their families. Mom could not get my father to leave our village and seek upward mobility. His rebuttals were always the same: "What people are running all over the world to find, I already have. That is, a home, land, family and the respect of my village." And so, in 1946 my mother left me and my sister with my father and his mother and set out for the city to improve her circumstances and make a better way for her two children. Mom started out as a shop assistant in her brother's (my uncle Hugh's) village shop in Thomas Gap off Westbury Road, near St. Leonard's Anglican Church in Bridgetown.

My father had the calmest personality of anyone you could ever meet. I have never seen him lose his temper, and he had the respect of everyone in our village, young or old. He loved his fellow villagers and they loved him.

He would cut all the boys' hair for free under our favorite mango tree, slaughter and butcher any neighbor's sheep, goat or pig, as well as castrate their young boars or turn their young rams and billy goats into weathers (males castrated for faster growth) – for free. He would calculate the amount of lumber that a neighbor needed to repair her home, and when he bought fertilizer for his sugar cane field, he would buy the same for the neighbor as well. If he had the time, he would help a young carpenter with repairs, for he was himself a competent woodworker, taught by my grandfather who had gone to help build the Panama Canal in early 1900 and had mastered both the carpentry and wheelwrighting trades.

On many occasions, my father would pick up a fellow villager's supplies and bring them in from the city in his jackass or mule cart, after selling and delivering meat (sugar-cane tops and other grasses) to his city customers. In those 1940s days, many city dwellers kept a dairy goat or cow in their backyard for the family supply of milk. In some cases, they reared Black Belly sheep, a native Barbados breed. For much of the time, my father was the parish dynamiter and rock blaster, providing most of the boulders and metal (rocks broken into different sizes) to build the local roads. My grandfather had also returned home with dynamiting and skills which he passed on to my father.

My father avoided the church like it was the plague. If he went to a funeral, he would stay out in the churchyard with the men of like spirit. He avoided priests, considering them agents of the colonial power. I never heard my father sing or shake a leg.

The Anglican church was an endowed institution, and the priests were paid and appointed by the government through the bishop who joined the governor and the colonial secretary in running the colony. My paternal grandfather broke away from the Anglican Church shortly after returning from Panama and formed his own church after my father was born in 1913. No wonder then that I got my exposure to the struggle for adult suffrage and the idea of national independence by the time I was eight years old. And no wonder that my father could boast that he never spent a night of his life out of his village.

When I became old enough to appreciate the subtlety, mother would tell me: "Of course your father could boast like that because he truly never had to leave the village any night to find what he really wanted ... he always found it in another house close by."

Until he was admitted to Queen Elizabeth Hospital in Bridgetown late into his seventy-ninth year, my father Edward Carlton could continue to boast that he never slept any night of his life outside his village. He did not make it out of the hospital, dying late in 1993, about a month before he turned eighty.

I got to daddy's bedside and visited with him several times before he passed away. He had a clear recall of everything I had done or accomplished in my career, some of which surprised me. I had remained in touch with him by letter throughout the years, and also by phone on major occasions. Whenever I reached a major milestone, I would go to Barbados to visit him and my mother, in 1959 when I left Nassau for Canada, in 1964 after completing my first degree, and again in 1969 when I had a master's degree, a wife and daughter.

During the almost seventeen years that I lived in Jamaica, I took my family to Barbados every two years. Our children often retell the story of discovering a family of green monkeys while exploring the woods and river course around my ancestral home, before the area became infested with the little apes. They must have felt at home in my Cane Garden. Two days after I got back home to Atlanta after visiting my father, I got word that he had died. Everyone swears that he had held onto life until I went to visit him. I did not go back for his funeral. "Pretty" was churched in the old ancestral St. Savior's and buried among our ancestors in the village graveyard. He was treated like a prince.

★★★

My paternal grandmother did not want me to have an academic education. My teachers, Messrs. Gay and Watson, were always in a battle with her to get me away from running her or her daughter's errands and make the time to take private lessons. By this time, my paternal grandfather had died, and my father was the sole provider for his mother in addition to his own family. My grandmother was aware of the benefits of higher education, for in her youth she had been a teacher at a school that her uncle had started in the village to teach the first two post-abolition generations to read and write. She wanted my father to send me to learn a trade so that I would not compete with her for larger portions of my father's income.

In the 1940s, high school was not free in Barbados. I recall having an almost three-year battle, from 1947 until the end of 1949, with my grandmother for my right to go to high school and not to be forced into a trade. The strange thing about all this is that my grandmother was the one who had been firing up my inquisitive mind all along. It was she who gave me books to read and discuss with her, the same person who made me read Bible passages aloud every Sunday. She had this big black Reference Bible, which led the reader from one related passage of Scripture to another, and by the time I was ten or eleven, I began to appreciate the structure of the Anglican /Roman Catholic lectionary.

A few years later, I learned that I had topped the island in scripture in my GCE "O" Level exams. My father did nothing to get me sent off to high school, even though he was a good earner and had extra cash flow every year from his sugar cane crop.

Mom was not twiddling her thumbs in Bridgetown. By the end of 1947, she came for my sister Thelma and set her up at school in town, and by the end of 1949 she came back for me, a very mature young man at thirteen. I knew something about raising small animals and had raised my own livestock. I understood crop cycling, how to grow food, slaughter, dress and butcher an animal and how to value things. I had been a pupil-teacher for a year and a half, a Boy Scout and a member of the Church Lads Brigade. I had exposure and experience in leadership, plus exposure to Latin and French, particularly their grammar. My elementary school teachers had launched me, their product, rather well.

When I was brought to the city right after Christmas in 1949, the first place we lived was on Fairfield Cross Road in the village of Black Rock, St. Michael, where my mother had rented a comfortable house in a nice area. Right beside her lived three young men who had just started in their careers at the end of the war. There was my mom's cousin Cleon Lynch, his brother Elson, and Purpose. A few chains up the street lived a boy of my age, Donald Armstrong, who became my friend and has continued to be my buddy up to the present. My mother cooked, did laundry, and kept house for the three young men.

Cleon's family had been bakers in neighboring St. Simons. He was one of the brightest boys to have gone through the Alleyne School, the Government-supported high school in our Parish. His performance in the Senior Cambridge Examination just before the end of World War II was held out to the students in St. Andrew as the model to follow. Cleon was now teaching Latin, French, and English at the Modern High School on Roebuck Street in Bridgetown. He was popularly known as Lynch Jr., to distinguish him from Louis Lynch, the headmaster and founder of Modern High School. Elson, Cleon's brother, worked in the family bakery and Purpose, who had recently returned from England after serving in the Royal Air Force, was an engineer with Rediffusion, the local wired broadcasting system. Six years later, after I had moved to the Bahamas, Purpose came to Nassau to work, and we renewed our friendship.

There was no radio station in Barbados in 1949, nor throughout my high school years. Only a few people could afford to buy a radio in those days, and then they had to pay an annual license fee to the government – and had to be able to afford electricity to power the radio. Those who could afford a private radio set listened to stations in Trinidad and British Guiana. All the radios were shortwave, and I fondly recall my favorite overseas signals, from Quito, Ecuador; BBC, Voice of America, Radio Australia, and sometimes Radio Moscow. Shortwave radio broadcasts of boxing matches came in from American Armed Forces Radio. That and cricket were the hottest items for the ears during my early teens. To this day, I have a shortwave radio in my home and still fool around the meter bands, looking for interesting stations and programs with no special allegiance. I treat TV the same way, playing around multiple channels until I find a satisfier. I often discover some real gems.

5. LOUIS LYNCH

My dear mother sent me to Modern High School in 1950. Unlike other parents, however, she did not take me to make enrolment arrangements. I personally negotiated the terms of my entry into the school in January 1950 with Mr. Louis Lynch over the form in which I would be placed and what fees I would pay. When I think of it now, I am filled with wonder. My parents, mother especially, always trusted and respected my common sense and judgment. They stoked a self confidence in me that has remained unflappable throughout my adult life.

Established in 1944 with only two students, Modern High eclipsed all the others in numbers and exam-passing percentages, and by the time I entered in the second term of 1950, there were twelve forms, each with at least twenty students and an overall student population of approximately three hundred. By the time I wrote "O" Levels in April 1953, there were more than five hundred enrolled. By 1959, there were 1,700 students on roll.

Lynch, who was a remarkable educator, counselor, and later, friend, placed me in Entrance A, an upper Second Form. I later deduced that the A stream was the stream for the brighter students. I must have represented myself well, for even though I was entering in the second term, he still placed me in the more advanced stream among the second-year students, with the school year having started in September.

Barbados had always been a place where education was revered. In the early years, and up to the beginning of World War II, only a few boys went to high school, and very few girls ever did. But during the war, most parents began to clamor for formal education for all their children. Government high schools could not accommodate the influx, fees for non-scholarship winners were very high and entry requirements difficult, a typical market phenomenon. Here was a tremendous business opportunity, and by the end of the war, dozens of private schools had sprung up all over the island. These were soon winnowed down in Bridgetown to Green Lynch, the Barbados Academy, and the Modern High School. St. Winnifred's Girls was another private high School, but I remember it as catering only to white girls.

Louis Lynch attracted a core of very competent and committed teachers, only one of whom had a degree, and that was a B.A. in Classics from the local Codrington College. None of them had any formal teacher training. We were all learning together, I guess, teacher and student alike. Lynch was irrepressible. Every year he would go off to the United States and secure funds from well-wishers to buy some facility for the improvement of the school. Unfortunately, he was not able to establish a science lab until after I had finished high school, and so I did not get any science exposure. It would later show up as a deficiency that I would have to make up.

A model for all, Louis Lynch, my Latin teacher in Form Entrance A, was tough but fair. For three days a week we had a Latin class, and we had a twelve-word vocabulary to study and remember. If the words were verbs, we had to state their principal parts, and if they were nouns, we had to go through their declensions. The class was held just before our lunch break, and it was always held outdoors in the circular entrance to the school. Any student failing to answer a vocabulary question, usually the meaning of the word, had to stand in front of the school for several minutes while the student population wondered around enjoying their lunch hour. Underprepared students invariably got the message, and the following year we were all reading *Caesar's Gallic War* by Livius. Many of us got the foundation to tackle Virgil, Ovid, and Livy once we got to the upper forms.

Lynch would eventually head sports and civic bodies such as the Barbados Olympic Association, the Barbados Table Tennis Association, the Lions Club and the Barbados Mental Health Association. He would go on to win a seat in the House of Assembly as junior member for Bridgetown and actually became mayor of the city in 1962. In honor of his contributions to sports and education, the VIP stand at Barbados' National Stadium and a school were named after him.

My old principal had been an excellent track athlete while a student at Harrison College, and he would coach aspiring athletes from Modern, often driving to their homes early on Saturday mornings to take them to the Harrison field for preparation. In my day he developed three very competent sprinters, Vernon Skeete, Clement Harper and Harold Chandler. I was not a good athlete, but I did become a competent competitor in table tennis, and after growing six inches between age fourteen and fifteen, I was able to play basketball for my school. I only got to play in one match, however, and I will never forget that night at YMPC grounds when I made both my shots on a penalty against Harrison College.

Lynch developed the finest group of table tennis players on the island during the early 1950s, including young men like Dalton Guiler, the Gregoires, and the Millers. One of the Millers went on to become Barbados champion. I played against them every lunch hour but got knocked out in every first round.

All of us as young blacks looked up to Louis Lynch. We saw how he kept his shiny car parked in front of the school. The gardener kept it washed and highly polished inside and out, the white-wall tires gleaming. While other black men cut their hair in mod styles, Lynch always wore the subtlest fades, something his barber must have maintained on a weekly basis. He was always clean shaven, and he wore a suit and tie with the finest dress shirts every day. He had short arms and a large neck, so he had to wear armlets to make his shirt sleeves conform.

He wore English-cut tropical suits, sometimes made of linen. Without saying a word to any of his students, he demonstrated to us that no one in the world was better than we were. People who looked like us were the professionals, the judges, the teachers, the tradesmen, the policemen, the parsons, the butchers and bakers, the athletes of our island. There was no room in our thoughts for fear or insecurity, for in every facet of our island's endeavors open to universal entry, we were the best performers. Business and commerce would change when we became self-governing and learned to put together capital. In the meantime, the West Indies cricket team was the best in the world, and five of the eleven players were Barbadian. All we needed was for the rest of the world to discover the joys of flying fish and cou-cou.*

I went through the high school curriculum so fast that I hardly remember the characters, students and teachers with whom I interacted. I do remember that during my first year at Modern, my uncle Hugh, who had been in the Merchant Marines during World War II and had opened a grocery shop after the war, went back to sea on Harrison Liners. He loaned me his bicycle to ride to school. It was a pretty good hike between Fairfield Cross Road and Roebuck Street five days a week, but Donald and I had been doing it every school day so we were a happy duo when I got uncle Hugh's Hercules. Humbers and Raleighs and Rudges were the bikes of choice for the more sophisticated, but Donald and I rode that tough old working-class Hercules with glee for a year and a half. I confess that I was surprised

---

*Cou-cou, a cornmeal-and-okra meal, is of African origin and was a common meal for slaves brought to Barbados. It is the Barbadian national dish.

when uncle Hugh came home from sea and took back his bike. To my chagrin, he came into the schoolyard at lunch break and took it, sans bell, lights, and gears, just as we had received it, but with a new paint job – even with stripes. It was good training for me, for I expressed more anguish then than I would years later when the pawn shop repossessed our car.

Some of my early friends were Lionel Goddard, Garfield Manning, Timothy Chrichlow, George Small, and Vallon Wharton. I particularly remember Aileen Porte. Before entering high school, I had no exposure to girls except those in my family circle. I had attended an all-boys elementary school. I was surprised at the brilliance of Aileen though, and I had to work hard to match hers. She and I would alternate with first- and second-place finishes throughout that first year at Modern High. Without knowing it, Ms. Porte prepared me for my encounters with brilliant females, and the respect I would have to pay women during the remainder of my high school years, and for contact with such women for all the years thereafter. I must confess that I fell short and am still stuttering over my answer when a female interviewer, after I finished college, asked me how I would react to a female boss. I didn't get the job, but I got a good life lesson in the bargain.

George Small, Donald and I had great battles swimming and racing from the end of the rum refinery pier at Brandon's. God can be kind to children and fools, for we used to "hit off" from the end of this pier, which jutted out into the sea and where the water was deep enough for ships to load and was often blackened from spilled molasses. We would race each other to shore, without fear or concern for any shark or barracuda attracted by the conditions.

★★★

I got a double promotion every year at Modern High School, going from Entrance A in January 1950 to 3A, to 4A, then 5A – all "A" stream forms, eventually writing "O" Levels in April 1953, passing in all six subjects entered. That's three and one-third years. There may be others who have done that, but I have not heard of them. I did not have much time to develop friendships in the middle forms, but in Fifth Form, I made some lifelong friendships. The late Ermine Holmes, Eudene Arthur, Bert Thompson, and Grant Proverbs, as well as extant colleagues like Hal Thompson and Ken Waldron in Alberta, Canada; Monica Daniel in Orlando, and Harold Chandler in Maryland, all come to mind.

My teachers were all untrained. A most memorable one was Marcelle Williams, a very young woman in her twenties. She herself had only recently graduated from Modern High School and was maybe only six or seven years older than her third-form students. She taught English composition and literature, introducing us to Shakespeare and sharpening my skills. I fell in love with her.

The play in third form was *A Midsummer Night's Dream*, which we read without appreciating what we were reading. Every year we read a new Shakespeare play —some years two — never really being sure of the material's significance. Three years earlier, I had won the all-island essay competition for elementary school students, so I had developed a limited idea about writing.

Ms. Williams was the first teacher who took me into her home socially. She lived with her mother and sisters in Nelson Street, in the middle of Bridgetown, the capital. They had a well-appointed cottage, almost unnoticeably located in a little nook on a quiet part of the street. I never knew that such normal living existed in the middle of a busy city with its seedy hustlers, pimps, prostitutes, as well as the fresh- and fried-fish mongers. This was a baptism for a boy born and bred in deep rural Barbados, and recently ensconced in the Bridgetown suburbs. My grandmother, who wouldn't allow goombay (calypso) music in her house would feel justified over her efforts to keep me away from the corruptive influences. Of course, neither my grandmother nor I had any conception of the challenges in the ideas to which professors could introduce a lad.

Ms. Williams invited me to picnic with students from more senior forms, and we explored beaches that I had only heard of before. We held beach parties at Sam Lord's Castle, Crane Beach, Silver Sands, Cable & Wireless at Oistins, and Accra Beach. We had the occasional school dance and gradually improved our poise and social skills.

Then there was Mrs. Callendar, who taught me scripture in every form throughout my high school career. She was the least inspiring teacher I have ever had. She was a woman who never displayed enthusiasm about anything, not even about her husband, who taught classics in the higher forms and who was the only teacher at our school who had a degree. Mr. Callendar had graduated from Codrington College, a local adjunct of Durham University in England that was set up to train Anglican priests and classical scholars. He moved on before I got far enough in school to benefit from his teaching.

I must have learned a bit more than drawing maps of St. Paul's

Missionary Journeys, and the *Beatitudes and Woes* from Mrs. Callendar, because I did extremely well in scripture in my matriculation exams. I was told that I had gained the highest marks among that year's "O" Level class.

Our cousin, Cleon "Lynch Jr." was one of the high school teachers who had a significant impact on my development. He taught me Latin, French and English in the third and fourth forms, but he was a model for me long before high school. Cleon was the first in our family in Barbados to have finished high School, as far as can be determined anyway. There may have been others in the USA, since family members had emigrated to that country before 1900, but we are not aware of them.

Cleon graduated from the Alleyne School, the local government high school in St. Andrew, our home parish, and distinguished himself in the Senior Cambridge Exams with second-class honors. This was before the University of the West Indies was established, and university places were only available to winners of the Barbados Scholarship. Only Harrison College and to a lesser extent the Lodge School had the sixth form levels and the advanced teachers to prepare students, only boys at that time, for the Barbados Scholarship Exhibition Exams. Winners would go on to Oxford or Cambridge Universities in England, fully funded by the government. And so, Cleon became a teacher at the Modern High School, while he struggled to achieve an external bachelor's degree from an accredited British university.

He was a good and engaging teacher. He never wore a suit jacket, only white shirts and ties. I had the advantage of closely observing his study and preparation habits, since he was our next-door neighbor, and my mother looked after him and the other two young men living in the house. Two encounters with Lynch Jr. stand out in my memory. He once gave my form an "unseen piece of Latin" to translate for a test, and there was one key word that would unravel the mystery. I felt confident enough to go to Lynch Jr. and ask him what the word meant, and he not only told me, but he put the information up on the blackboard. The other encounter is more personal. My mother thought that if she got Cleon to give me private lessons, I would be greatly helped, and so she sent me to him. After two lessons he told her, "Leslyn, don't waste your money. Let the boy go play with his friends. He doesn't need any private lessons."

Mr. Ward, called "Moby Dick" behind his back, was another man who left a lasting impression, teaching me mathematics in form 4A.

He was small of stature, highly opinionated, but not offensive. He wore the best tailored suits of anyone that I can recall, always as neat as a pin from the top of his head to his highly polished oxfords. He had a penchant for tan tropical-weight suits. I was aware of the weight of fabrics, and of good tailoring from a very early age because my aunt's husband was a master tailor in our village, and he lived in my grandmother's extended home. Uncle Willie made suits for all the leaders far and wide, and I not only was aware of the cuts, but of the appropriateness of the colors and weights selected. This orientation was to come in handy later.

Moby Dick fancied himself a soccer player, and would sometimes take his jacket off, don a pair of soccer boots and get among the senior boys to demonstrate his skills. I believe that it was out on the field that he and Ethelbert Thompson, our head boy, got into it, and Ethelbert derogatively referred to Moby Dick's height. This led to the biggest crisis in my high school years: we were about to write our graduating exams; Ethelbert was arguably the brightest boy in school, maybe only behind Grant Proverbs. He was the model for the entire school, especially for us as prefects.

Ward was a good teacher and hard to replace, so the headmaster ordered a public flogging for Ethelbert. The options were six lashes with a leather strap administered by Lynch himself before the entire assembled school – or dismissal. Everyone, teacher and student alike, counted the lashes. The school remained hushed, like a village in mourning, for about a week. Ethelbert went on to teach with me at our high school the following year, and later earned top academic credentials overseas.

During my penultimate year in high school, Louis Lynch began bringing Barbados Scholars and other sixth form Exhibition Scholars from Harrison College to teach at Modern High School during their gap year. I had the benefit of being taught by and socializing with brilliant young men such as Henry Ford, who went on to be a leading minister of government, acting prime minister of Barbados, and an outstanding lawyer; Mickey Waldron, who became an outstanding surgeon and professor of medicine; Blues Trotman, a brilliant mathematician at Cambridge University and Nickey Sealy, with whom I would later reunite overseas. Nickey later became chief engineer and head of the Barbados Water Commission, and I got a chance to meet his wife. I recall passing her father Dr. Payne's home and dental clinic on Country Road off Roebuck Street on my way to and from the Modern, every school day. Later in life, when I was a bank manager in Jamaica, I got to meet three of Dr. Payne's sons, two of whom were PhDs; the other was a bank manager. Mr. Lynch also brought us Rudolph Hinkson, who later became an outstanding solicitor at the Barbados bar.

Louis Lynch also brought Cameron Tudor to us. He was a top student from the previous generation, a distinguished graduate of Oxford University, and the first student from the Caribbean to become president of the Oxford Union, that distinguished debating society. When Louis Lynch started a sixth form at Modern in 1953, I was one of the first students, and Cameron taught a course called British Constitution in a program called Modern Greats. It is worthy of note that my professor of Political Science 300, political theory, at the University of Alberta, Edmonton, in 1961 was Dr. Neville Linton, a Guyanese, who had been taught as a high schoolboy at Queen's Royal College in Guyana by none other than Cameron Tudor. Tudor and his sister, along with Errol Barrow, who in later years was often my guest in Jamaica, and Sleepy Smith, who hailed from my home parish of St. Andrew, and whom we had the pleasure of entertaining in my home in Jamaica, were among the founders of the Democratic Labor Party of Barbados. The Democratic Labor Party was the instrument used by these leaders, with Errol Barrow as prime minister, to gain independence for Barbados.

I truly believe that Lynch's motive for bringing these young luminaries among us was much greater than merely getting us to pass exams. He wanted to demonstrate to us that these specially selected young men were not any different than we were. They were mostly all coming from more privileged backgrounds, but we could catch up through exposure, and he would give us that exposure. Having these select of the establishment among us and observing their habits and comportment would improve our self-confidence and reinforce the desire for excellence that Modern High School was instilling in us. Such was the impact of Louis Lynch's life that upon his passing, the *Advocate News* made it their front-page headline.

Every Saturday morning throughout my high school years, I would leave the city and go home to the country. This became a tradition that I have been able to maintain for much of my life – at times in more pretentious ways than others, but always with the effect of recharging my batteries. Going home to Cane Garden and Fruitful Hill on weekends served many purposes: I was able to run around barefoot, climb our mango and guava trees, and eat more fruit than proper meals. I was able to play games with my mates in the country and maintain a relationship with boys and girls who were now on a different social path than I was. More importantly, I could continue to participate in the Boy Scouts movement and the Church Lads Brigade. The discipline and leadership knowledge that I gained in these two organizations have served me well throughout my entire life.

I also looked forward to the comforting joy of sleeping in my grandmother's bed, made in the colonial style, of mahogany topped with fringes. It stood high off the floor with its necessary footstool for mounting. The mattress was homemade of ticking and stuffed with khus khus grass, grown in our own pasture, cut and dried in our own yard. The smell was heavenly. Aunt Dru's was the most comfortable bed that I ever slept on until I became a manager and my wife established our home some sixteen years later – and believe me, I've slept on some Hobson's Choices along the way. Her bed remains the memorable one.

★★★

I went back to Cane Garden from Bridgetown every weekend, and that was to bring back food for my mother, who had very little money. Regardless, she had to feed three of us in the city every week, in an environment where she had to buy everything and there was no space to plant or rear anything. My father, on the other hand, made much more in the country from his various endeavors, and he grew all the food that any family needed, so after loading me up on Sunday evenings, Daddy would personally take me to the last bus leaving Cane Garden for the capital.

The conductor always helped me find places to store my crocus bags and baskets. I would be packed to the gills with potatoes, yams, breadfruit, cassava, peas, beans, carrots, beets, sugar cane, mangoes, green and ripe bananas, fresh cashews, various fruits in season, paw paws, coconuts, eggs wrapped and packed protectively, and often, a live fowl. I would have enough food to feed our family for more than a week and to share with any needy person who came by. If you think that boarding the bus was a challenge, you would sympathize with me when I had to gather up all those packages when it was time to get off at Eagle Hall. Sometimes the chicken would relieve itself in the basket, adding to my agony. Of course, my mother and sister had to come meet me at the bus stop to help get our bounty home. All of this was done without the benefit of telephone calls or other means of communication, but somehow I was always met when I arrived in the city.

6. MY BARBADOS, WRONG OR RIGHT

The social structure of Barbados was just beginning to change when I entered high school in 1950. Grantley Adam's efforts as leader of the Barbados Labor Party were becoming more aggressive and beginning to effect meaningful change in the island.

From a very early age, I was an observer of the political and social structure of my island home. I grew up attending St. Savior's Anglican Church and had a front-row seat to the process of governance and social structure of the island, and the parish of St. Andrew in particular. Throughout my entire time at elementary school, the parish was run by the vestry of the Anglican church. Only male landowners could be elected to the vestry, which was responsible not only for the ecclesiastical boundaries of the parish but the political boundaries as well.

Vestrymen held immense local power, but it was the priest who was all-powerful. He was usually white, male and English, controlling all hiring on the government's behalf through his grip on the local vestry. No meaningful contracts could be won by anyone without the consent and knowledge of the local priest. I have learned along the way that up to 1947 or thereabouts, there was only one black priest who was a rector in the Anglican church in Barbados. The power of the Anglican church was even more entrenched than I have thus far indicated, for the bishop was one of the three white men who sat on the executive council and ran the affairs of the colony of Barbados, directly reporting to the British cabinet through the colonial secretary's office.

The Anglican church was the Establishment Church, and there was no separation of church and state. There was only one Roman Catholic church on the island in my youth, and a special dispensation must have been given for its establishment. There were also one or two Methodist and Moravian churches. Pentecostals and other fundamentalist groups appeared late in World War II as part of the arrangements that the British made with the Americans under the Lend-Lease programs.

During these early days and even after 1950, some churchgoers paid for special pews and had their names affixed to them, and no unauthorized person would go sit in a bought pew. These chosen took communion first, and from their positions of general privilege and prominence in the island, it was generally felt that they would have first shot at entry into heaven with reserved seats.

Blacks were not excluded from these privileged ranks. For example, one of my great uncles, Joe Foster, was a vestry member in St. Andrew during my boyhood and maintained a private pew up to his death. I would be remiss if I failed to mention that Uncle Joe was a fair-skinned black man. The racial intricacies of the period will keep featuring prominently.

There was almost no social activity between the two key racial types on the island during my boyhood. The whites were the managers and bookkeepers on the sugar plantations, and the blacks were the workers on the plantations. The whites rode horses and the blacks walked. In the city, whites were the bank managers and the department store managers, and a few light-skinned blacks got jobs as clerks. Most of the clergy were white. All skilled tradesmen were black, and they worked for both races. All teachers were black, as were most lawyers, magistrates, civil servants (heads of departments were Englishmen), policemen (except gazetted ranks), nurses – not doctors – fishermen, bus drivers, and butchers. Except for a few black men who owned a few acres of land, small grocery stores and rum shops, all capital was owned by whites, and except for one or two black families, only whites had access to loans from banks.

In sports, there was open and active competition between blacks and whites, but the structure of the club system said a lot about Barbados in general. There were white clubs and black clubs all playing cricket, football, rugby and table tennis in the same leagues – but not on the same club teams. Wonders Cricket Club was white, and so was Pickwick, Carlton, and YMPC. Empire Cricket Club was for blacks, as was Everton, Spartan, and Police Cricket Club. The island was so comfortable with its social distinctions that each one of the clubs mentioned, white and black, had its quietly understood and accepted membership criteria.

At graduation, boys who played for high school teams went to the club that matched their social status. There was absolutely no rancor or animosity, just fierce competition. Cups changed hands with regularity at the end of each season, and the honor of being selected for the West Indies cricket team, one of the best teams in the world, typically went to the best players. However, it was not until the mid-1960s that the West Indies Cricket Board of Control selected a black man to be team captain. Sir Frank Worrell had been a great cricketer and budding leader since his high school days at Combermere, but he was continually overlooked for the captaincy of the West Indies test team for over fifteen years while many less talented white and near-white players were given the honor.

Our system could rightly be referred to as voluntary apartheid. In Barbados politics, 1944 was a red-letter year, the first time that the general public's interest was ever truly captured by national polls. The general elections that year allowed that all men over twenty-one would have the right to elect members of the House of Assembly. For his part, my father took me to every political meeting he attended in our parish. I was only eight years old, but I remember every minute of my experience, especially those meetings that took place at the major corner in Cane Garden.

Grantley Adams was our great champion. He carried the torch for the black masses against the hegemony of the plantocracy and their alliance with the colonial office in England. Adams was one of those brilliant young men that the colonial educational system had a knack for identifying and educating towards excellence and future leadership, often after a term of imprisonment. Despite the deprivations that the British colonial system wreaked on the masses, it somehow managed to select the very brightest among us, prepare them for Oxford or Cambridge University in England, and allow them to prepare themselves for whatever careers they chose. The color or race of the celebrated student mattered not in those days, but the gender did – boys only.

As the son of one of the leading primary school headmasters on the island, Adams was born and bred for the role. He was specially tutored by his father at St. Giles Boys School and entered Harrison College on scholarship. He won the Barbados Scholarship in 1918 and entered Oxford University in 1919. Adams spent six years studying in England and returned to Barbados in 1925 with a bachelor's degree from Oxford and a law degree from the Inns of Court in London. He quickly built up a thriving law practice and held briefs and retainers for many local businesses and plantation owners. Adams quickly recognized what many later blacks took a long time to recognize, in that they may be successful in their isolated status as professionals, but they were not respected in their country, because their people had no true power and were not respected. To self-actualize, men like Adams would have to instill in their people a sense of self-worth and national identity, so that they could be recognized as a force to be reckoned with politically.

Along with other Barbadians of like mind and experience, Adams became one of the founders of the Barbados Progressive League. He had become a Fabian Socialist in England during his university days, and he started the process of educating the public about citizens' rights, especially their right to fight for the vote and select those who would govern them. In less than ten years, Adams lost all his major briefs, and it was only through the generosity of one rich supporter that he was able to keep his home.

In 1938, labor unrest exploded throughout the West Indian islands. As there had been in Jamaica and other places, there was a major riot in Barbados, and the Barbados Progressive League became the Barbados Labor Party with Grantley Adams as leader. Adams, like labor leader Bustamante in Jamaica, now had a firm platform to stand on and a cause to champion. For these two men, workers must advance from simply being union members to being full participants in the political process through Universal Adult Suffrage. By 1944, the people of Barbados had achieved the right of adult males to vote, without the earlier property restrictions, and this is where my earliest personal exposure to political processes began. This is a very early awakening for an eight-year-old.

I believe that the Barbados Labor Party won seven seats out of a possible twenty-four in the House of Assembly during the 1944 elections – just enough to get noticed. I also recall that, ironically, many black voters backed the white managers and plantation owners, the same group that was hitherto regarded by many as the oppressor.

By 1948, women had won the right to vote. The Barbados Labor Party under the leadership of Grantley Adams won the most seats, and he was the one asked to form a government, albeit with limited ministerial powers. The British governor of the island was still in charge as head of the executive council, on which the colonial secretary and the Anglican bishop served. Adams and three of his Labor Party members were given seats on the legislative council, whose job it was to propose legislation to the executive council for passage into law, but only if the council saw fit. This experiment of continuing the British Raj, with elementary representative government, with Adams as premier and limited cabinet responsibilities, went on for my entire time in high school and was still in force when I left Barbados in April 1955.

7. PORGY'S [P]LUCK

Islandwide, my high school graduating class of 1953 was the largest-ever group of young people to graduate from the high school system in Barbados – all with five or more subjects at the GCE "O" Level. We were the product of our parents' exertions at the end of World War II, when the middle-class sense of conspicuous consumption, homeownership and political freedom overtook the entire western world. Before and during the Second World War, only children of richer parents, those with regular and predictable income, or the super-achieving students, went to high school in Barbados. Secondary education was not free, but after the war, most parents made the effort.

The society in general, particularly the government, made no plans or provisions for assimilating the influx of new high school graduates into the workforce. This is not surprising, considering that Barbados was under colonial rule at that time, and the essence of colonial policy was to extract primary products as cheaply as possible for export to the mother country for manufacture and re-export to the colonies and other world markets. The welfare and improvement of job opportunities for local populations were not high priorities for the Raj.

And so they dumped us on this little rum- and sugar-producing island with nothing to do. Very few of us thought of going to a university to continue our studies, and our only university was 2000 miles away in Jamaica, albeit established just five years before amidst circumstances of questionable viability. Additionally, university entrance in our system was based on Oxford and Cambridge Advanced Level certificates, and we were all graduating mostly with Ordinary Level certificates. Most of us, including myself, had never given any thought to what we wanted to do career-wise, and we had never heard of a career counselor, much less seen one. We were a neglected species thrust upon society and left to find our way, male and female alike.

I had by this time turned seventeen. Under the tutorship of Cameron Tudor who later became Barbados minister for foreign affairs and Henry Ford who read British Constitution with us before he went off to Oxford on a Barbados Scholarship – later becoming Attorney General and a leader of the Barbados Labor Party – we set out on a path to higher achievement. This was short-lived, for by Christmas 1953, Modern High School had become a victim of its success and had grown enormously in the lower forms. Louis Lynch turned my entire class population into teaching staff.

While I was happy to be a teacher, looked up to as an intellect by the student body and called "Mr. Weekes" by all and sundry at seventeen years of age, I was sufficiently concerned about my inadequacy to tell Principal Lynch that I honestly did not know my subjects well enough to teach them. He informed me that I did not have a major problem, for "the best way to learn a subject is to teach it". I therefore set out to learn and teach, and so I taught Latin, French, and English Language and Composition in the lower forms for four terms. My remuneration was the princely sum of thirty Barbadian dollars per month, the equivalent of fifteen dollars in United States currency.

As would be my lot for all my life, my colleagues selected me to make representation to the Principal on their behalf, and this time, it was about the paucity of our salaries. Lynch treated me like an adult although I was not yet eighteen at this point, and we talked for about twenty minutes before he brought up the subject of my visit.

"I think that we need to be paid more, sir." His answer threw me completely off guard.

"Salary, Mr. Weekes?" he responded, incredulous. "What are you talking about? I am not paying you a salary. I am giving you a stipend while you prepare for and make yourselves aware of the benefits of higher education!"

When I reported back to my colleagues, we all had a good laugh, but in less than one year after that, we were all out of Barbados trying to find our way to advanced education and careers. In the interim, I had bought my first watch, a beautiful gold Bulova, and my first new bicycle, a Humber.

In September 1954, I got a call to fill a temporary clerical appointment in the Barbados Civil Service. I resigned my position as a teacher at Modern High School and reported for duty, assigned to the department of education located at the Garrison Savannah in the area since occupied by the Hilton Hotel. My supervisor was Horace King, a spin bowler for Empire Cricket Club and Barbados. My major recollection of this assignment is that I had to travel through the northern parishes by car with a police escort to pay the teachers in the government elementary schools. I had a briefcase full of cash, and the policeman carried an empty rifle. Our first stop was St. James, then St. Peter and St. Lucy in the North, then around the bend to my home parish of St. Andrew, finishing at Holy Innocent's Elementary in Welchman Hall, St. Thomas. I can still remember the sense of accomplishment and elation I felt when I delivered the pay envelopes to the teachers at St. Savior's, my old elementary boys' school, and the institution that first excited my appetite for learning. I'd only been gone for five years, but already it seemed like a lifetime.

After a couple of months, I was transferred to the Registrar's Office to work as a scribe. My job was to write up documents from the official records as requested by the public, then take them to the registrar for his signature. I mostly wrote up birth certificates, but sometimes there would be wills and testaments, land deeds, copies of trusts and other recorded items.

Two striking things remain etched in my mind from those three months. The first has to do with Garfield, now Sir Garfield Sobers, but at the time he was just one of so many of us regular boys, knocking about Bridgetown and looking for a way up and out. Gary was called up to play for the West Indies cricket team in what would be his first test match. The MCC (Marylebone Cricket Club) of England, which keeps the official records for test cricket, wanted Sobers' birth certificate, and Mr. Williams, the father of Boogle Williams, another Barbados cricketer, asked me to prepare the document. I have no doubt that the Sobers certificate in my handwriting is still the one in the official records at the MCC.

The second significant event emanating from my stint at the Registrar's Office is far more important. One day after presenting a document to Williams, the chief clerk, he asked me to stay for a minute or two. He then said "Weekes! What are your plans for your future? What do you intend to do with yourself?" I was taken aback. On the one hand, I had given no thought to what I wanted to do. On the other, none of my teachers – and certainly no-one in my family – had ever asked me that question so pointedly. My dear mother always preached to me that education was my way up and out of the cycle of underachievement, but she never asked me to identify a career. Maybe she wanted to shield me from frustration, or maybe she just wanted me to be led by the Spirit. In any case, I had no answer for the man.

I was struck by the fact that he took such an interest in me, considering the social and economic structure of the island at that time. Blacks and whites had very little social intercourse, and each group seemed to exist quite comfortably in its own milieu, as I have alluded in an earlier context. Williams was of that straddling group of Barbadians who were white enough not to be treated as black, yet black enough not to be treated as fully white. Williams' group would be the first out of the chute. They got the better jobs at the earliest stages of our history, and many Barbadian black families who I knew in my youth typically had members like Mr. Williams who had been similarly favored. In my time, not many of the privileged imparted advice to children of the future.

Shortly after my exchange with Mr. Williams, I had to take a document to Registrar Randy Douglas himself. After signing the document, Douglas said to me:

"Young man," he said, "you need to go away to university and study."

"I have no funds for that," I replied helplessly.

"You have to find a way," he shot back.

When I got to Jamaica fifteen years later, one of the law firms with which I did a lot of business was a firm that Sir Randolph Douglas had just left to return to Barbados as Chief Justice. I regret that I never got a chance to thank either man for his inspiration. I have, however, met one of Williams' sons, himself a former Chief Justice of Barbados, and was able to tell him of my respect for his father and my gratitude for his interest in me.

8. BAHAMIAN ODYSSEY

In March of 1955, I was laid off by the Barbados civil service. Then one day in early April, while hanging out with several other unemployed and undirected young men, something momentous happened. We were mostly all Modern High School graduates, with Vernon Skeets, our host, being the eldest of the group. He was our basketball team captain and we gathered at his yard on Westbury Road in Bridgetown. Vernon's girlfriend, Velcie Critchlow, was visiting. She was a very mature young lady who had graduated a year before most of us and we all held her in very high regard. For reasons unknown to me, she had clipped an advertisement out of the *Barbados Advocate*, our leading local newspaper, and slipped it into my shirt pocket.

When I left Vernon Skeets's, I rode my bicycle straight to Cave Hill, where I'd been staying at my uncle Hugh's home. This new state of affairs was brought about because I'd had to leave my mother's house since her live-in gentleman friend and I were not taking tea. I had grown accustomed to being the only man in the house for many years but was now not a strong enough bull to control the pen, so according to natural law, I had to move on. Mom was only thirty-six years old at this time and had devoted her life to seeing me finish high school and bringing me to young manhood. I guess it was fitting that we should both get on with our lives. Mom cooked and washed and ironed for me just as before, and I would go by at mealtime, eat, take my clean laundry and leave before the big bull got home.

In the evening when uncle Hugh returned to his house, I remembered the clipping that Velcie had slipped into my shirt pocket. I took it out and learned that the assistant commissioner of police for the Bahamas was in Barbados to recruit twenty-one young men for their colonial police force. Interested young men were required to appear in person in two days at 9:00 a.m. at District A Police Station. Among the requirements was that applicants had to be twenty-one years of age. When Uncle Hugh asked me what I was reading, I told him and protested that I was only 18 years old, three years short of the requirement. He advised me to go and apply anyway.

"You go and stand in that line," Uncle Hugh had commanded; "the officer will not be able to go by without selecting you." On the morning of selection, I rose early, took my cold-water bath, got dressed in my blue blazer, gray flannel slacks, white shirt and Modern High School colors – my black and white striped tie – with black

Oxfords shining so you could comb your hair in their brilliance. I rode my Humber the two miles to District A Police Station, not forgetting to sport my gold Bulova wristwatch, and joined the line with a yard full of other fine young men, the pride of Barbados' youth.

It was a very simple procedure: we were placed in rows. I was early, so I was placed in what became the front row. A local police inspector introduced Major Spencer-Harty of the Royal Bahamas Police Force, and they proceeded down the rows. When the entourage was just two men away from me, I came to attention with my eyes fixed straight ahead. I was tall and slim and had gone through Cub Scouts, Boy Scouts and the Church Lads Brigade, so I knew how to command attention with my posture.

Uncle Hugh was right. The officer could not go by without selecting me. I was the second man picked. I was not at ease, however. I was sure that I would be rejected when I disclosed that I was only eighteen. In any case, I was resolved not to lie at any stage of the operation. At the next stage, I had to give vital details like age, address, education and so on. They kept moving me along the process, and by the time I got to the medical exam, Dr. Cato claimed that I had fallen arches and he would be failing me. Dejected, I went to see my old high school Principal Louis Lynch. He listened to what had happened, then got on the phone right away.

"Cato!" he shouted into the receiver. "One of my boys was selected to go to the Bahamas police, and he says you turned him down, claiming that he has fallen arches." I could not hear Dr. Cato's reply, but Lynch's next statement said everything.

"Cato, man, Irvine Weekes is one of the brightest students to come through my hands. I don't expect him to be walking a beat long enough for flat feet to be a problem, and you should not either."

He held the receiver so that I could hear the doctor.

"Tell Weekes to come back and see me to pick up his passing paperwork," came the reply.

I rode from Roebuck Street to Government Hill at bird speed, picked up my documents from Dr. Cato's office and was down at the Main Guard in Bridgetown that afternoon to apply for a passport. This time, I was sure that I would be cut because there was no way that my age could be mistaken or overlooked now since it was going to be placed in an official Barbados document. I was not even tempted to lie, because my baptismal certificate was there in evidence. In those colonial days, baptismal certificates were more widely accepted as official documents than birth certificates, for the priests were more readily trusted than the local police diary duty officers. I thought I was cooked but received my passport that day anyway. Within twenty-four hours, I was aboard the *Jenkins Roberts*, a slow rum-carrying cargo vessel bound for Nassau on New Providence Island, the capital of the Bahamas. With me were twenty other young Barbadian men.

★★★

My father came to see me off. My mother did not. I only learned later that it was a tradition in my mother's family never to say goodbye. I surmise that it was a carryover from the painful days of farewell during slavery. I had the princely sum of five Barbados dollars in my pocket, and a valise so light that I could run with it for a mile without being exhausted.

I was leaving my home like a true Christian heading off into the unknown without fear or plan, knowing that he was going to enter the Promised Land and that his God would look after him. I was not thinking of God though; I wasn't thinking at all. I was euphoric, for even though I had given no thought to what I wanted to become, or what I would do in life, I instinctively knew that I would find my way.

The scene at the careenage was chaotic and somber at the same time. In those days, the boats with small draughts and the schooners that plied the islands were able to come into the inner harbor and berth right alongside Harbor Street in the very heart of Bridgetown. The traffic comprised pedestrian, motor and animal-drawn varieties including bicycles moving up and down beside the boats and yachts, and people on shore would often reach out and touch boatmen that they knew. As always, whenever there was an occasion like young men leaving to improve their lot, folks from all over would gather to celebrate.

There were young women and mothers crying, parents laughing and crying, and friends in a party mood. I had no celebrants or mourners, no girlfriends or colleagues to see me off, just an unemotional father who knew that there was enough in me to be trusted with my own future.

We left Barbados in the late afternoon and headed northwest for the 2000-mile voyage to Nassau. I do not believe that too many of us knew that we would be at sea for ten days. The *Jenkins Roberts* was only capable of about seven to eight and a half or so knots (8-10 miles an hour) covering between 190-200 miles per day. She was carrying a cargo of rum to Nassau, a regular run for the vessel. Owned by a well-known Barbadian and later politician, Captain Fergusson, the vessel was skippered by a young Barbadian, Cheeseman, who had recently obtained his master's ticket. She was old but steady, and for the ten days that we were on board, those old slow-moving diesel engines never missed a beat, maintaining a low growl hour after hour. This was annoying at first, but reassuring after two or three days and nights at sea.

The crew was very small. Other than the captain, who looked no older than I was, there was Massias, the chief engineer, and a boatswain who served as cook and general dogsbody. I'd had the experience of being in close contact with large numbers of strange boys before, but I had no preparation for being stuck in close quarters with these twenty young men for ten full days, with no avenue for escape, personal pleasures or simple reverie. The bunks were all below deck, but my first inspection turned me off, so I took my nightly rest on deck lying on a groundsheet, counting the stars and listening to the diesel engines.

My companions, who were all older than I was – one or two of them were about thirty years old, and most were between twenty-one and twenty-six – hailed from all sections of the island. There were men from Bridgetown, like Doc Strachan, Lloyd Headley, Milan Gittings, Gussie Bolden, Braithwaite, Maxwell, Babb and Codrington; men from St. James and the northern parishes such as Emerson Thompson and Goodridge, St. Elmo Blackett, and Merville Bradshaw from St. Andrew; Carrington from St. Joseph; Ken Brooks from St. John; Earl Alleyne, Keith Mason and Thompson from St. Phillip; Victor Callendar, Summer Bannister and Ennis from Christ Church, and me, the St. Andrew boy living in the city of Bridgetown. Most of us had finished high school and all of us had high school training. Most feared God and a few were decidedly ungodly. Some of us were disciplined and of good manners, but some did not give a darn about God or man.

I was completely blown away when I heard young colleagues raging at the seas when the weather got bad, imploring God to take the old boat down and take us all, not because we were in imminent or especial danger, but just out of pure worthlessness. I knew that I had to grow up fast, for I was but a choir boy amongst more than a few street boys and thugs. Of course, there were fine mature young men among us, like Goodridge who read his Bible constantly, Emerson Thompson, who was more mature and balanced, and Ken Brooks, a peach of a guy who never seemed perturbed by the behavior of the misanthropes.

As we traveled northwest, we stayed on the inside route and remained in the Caribbean sea for the entire trip. The first islands we passed were St. Vincent and St. Lucia. We caught a dolphin fish that day and the cook made a delicious meal of it with rice. We went to town on that meal, those of us who were not under the weather and could still eat. Barbadians love dolphin fish, especially the head steamed with vegetables, spices and plain rice. There was not a scrap of that fish left.

Up around Martinique, Dominica and Guadeloupe we caught a shark. Barbadians love shark meat too, but most of us never see a shark's head, for Barbadian fishermen always remove the head before they make for shore. It's not a pretty thing. Steamed shark and mashed potatoes make a delicious meal, however, especially with hot pepper sauce, mustard, turmeric and limes. Better still if the peppers are Scotch bonnet, with one or two bird peppers ground up and added for more fire. The memory alone makes the top of my head sweat.

The trip continued uneventfully as we settled in and accommodated ourselves to each other as we sailed past St. Kitts, noting St. Martin and Saba in the distance. We felt a change in temperature as we went through the Mona Passage between Puerto Rico and the Dominican Republic. By this time, we had broken the back of our journey and had eaten our main meals mostly from the sea. We had caught dolphin, shark, barracuda, swordfish; with a little lard oil, flour, cornmeal and rice from the boat's stores, we were generally well fed. The cook and small crew had to do very little.

One early morning after ten days at sea, we arrived in Nassau Harbor. It was the end of April 1955 – and it was cold. No one told us that it got cold in the Bahamas. Not that it would have mattered; there was one lonesome policeman dressed in night-duty winter blues on the docks. He turned out to be a Barbadian named Worrell who was recruited from home like we were, back in 1953. He went to the barracks and reported that we had landed and a truck had been dispatched to pick us up. There was no customs, no immigration, no entry protocol. Her Majesty's own had entered Her Majesty's extended kingdom.

***

The Royal Bahamas Police was ostensibly a civil force but was much more than that in 1955, only ten years after the end of World War II. The only piece of the old empire that had been shed to date was India in 1947. To the extent that she could, Britain was hell-bent on keeping the empire intact. Therefore, in colonies where there was no military, the police had to be trained for military enforcement. Such was the case in the Bahamas. Our program went even further, encompassing fire brigade training and responsibility.

Except for married men and a few single men specially exempted, all policemen had to live in barracks at headquarters on East Street. There were no females in the Bahamas police when I enlisted. Headquarters also housed the offices of the commissioner of police, the deputy commissioner, three senior superintendents, one white Bahamian superintendent, three inspectors, and the sole fire station on the island. There was only one black inspector and one black superintendent of police. All the other officers were white Englishmen.

The barracks comprised a self-contained garrison at the highest point of East Street, which ran south from the harbor. The street turned downhill to an area appropriately known as Over The Hill. North of the barracks, all the way down to Bay Street and the Nassau harbor lived the more successful Bahamians, mostly white or of mixed race, with Bay Street as the major business, shopping and professional area. South of the barracks in the Over The Hill area lived the poor and lower-middle-class blacks amongst their nightclubs, cheap hotels, grocery stores, barbershops, beauty parlors, rum shops, churches, theaters, general trades, and undertakers. Along the eastern side of the Over The Hill area ran a wall separating the poorer economic area from the more successful area along Collins Avenue.

All the officers except the one black man had homes on the barracks compound. In addition, there was a large parade square where recruits like me learned to drill. Here, guards of honor were prepared for special events like the Queen's Birthday parade or the opening of the Assize Courts. There was a manicured field where we had morning exercises, a garage area for fire trucks and police vehicles, a firing range where we had weapons training, and a quartermaster building where stores like uniforms, boots, weapons and ammunition were kept.

The quartermaster in my time was a little Scotsman with the rank of inspector. He was generally a fair and honest man, but he was very noticeably sensitive in his interaction with the Barbadians in the new contingent. I guess he recognized that we knew that he was a lance sergeant from some British outpost, and my batch of recruits were better educated than he was. Other things being equal, we would probably reach higher levels of achievement than he did.

The barracks building where we would live was a long, rectangular three-story building. There were sleeping quarters on all floors, and at one end were showers and toilets on the upper floors. Below was the galley and dining room, and on the other end of the ground floor was the classroom.

Since it was breakfast time when we got to the barracks on this first morning, all of our little suitcases were placed in one corner on the first floor while we were treated to the morning meal. We were in for culture shock. First, Barbadians are not great breakfast people. Our big meal was normally served between 11:00 a.m. and noon. Secondly, none of us was accustomed to Bahamian cooking. Thirdly, Johnny Saunders, the kitchen contractor, seemed to know very little about cooking food, from Bahamian, Barbadian, or any other culture.

Breakfast on that first morning was grits and boiled fish. None of us had ever heard of grits, and Bajan people never boiled fish, certainly not the kind that bled when cooked. We steamed our fish in one form and fry it in another. When the breakfast came, there was this mess of white ground corn on a plate with fish swimming in a watery grave.

A harmonious groan escaped us with one accord, and then one brave soul stuck a fork into his fish. The unfortunate creature bled. This poor recruit raised his displeasure to a shout of terror, leading to general pandemonium with bloody fish, both true and imagined, turning up all over the dining room. A mini-state of emergency was declared by Corporal Johnson, our appointed physical trainer and drill instructor. He not only mollified us but saved a frightened Johnny Saunders both from being mauled and losing his food contract.

Saunders made every conceivable promise of future good meals, even to the point of making cou-cou. Why would anyone take good cornmeal and turn it into inedible mush when a few okras and boiling water added skillfully to the mix, cooked slowly and lovingly and turned with a wooden cou-cou paddle, could produce an epicurean treat? And how could a cook not know how to steam beautiful Bahamian grouper? It's the easiest thing in the world: a little water, a dab of butter, salt, black pepper, scotch bonnet pepper, thyme, chives, onion, a grouper properly cleaned with limes, all placed in a covered saucepan and steamed or sautéed until ready, truly ready. And to think that we had to endure six months of this. Little did we know then that this insipid food would be the least of our concerns. The mental and physical challenges took over our minds, the competition intensified among us, and as we learned our strengths and the capabilities of our colleagues, Johnny Saunders and his unappetizing meals were not even noticeable. One of us even earned the nickname "Heavy Grits", an allusion to his penchant for asking the server to go heavy on that alien food.

Barracks living turned out to be like living in a glasshouse. All the recruits went into semi-shock when they saw the rows of beds set out in enormous dorms, with no curtains, no individual cupboards or closets, and in our case in the tropics, no doors to lock. We must have had a locker someplace, but I can't recall now where we stored our few belongings. Additionally, since the beds all looked alike, there must have been some built-in homing device that led us to our bunks during the early weeks. Since privacy is non-existent in barracks you learn to complete your movements quickly, especially in the showers. In our case, the toilets and showers were doorless, as was the entrance. There were benches to stand on for drying one's body and probably mirrors for shaving, a provision that I had no concern over since I had not yet begun to shave.

We noticed that the older policemen moved around the showers with naked and immodest ease, I suppose as part of our unofficial initiation into the world of natural living. I never did shed my inhibitions entirely but had no choice but to perform my ablutions under the prevailing conditions, never really getting accustomed to the setup. I did, however, learn to shower, shave, shit, brush my teeth, clothes and shoes, get fully dressed in the necessary outfit, and be off to my assignment in less than thirty minutes. It's a habit that I have followed conscientiously every day since entering the Royal Bahamas Police Force.

That first morning in barracks, we were escorted to the quartermaster's stores and issued with black military boots, blue physical training shorts, gym shoes, fatigue trousers, blue uniform trousers with a large red stripe down the outer sides, two casual tropical uniform shirts, a whistle and lanyard, a uniform cap with a Bahamas police insignia and a rifle without ammunition. We also met Inspector Caytes, our Quartermaster. Caytes had been a member of the Royal

British Marines, and it was he who put the British Marine stamp on our squad by changing the old drill movements to suit his preferences. For example, the normal way of making a turn was to raise the trailing leg and bring it to the ground sharply, the army way. For Caytes, to complete a turn, you did not raise the trailing leg, but rather brought it home parallel to the ground, a couple of inches high, and finished with a British marine click of the heels, not an army crack on the ground. Sounds crazy, I know, especially to former cadets or Boys' Brigadiers, but extremely smart when done by a coordinated guard of honor of fifty or more men wearing dress uniform.

Our next assignment was to meet our academic instructor, Inspector Alleyne, under whose tutelage we would spend six months of class time. Alleyne was a retired member of the British colonial police. He was the perfect example of the well-trained administrator or technical expert that the British liked to select and train in their colonial exploits, for the further protection of their interests in the colonies, as British leadership manpower became thin after World War II.

Alleyne was a Guyanese or a man from "B.G." as we called that country at the time. His parents were from Barbados, and he encouraged us to live up to the Barbadian reputation of scholarship, enquiry and fair play. By this time, two Bahamian recruits had joined us, and under the tutelage of Mr. Alleyne and Corporal Edney Johnson, our P.T. and daily drill instructor, those two young men, Bullard from Cat Island and Watkins from Long Island, were holding their own with twenty-one Barbadians and sometimes even kicking our butts. They could say "not for shite", or "cor, blimey" in context as readily as any of our bad boys could, but none of us Bajans ever got the hang of turning our "v's" into "w's" in the way that was natural to Bahamians.

Inspector Alleyne taught us courses in police duties and responsibilities, English common law and Bahamian practice, criminal law, powers of arrest, methods of observation, civil policing and military policing, psychology, report writing, maintenance of a police station diary, rules of evidence, British court practice, and Her Majesty's court structure. Almost every day since I graduated from Inspector Alleyne's class in November 1955, I have found some useful tenet learned from his teaching that guides my thinking.

As recruits, our days began with "Reveille" at 6.00 am. When that bugle blew, there was a mad dash for the bathroom, for every man had to be on the physical training grounds by 6.15 a.m., dressed in white tee-shirt, blue running shorts, and standing in gym or tennis shoes. After fifteen minutes of calisthenics, topped off with five sets of ten pushups – more if you could manage it – we would go for a twenty-minute run to one of several beaches, swim for ten minutes, and run back to barracks, always as a squad in strict formation. During these runs, we would encourage and motivate our colleagues if they showed weaknesses, for Corporal Edney Johnson always seemed to be looking for opportunities to berate and belittle the weak. The problem was greatest on Monday mornings, for those who liked to exercise the least loved partying the most, and Saturday and Sunday nights were party nights. We had to be in barracks by 10:00 pm, so a lot of doubling up on drinks took place. Fate is a joker, for years later I learned that our weakest recruit at P.T. – and not great on the Parade Square or academically either – went on to become commissioner of police in the Bahamas.

From 7:25 a.m., we did all our ablutions, had breakfast, shined our boots and belts, cleaned our brass, pressed the uniform shirts if necessary, brushed our caps and pants and appeared promptly on the parade square at 8:45 a.m. for inspection. Failure to pass inspection resulted in extra pushups the next morning. I never had to go through the exercise of pressing my uniform trousers during the week after ironing on Sundays, because every weeknight, I placed my uniform trousers under the mattress, creases in line, and slept on them. Trousers were properly tailored in those days and so all the seams were already properly aligned and easily kept that way.

Our classes were of one-hour duration with fifteen-minute breaks. We had two classroom lectures in the forenoon and military drills between sessions. Lunch was from noon until 2:00 p.m. Lectures in the classroom went from 2:00 p.m. until 3:00 p.m. and weapons training took place for an hour from 3:00 p.m. until 4:00 p.m. at day's end, Monday to Friday for six months without variation. One could leave barracks any time after 4:00 pm, but you had to study and rest, and be back in barracks before lights-out at 10.00 p.m. Violations were met with fines. It was not a joking business; we lived in a military compound. There was a sentry at the barracks gate, and the corporal in charge recorded every violation, which later went up the ranks for action.

Despite the toughness of the training, there are a few things that I fondly remember. There was only one submachine gun available to us for training, a Bren gun of World War II vintage. I got so familiar with that weapon that I was able to strip and reassemble it blindfolded in less than the time allotted. Another memory is that of the speed that we could get into fire-fighting gear and mount the fire truck when an alarm was raised. The best memory of my training, though, was preparation for a guard of honor.

I was honored and privileged to have been a member of every guard of honor that was assembled during the four years that I spent in the Bahamas Police, wearing that white helmet with brass chin strap, stiffly starched white long-sleeved tunic with brass buttons, black trousers with red seams, black boots gleaming like mirrors in the tropical sun, brown leather belts highly polished, with brass buckles, silver whistles attached to white lanyards, rifles clean and gleaming with long, World War I-type bayonets menacingly affixed. Every available civilian turned out to see us, some even came to see individual members. One of our Bajan lads, Drum Major Braithwaite, I believe, was a special draw, but there was nothing sweeter than when the parade commander gave the order to *preeesent arms!* and as one man, without missing a beat between movements, the entire group completed the order with that marine-style crack of heels on the pavement.

9. THE NASSAU SCENE

Halfway into our training period, we got a new commissioner of police. His name was Colchester Wemys (pronounced 'Weems') and his previous posting was the Solomon Islands. He was an Englishman of a complexion turned lobster-red by constant exposure to the tropical sun, and his visage was closed and uninviting, a mechanism meant to hide an otherwise considerate nature. Wemys' wife was a white Barbadian, and we soon discovered that he understood West Indian habits and inclinations, certainly much better than the typical British officers and Bahamians themselves often did, since Bahamians did not consider themselves West Indians at that time, either culturally or geographically.

The Bahamas police force in mid-1955 comprised about 300 men, of whom fifty were Barbadian, fifty were Trinidadian, about ten were Guianese, three were Jamaican, and one was from the Turks and Caicos Islands. Just about half of the force was from the British West Indies. I have always wondered why there were no Jamaicans recruited, considering that Jamaica was much closer geographically to the Bahamas than the Southern and Eastern Caribbean from which so many of us hailed. It was even stranger when I discovered that the three Jamaicans in the force happened to have been living in Nassau at the time they were recruited.

West Indian males love cricket and soccer and dance parties. Like the English, we love our clubs. Allegiance to one's favorite club can take on religious fervor, as for the British, so for us. Under Colonel Wemys' encouragement, we formed a police cricket team and a police football team. We then worked with the local community leaders to create where necessary, and to revive cricket, football and athletic clubs all over New Providence. Vernon Fenty, a neighbor from my country village in Barbados and Cyril Joseph from Trinidad, two policemen from a previous recruitment to ours, were chiefly responsible for organizing the different teams into leagues. These efforts and the enthralling competitions that resulted among us humanized the police and brought us into more positive, non-confrontational engagement with the public.

While we had football fields and cricket pitches to play on around Nassau, the police had no clubhouse, so Commissioner Wemys got the funds to build us one. There was adequate space at the back of the barracks compound and in a very short space of time, police had the most modern and well-equipped sports facility in the entire Bahamas. It was equipped with a games room, exercise room, showers, a large ballroom, and an enormous bar. Everyone drank in our Caribbean culture, so why not have a beautiful place of our own to take in your "waters", especially for Her Majesty's Finest? There was also a room where I was introduced to the art of fencing (a sport that I grew to love and to be reasonably competent at) in addition to a tennis court and volleyball court – both grass – out in the back.

Our police club became a gathering point for men of prominence in local society. Soon many lawyers, doctors, accountants, engineers, top civil servants and budding politicians would come after work to play pool or tennis, or ping pong, chat and have a couple of drinks and conversation before going home to dinner. By the time I graduated from training and hit the beat, I came to personally know many of these professionals and future leaders of the Bahamas. I particularly remember the Adderley brothers, Paul and Francis, lawyer and doctor; Lynden Pindling, the future and first Prime Minister; Randol Fawkes, Kendal Isaacs, magistrates Johnson and Maxwell Thompson, and future Governors-General Sir Gerald Cash and Orville Turnquest.

Sir Gerald was the most congenial of all these likable men. For some inexplicable reason, he was more like us, West Indians from the Eastern Caribbean than any of his Bahamian colleagues. The other men were at ease with us, but Sir Gerald was entirely one of the boys. Perhaps it was because his wife was Jamaican, because he could talk trash on the tennis courts, run pekong* with the Trinidadian fellows, have a beer with anyone available, and be as comfortable as you please. Not so for Lynden Pindling, for although his father was Jamaican, he was as adamantly anti-Jamaican as Dudley Hanna, who would later become responsible for immigration affairs in the Pindling governments.

During the latter part of our training, we began the tradition of the Annual Police Ball. Young men in full formal dress uniform are a sight to behold, and the ball was going to become the big social event of the year. We police recruits all wore shell coats, white formal shirts, black cummerbunds, black bow ties, and red-seam uniform trousers with black shoes. Those of us who were lucky enough to have made a connection with girls brought them out, but in those early days, most of us had no dates. This was of no special concern, for we mostly

---

* A Trinidadian term describing the use of insults for fun, using barbs about rivals' attire or derogatory comments about one's physical attributes. In this respect, the form is similar to that of the modern rap battle.

wanted to nurse our two beers for the evening, hang out at the bar or strut around, showing each other and the guests how pretty we were. It was utterly remarkable how quickly we young black bachelors in Nassau, who only earned ten pounds and ten shillings per week in the mid-1950's (about US$ 25.50), felt that the world was our oyster, and strutted like peacocks.

★★★

The following excerpt was lifted in its entirety from the current website of the Bahamas Government:

Prior to 1959 only males who had British citizenship were permitted to run for the House. In addition, the male had to be a resident in the Bahamas for three (3) years and own property, rent or personals of the value of 200 pounds above all debts and mortgages.

The right to vote also was restricted at first to white males who were twenty-one (21) years or older, and who were resident in the colony for twelve (12) months. The skin color restriction for males was removed in the mid-nineteenth century. The male voter also had to be a tenant or householder paying an annual rent of 2.85 pounds.

In addition to these restrictive measures the electoral process was antiquated and unfair. Voting was conducted openly in the presence of the candidates or their agents. This system was oftentimes subject to intimidation and corruption and candidates who were defeated often correctly alleged that the results of the elections were undermined by payments to voters by wealthy candidates.

Elections were held over a period of weeks with voting for each district being held on a separate day. This facilitated the unfair and inequitable system of plural voting.

In 1939 the House passed the 'Ballot Act' which provided for secret balloting, but its provisions were restricted to the four New Providence Districts and were temporary as they fell away after five (5) years. Sir Harry Oakes, a wealthy Canadian, resigned his Western District seat in the House in October 1939 after only a year in the House. A by-election was held to replace him in November of that year and Milo B. Butler won that ensuing by-election and thus became the first person in The Bahamas to be elected by secret ballot.

A new Ballot Act was passed in 1949 and the general elections later that year were the first to be conducted by secret ballot.

Such was the general framework of political development when I entered the Bahamas in 1955, and it was still there in a broad sense up to the spring of 1959 when I left. To a great extent, it was déjà vu for me. Earlier in this memoir, I spoke of attending political meetings in Barbados with my father and listening to Grantley Adams educate voters on the almost criminal structure of the voting system that obtained there up to 1944. I will not fall into the potential trap of comparing the Bahamas with Barbados, for my objectivity could be impugned, but it was now as late as 1957, and I was 21 and could view things through more mature eyes.

The social and political system in the Bahamas was atrocious. Before and up to the time of Randol Fawkes's trial for inciting rebellion, most residents of the colony seemed resigned to the status quo. The blacks had their separate social and economic life almost exclusively 'Over the Hill', and the whites had their social and economic activity along Bay Street and Shirley Street in the north of the city near to the harbor. The only business activity for blacks on the north side of the city was the native straw market and fishermen's wharves. The Family Islands were like places out of the Robinson Crusoe: idyllic, hardscrabble and neglected, with lovely, good fishing, and enough arable land to feed your family.

There was hardly any social interaction between blacks and whites. There was one theater on Bay Street where only whites went; blacks attended the one cinema Over the Hill. The mulattos sat between the two stools, with predictable historical outcomes. There were two vibrant newspapers, *The Guardian*, which was white-owned and *The Tribune*, which was owned by the Dupuch family, who at that time seemed uncomfortable about embracing their brown-skinned blackness and would rather make petition to be welcome amongst the dominant Bahamian whites. Several other families were fair-skinned enough or of a high enough social standing to participate in the white rapaciousness and compromise any pangs of social justice that they may have had from time to time.

I was only aware of one government high school and one Catholic high school in 1950s Bahamas, and neither was free. There was no income tax then, and correspondingly very limited social services. At least there were public wards in the single hospital on New Providence for those who could not pay.

From time to time, I have allowed myself to wonder why Britain grew so enamored with the Bahamas. For the sake of resources and exports, they should logically have been more interested in Jamaica and the Southern United States, and to a certain extent Cuba. Places like the Bahamas, the Cayman Islands, and Turks and Caicos Islands, it seemed, just fell into British hands without loss of treasure.

In a sense, the Bahamas was especially blessed. The most select of these blessings comes from its proximity to the United States, and the first material economic gift was the sponge beds, harvested plentifully and profitably before artificial sponges came on the market. Immediately after the sponge beds were depleted, Prohibition became law in the United States in 1919 and liquor smuggling became a popular way for connected Bahamians to get rich. Many local family fortunes owe their establishment to rum and whiskey running between the Bahamas and the Florida Cays. After all, Grand Bahama is only a quick boat ride from Florida, and Bimini is just about whistling distance from Key West.

When the Twenty-first Amendment to the US Constitution finally brought Prohibition (and rum-running) to an end in 1933, tourism was the logical next industry to take hold. The Bahamas has lovely beaches, a very liberal tax policy and an oligarchy with whom to make unaccountable deals, allowing hotels to spring up all over the place with Americans brought in at publicly affordable rates to fill them. Money flowed easily. People did not need high or particularly good schools to be productive at the available jobs, and there were a sufficient number of families who could afford to send their children abroad for the education necessary to fill the jobs requiring higher education. The country could always recruit young men from the Eastern Caribbean to fill gaps when necessary.

As I grew and observed, I gradually appreciated Britain's interest in maintaining its colonial hold on the Bahamas. A colony was attractive for producing primary products for export to the mother country, in turn creating manufactured products for export to the world. Classic primary products come to mind, such as sugar, cotton, cocoa, ores, timber, crude oil and so on, but the Bahamas has no capabilities in this traditional sense. I believe that what they do have is the ability to attract net flows of capital and if the mother country can maintain control of those net flows of capital, it can finance its home development and also positively influence economic and political development in other parts of the world. If the colonial power can find a controllable partner in the colony to keep political power and aspirations away from the masses, then that created an oligarchy with whom the colonial power could work for mutual benefit. The British found that partner in a group called the Bay Street Boys. These locals, led by Stafford Sands when I was there in the 1950s did not report to the British cabinet in London directly; they reported locally to the governor, who maintained control along with the colonial secretary and the Anglican bishop.

The unholy alliance between the British and the Bay Street Boys went on happily and became more entrenched as the Bahamas became a leading tax haven for offshore dollars. Many were the times when I was on beat duty along Bay Street and wondered about those tall plaques on law office doors with the names of firms inside. Indeed, I never saw any staff coming out at lunchtime, and only noticed a few mostly white men heading to their cars in the afternoons.

Nassau was replete with dollars. I am still amazed at how much American money there was in circulation. One could routinely pay a vendor in Bahamian money and get US dollars as change since nobody observed exchange control regulations. The Bahamas could not use those dollars, certainly not with the safety and level of return that the owners demanded. More likely, the colony provided cover for a bookkeeping entry for dollars invested elsewhere, fees paid to local agents and, of course, to the Crown.

Bahamians displayed an inexplicable uneasiness about other West Indian islanders, especially about Jamaicans. I never grew to understand it. Bahamians never even considered themselves West Indians. Maybe the tendency of West Indians to strut was too off-putting, and maybe God's gift of easily accessible resources to the Bahamas islanders was too heady. Somewhere within these concepts lies the answer.

It's a cliché, but politics makes strange bedfellows, for I later learned that during the days of particularly restrictive immigration activity, especially against Jamaicans and other Caribbean blacks, Dudley Thompson, a brilliant Jamaican lawyer and parliamentary scholar was running Mr. Pindling's law office and advising him on statecraft. When Randol Fawkes, the first of the new Bahamian leaders to openly challenge the Raj needed a legal defense, the emerging political parties sent for Vivian Blake, an outstanding Jamaican defense attorney, to lead the defense. I had a front-row seat in all this as a member of the guard of honor that opened that particular Supreme Court s ession, and I also formed part of the guard of the prisoner in the dock.

Among my earliest exercises in observation was to attend political meetings, make observations, and report on mood and expressed sentiments. I had heard of sedition from my early days of attending Grantley Adams' political meetings with my father back in Barbados, for it was a weapon with which the British Colonial Office threatened challenges to its authority. I never dreamed that as a policeman, I would become a part of British Colonial enforcement policy. I was not yet twenty.

The ensuing event spoke volumes about the British legal and trial court system. Early in August 1958, trade unionist and lawyer Fawkes was arrested for sedition stemming from a speech he made to lumber workers at their invitation. He had written to the Bahamas Lumber Company in the previous year, requesting compensation for seven laborers who had variously sustained broken legs, arms, jaw and skull while doing dangerous work over long hours. Conditions were generally appalling for the workers, who had poor sanitary facilities and had to live on filthy premises among the sawdust, receiving company store credit instead of actual wages. Threatened by the company's owner, Fawkes took the opportunity to stage a huge rally in which he criticized Bahamas Lumber – and denounced the government.

The chief justice in the Randol Fawkes sedition case was a white Englishman, Sir Guy Henderson. Fawkes, the defendant, was a black colonial, as was Vivian Blake, who at the time was the youngest Queen's Counsel in the entire British empire. At stake was an opportunity to make a crack in the power structure. Most non-whites on the island recognized Mr. Blake's erudition and were proud of the way he marshaled his facts and challenged the prosecution's postulates and conclusions, but in our hearts, we did not expect the conclusion of the Chief Justice, who found Fawkes not guilty, but he chose not to stop there. My skin still tingles when I recall the tenor of the Justice's remarks. He took pains to congratulate Mr. Blake on a brilliant defense and further stated that it was a pleasure and very enlightening for him to have had the honor to preside over the case and to witness such a brilliant exposition of the law relating to the serious charge of sedition. Nassau went completely mad. The drums 'Over the Hill' boomed all night, and politically the Bahamas was never the same again. I was a front-row witness to the cataclysmic event that would eventually lead to Bahamian independence.

As I recall, there were no political parties in the Bahamas until

Randol Fawkes formed the Bahamian Labor Party in about 1957. There were elections that year, and the group of independents loosely known as the Bay Street Boys won the majority of the seats. The atmosphere in Nassau became very tense and the commissioner of police formed a riot squad of thirty specially selected men – including me. A retired soldier named Captain Granger, a black Bahamian who had reached that rank during the war, was brought out of retirement to train us, and Edney Johnson, a sergeant by this time, who just a couple of years earlier had been my physical trainer and drill instructor had the job of getting us into shape. I thought that the training was tough for police recruits, but that was like preparation for what we were put through in the riot squad. Now there was serious weapons training with the use of live ammunition, tear gas, shields and batons, as well as instruction in crowd control methods, mass arrests and removal from scene, teamwork and hand-to-hand sparring. And there were pushups. Lots of pushups. The riot squad was in top shape in about six weeks, just in time for the uprising in Grand Bahama.

By 1957 or 1958, Lynden Pindling was back home from his legal studies in Britain and following the wave of sympathy for Randol Fawkes after his acquittal, Pindling was moving heaven and earth to organize and establish a political party of wide appeal and acceptance by the masses and the black middle and upper classes, with whom he did not have good support. I had been a witness to Grantley Adams' success in making the Barbados Labor Party a force to be dealt with in Barbados ten years earlier, and I was very much aware of Norman Manley and Bustamante's success during that same period in Jamaica. But Nassau was different. Here, the professional blacks were very late in supporting Pindling. Even the *Tribune* newspaper, independent, black-owned and well supported by the masses, saw no grounds to publicly support Pindling in the early going. The Dupuch family-owned *Tribune* leaned toward the Bay Street Boys side more than to that of reform, since one of the brothers, Eugene, was an independent member of the house at the time.

A snap election was called, I believe in 1957. Running as independents, the Bay Street Boys won the majority of seats and formed the government. Randol Fawkes was the only member elected under a party banner; Stafford Sands and his group were sufficiently emboldened to conclude a deal which in the eyes of the people of Grand Bahama represented a complete giveaway of the prime property on that island to an American group led by Wallace Groves. The people on Grand Bahama protested vigorously, so much so that the British authorities felt that a riot would erupt. My riot squad was summarily shipped out to Grand Bahama.

I had been to the Out Islands before, as the Family Islands were then called, but nothing prepared me for my first visit to Grand Bahama. Surprisingly, there were no facilities on the land for the riot squad to defend. We had to set up tents for sleeping, sanitary facilities, tents for rest and off-time activities, and the supply of meals. All of these challenges we found manageable, but we could not handle the mosquitoes, which on Grand Bahama seemed to be the biggest in the world. You stumbled when they hit you, and when you killed them, they left splashes of blood, not drops. There wasn't a man among us who planned on shooting any of the people of Grand Bahama, but many of us felt that we might have to shoot some of those insect monsters.

We spent ten miserable days on that god-forsaken island. The uprising subsided, and the Bay Street Boys did their deal with the American group. Twenty years later, I was privileged to return to Grand Bahama for a directors meeting held there by one of the boards on which I sat. My hotel room, on the same ground that my riot squad had set out to defend twenty years earlier, was luxurious. The mosquitoes were gone, their land usurped for progress.

In the aftermath of the Grand Bahama uprising, Pindling consolidated his group into a fully-fledged political party known as the Progressive Liberal Party, and the Bay Street Boys organized and transformed themselves into the United Bahamian Party. Randol Fawkes was still there with his Labor Party. I left the Bahamas in 1959, just before all the monumental changes that would take place there during the early 1960's.

Even with the establishment of Universal Adult Suffrage in 1961, the UBP was able to win the elections in 1962 with fewer votes than the PLP, and to gain the majority of votes cast in the 1967 elections. The PLP did win the same number of seats as the UBP in the 1967 election but was able to form the Government when Randol Fawkes's party, which had won only one seat, sided with them. The Bahamas would never be the same again politically.

10. WILD OATS, RUM & GINGER

My experiences in the Bahamas were not limited to policing and political observation. I took the opportunity to visit several of the Family Islands, with a strong preference in the archipelago for Eleuthera. To be sure, the Bahamas is replete with beautiful beaches, but none, in my opinion, match the pink sand found at Rock Sound and Governor's Harbor Eleuthera. I continue to be amazed at their regularity and firmness sufficient to accommodate a motor car ride.

Harbor Island rekindles thoughts of an exciting vacation. I believe it was in 1956, when one of my buddies, Lloyd Beach, an older police officer of Tobagonian and Trinidadian origin, invited me to go there to spend a vacation. Beach was posted as the only police officer on the island. He was quite pleased with the job that I had done in getting him trim and fit in the gym so that he could look good at his wedding. At nineteen, I'd fancied myself quite the bodybuilder, and many of us wanted to look like Joe Weider or Steve Reeves, the leading bodybuilders of that era.

And so I took the MailBoat and journeyed to Harbor Island. After about a week of hanging out and scouting around, I established r elations with a captivating island beauty of about eighteen years of age. We would meet and frolic on beaches of paradise, gradually building our teenage juices to points that needed safe places to explode. My host and friend Lloyd Beach lived alone in a beautiful house, and since he was out on bicycle patrol most of the time, it seemed perfectly logical that I should invite my island nymph to visit me in my lair at his home. Maria came, and just at the point when I thought that the entrance to Elysium was about to open and I would enter with joy and conquering glory, a different entrance opened when Maria's father and three brothers burst in the front door of the house.

I froze but was not afraid. After all, I was a trained police officer and known to be a good talker. I thought that the family would get violent, so my first response was to calm them down and get them to talk with me. In the interim, idle villagers started to gather at the front of the house to get first-hand information for the local gossip machine. I found that I felt a little safer with this surrounding throng, for the actions of an irate family would be tempered by the presence of so many witnesses. It turned out that Maria's family did not want to lynch her new-found love, but rather to get him to do what they considered the honorable thing and agree to marry her. I agreed that

I would and that I would make an official visit to their home the next day to demonstrate my acceptance by the family. Maria and her folks withdrew along with the idlers, leaving me to ponder my predicament. I went in search of Beach, my friend and host. He and I planned our strategy: I went back to the house; he continued his patrol. At four o'clock the next morning, he delivered me to a local fisherman at his moorings and by six that same morning, I was on the Mail Boat at Abaco Island. By evening, I was back in Nassau, safely in the police barracks and under the protection of Her Majesty the Queen. Harbor Island remains an exciting memory.

★★★

One of my earliest hangouts in Nassau was the Shalimar Hotel. The owner and manager was a charming lady of about sixty named Nellie Granger, a mixed-race lady who bore her age gracefully and was very familiar with Bahamian culture and traditions. I started eating lunch there every day once I was no longer compelled to eat Johnny Saunders' offal. The Shalimar served the most delicious liver and bacon, and for a change-up, I would get into their macaroni and cheese. I spent many an hour talking with Mrs. Granger, who willingly shared some of her knowledge and experiences with me. Her late husband turned out to be the brother of Captain Granger, the man who commanded my riot squad. Nellie's current lover was a young Bahamian man of linebacker build whom her late husband had given to her as her chauffeur and bodyguard so that he could be free to pursue his other women. The chauffer guarded Nellie very closely, leaving room for young bucks like myself to get no further than her delicious meals.

The Silver Slippers nightclub was a few doors down the street from the Shalimar, and I spent so many nights there that I had my own seat at the bar. I did not go there only to drink, however. One rum and ginger lasted me however long I stayed because I was there to see the art of movement that was Mitzi. She was a young dancer from Andros and could do things with her backside that no bootsie shaker on the island could. Men and women loved her and later had her, but I adored her. I worshipped at her altar for months, pleading for a night of personal pleasure. It seemed like forever before she let me take her home. The joy was in the chase and the anticipation, I guess, because with me Mitzi was like a dead fish. There was absolutely no passion, no juice, no spark. Where were the moves of the dance floor? Where was the controlled fury of the temptress? I kept doing my best, from mouth to breast to mound but accomplished nothing but resignation. I managed to enter, became bored, withdrew, got dressed and walked to barracks contemplating my folly and lessons learned.

★★★

The Crown Lands Department of the Bahamas Civil Service recruited several land surveyors from Dominica and Grenada, and they often came to our police club to pass the time. It was here that I renewed my acquaintance with Alfred Bellot, who was from my village in Barbados, and our families knew each other over hundreds of years. Alfred and I had attended the same St. Savior's Boys' Elementary School. He was about seven years older than I was, and had been the leader of my scout troop, the 51st Barbados. Alfred's father was a Dominican of French origin and took him to Dominica when he was about seventeen or eighteen years old. I had not seen Alfred since I was about ten. You can imagine the joy we both felt at reuniting.

Alfred invited me to his home to meet his wife Agatha. She was twenty, a year older than I was. They had a one-year-old son, Clarence. We liked each other from the get-go, and she, Alfred and I remained close friends until their deaths, Alfred in 1984 and Agatha in 2006. The Bellots introduced me to their wide circle of friends, including all the young land surveyors, lawyers, doctors, magistrates and budding politicians, elected and aspirant alike. I went to all their parties, socializing with them and with visiting top colonial civil servants as they came through from British Honduras, Bermuda, or the Turks and Caicos Islands. I met Norman Manley, Premier of Jamaica at the time, George Price, Premier of British Honduras (now Belize), and Claude Magloire, President of Haiti, until he was replaced by François "Papa Doc" Duvalier.

The Bellots also introduced me to the Davis family, one of the most respected, highly professional, low-keeled and successful families in all the Bahamas. My family has maintained a close relationship with three generations of the Davis family so far, and a nodding relationship with a fourth. I consider myself to be extremely fortunate to have been able at that stage of my life to socialize with folks who had this level of success. They didn't seem concerned that I was just a police constable; I was the only one who seemed to notice. They engaged me in conversation, and I engaged them, as was my wont. It was I who was making the big discoveries, not they. I had to get abroad and study. It didn't matter what I studied, for I knew that I would not necessarily make a career where I started. I resolved to save more of my salary.

Susan Johnson remains one of the kindest and most practical persons who have influenced my life. Miss Sue made a living preparing Barbadian and Bahamian meals for young men like me, feeding and counseling several of us. After a while, I grew tired of eating at the Shalimar Hotel and was glad to have a regular home-cooked meal. Her husband was a Bajan machinist who had been living in Nassau since the 1920s when he left Cuba after the sugar mills were fully established. Miss Sue lived Over the Hill, of course, and as we sat and enjoyed her one-pot crab and rice, or her macaroni and cheese with fried grouper – Bahamian specialties – she would give her counsel on what was expected of us. When Miss Sue was particularly moved to do so, she would make black pudding and souse on a Saturday evening. You can't get any more Barbadian than that unless you knew how to prepare sea eggs and steamed white rice, which would have been quite a stretch for a Cat Island woman.

We all tried not to stay too long at Miss Sue's on a Friday or Saturday night. For reasons hard to explain, the men from Over the Hill, in the Grant's Pen District, especially on Miss Sue's street, seemed to beat their women every Friday or Saturday night. Sometimes when the women got tired of crying and begging for mercy, they would rush over to Miss Sue's house hoping to find a police officer to protect them. If we were fortunate enough to have weekend nights off, we were not too anxious to lose our free time having to make arrests and write reports for prosecution the following Monday. There was also the fact that we would get our clothes bloodied and sometimes torn without compensation. When we were on duty, it was a different question. Sometimes we would arrest the men by the paddy wagonful on Friday and Saturday nights for these unbelievably regular assaults.

Why, you may well ask, did these one-sided family fights occur, mostly on pay weekends? Could it have been that the men got drunk on payday, and out of frustration over the trap that they felt themselves in, took it out on their women? Or could it have been attributed to demon rum? I never heard a plausible explanation, but there sure were blows flying through the poorer classes on Friday and Saturday nights

Over the Hill in Nassau.

***

In early 1956, the American pop singer Roy Hamilton was featured at a concert in Nassau. He appeared at the Cat & Fiddle nightclub. All the rage at that time, his rendition of the song "Unchained Melody" was top of the charts and every young swinger in Nassau simply had to be at that concert. I considered myself high among the swingers, so I could not let my boys down; I had to be there.

In those days, male and female swingers alike dressed to the nines to go to nightclub concerts. One had to hit the floor hard, looking good and dancing beautifully. The girls were going to notice and dance with you when you asked, and the guys were going to copy your style. For this concert, I wore my very first white dinner jacket and black tuxedo trousers with satin stripes on the outer seam, white pleated evening shirt, red bow tie, red cummerbund, and black dress shoes. My tailor, Hiram Newbold, cut and fitted my dinner jacket beautifully.

None of us in my group had a date. We were not taking females to the club and we did not know many. We were going there to meet women. After all, one doesn't take coals to Newcastle. After getting my now-familiar rum and ginger at the bar, I cruised around and between tables, studying the crowd to determine which ladies were without dates and indicated some openness to an approach. Players can tell; they never get insulted. They may be rebuffed, but never rudely. I was not yet a player, but I was bold, born with abundant self-confidence, and I knew that I looked good. What the heck, man, at twenty years old, a fully trained policeman, one of the few people in that club with powers of arrest, I was not going to be afraid to walk around and look for an open face. I soon found it. Not one, but three beautifully well dressed, sophisticated young women were all alone at their table. I approached as Sondheim wrote, "making my entrance with my usual flair" and met the Gibson girls, three of the most beautiful and desirable women in the Bahamas. They were extremely gracious and invited me to join them.

One of the first things we learned in my youth was the art of conversation. Few girls would ever go out with you or dream of inviting you to meet their parents if you could not carry on a conversation. Secondly, you had to be able to dance well and to dress even better. In two two's, I was off the mark and running with these beautiful women. I needed help, especially if I were going to be successful at isolating the one that showed the most interest in this young man from faraway Barbados. My boys were all in the wings, so I found Doc Straughn, and Slicky Ifill (who claimed to know my new friends) to join us at the table. Freddie Mullings, an amazingly accomplished local jazz clarinetist, kept the club rocking and grooving, and we had things so well covered that not a man tried to horn in on us. Then, Roy Hamilton hit that first line of his signature song:

Oh my love,
my darling,
I hunger for your touch

We all slid onto the dance floor, me with Paula in my arms, and the world melted away. My life changed that night and I would never be the same again.

I started dating Paula from that night on, and for the next three years until I left Nassau, she was my only serious girlfriend. I had many female friends during our relationship, some of whom are my friends up to this day, but those friendships were all platonic. Paula was my woman, and unassailably so. She was a beautiful woman, of medium height and well-toned body. In addition to being highly intelligent, she was well informed and extremely generous, never hesitating for a moment to bring me into her circle of family and friends. Paula was a good dancer, loved a party, loved her family, and was very proud of her heritage.

An accomplished cosmetologist with her own shop, she also had the reputation of being one of the leaders of her profession in the Bahamas, later becoming a doctor of cosmetology and a teacher to many in that field. Teaching was the family business, it seemed, for her father was a famous headmaster in Nassau schools and a music teacher to many performing artists in the country, including the first prime minister. Her mother was a school teacher for many years until her retirement.

Nature always presents challenging juxtapositions. Paula turned out to be a twenty-six-year-old divorcee with three children aged eight, six, and four and still lived at home with her parents. I was a few months short of my twentieth birthday, and at best what was in the jargon of the culture, nothing more than a forced-ripe man. We never discussed all this, and none of our friends ever mentioned it – nor did her parents.

Paula had got married when she was eighteen and started having children immediately. Before she even had time to enjoy the height of her teenage years, she had a family, and five years into her marriage she was divorced.

Her family was truly an extended one. Three generations of them lived in this long, narrow and beautiful shotgun-style house, with its courting veranda, just a few chains from the Atlantic ocean near Western Beach. There were Paula's parents, her single sister, her married sister with her two children, then Paula and her three. If there was conflict I never noticed any, for the constant sound of piano music and musical composition drowned out any disharmony that may have existed. Daddy O – or was it Daddy G – was always composing. Years later, I learned that Timothy Gibson had composed the country's national anthem when the Bahamas gained independence from Great Britain in 1973.

From my vantage point of several years later, I think that Paula was able to enjoy with me the teenage experiences that she had lost by marrying so young. We went to lots of movies and we drove all over New Providence in her father's car. She was a good driver, and her father would let her have the car whenever he was not using it. I was still at the bicycle level, and that apparatus was not the right instrument for this level of romance. We swam a lot – at least I swam a lot, because Paula never went into the water. We visited with her few close friends, and we partied. I believed that we were known at every nightclub in Nassau. I certainly was, especially at the late, late, after-hours clubs. Our favorite hangouts were the beaches, especially at night, and became our bedrooms and lovemaking spots. We had our hidden coves at Montague Beach, at Western Beach, and Cable Beach.

In these places and without external stimulants, we took each other to heights of ecstasy that were mind boggling. This was my first woman and if I were able to hold her and to satisfy her, either she was a good teacher and I was a good student, or I was a natural for the game. Sometimes I would think of Odysseus being driven mad by the sweet voices of the sirens as he was strapped to the mast crying to be set free. But I had one up on old Odysseus for I was in bed with my siren. I was not only hearing her sweet voice; we were making the music and singing together. Dylan Thomas could complain that his back was sunburned from too much lovemaking in the sun, and now it is my turn to state that my ass was sandbagged from too much lovemaking in the sand.

I once had a magnificently exciting night with Paula, capped off by a session of multiple couplings and mutual comings. I was completely transported and got to barracks after midnight curfew.

All single policemen had to live in barracks at that time. We were a civil and military police force and were subject to very strict codes. One had to get special permission to be out after curfew; in this case, I did not. The corporal in charge of the guard at the barracks gate challenged me and threatened to write me up and put me on a charge. I was on a high. Here was I, a moment ago supping with the Gods, and in the twinkling of an eye, I had to face this nincompoop. I proceeded to let him have it, gently reminding him that he had been recruited from Barbados the same year that I was born, and the best he could do after twenty years was to be a corporal in charge of the gate in this mother-sexing country. He wrote me up, and I went to my floor and to bed. I was charged for insubordination, among other things and given fourteen days' confinement to barracks, the indignity we called "CB".

For the next two weeks, my only release was going to work. After my eight-hour shift, I had to be driven back to barracks to do any menial work that the sergeant in charge wished to assign. It felt like being a low-level criminal in a concentration camp; work and no play, driven to and from work and confinement to barracks in between, with no social intercourse or recreation time. I never knew that there were so many toilets in our compound, or that our barracks yard was so large, or that so many people smoked so many different brands of cigarettes, or that I could keep finding butts to clean up as I carried out my assignment to keep the compound clean. I could not be seen conversing with anyone, or we would both be punished. My orders were not complex: beat duty for eight hours, CB for the next sixteen hours, eight of which were reserved for menial tasks and the remainder for rest and sleep. Oh, the agony and the longing for my woman, the shame and disillusionment, the resolve to rise above it all, to build from this self-inflicted low point. Those two weeks were an eternity.

I came out of confinement to barracks a more serious and contemplative individual. The three people whose counsel I had always sought most were my friend Alfred Bellot, his wife Agatha, and Paula's mother, Mrs. Gibson. I now talked with them more earnestly. Mrs. Gibson and I would have long and interesting talks during the evenings that Paula had late-arriving clients. She had never traveled further from Nassau than to her native Rock Sound in Eleuthera, and she would ask me all manner of questions about my native Barbados and the islands in the Eastern Caribbean. Her questions were very probing, forcing me to be more aware of the self-revelations in my answers. I gradually became aware of the fact that she was confirming her impressions of the sociopolitical development of her beloved Bahamas as compared with what was happening in other neighboring British colonies, and like the teacher that she was, she was making me more cognizant of what lay ahead for my generation.

Suddenly one evening, as if to bring things back to earth, Mrs. Gibson asked, "Why did you have to choose Paula and not my youngest daughter Faye, who is more your age group"? When I think of the answer that I gave her, I am amazed at my maturity at the time.

"Faye," I answered, "would have been interested in more dashing playboy types than I am. She wanted the challenge of taming the lion. Paula wanted quiet dependability".

"Young man," she replied, "you have to go away and study. You have too much talent to settle so early."

Years later, whenever I earned a degree, I would pass through Nassau to see Mrs. Gibson, among others, and when I became a bank manager in Jamaica, I would take my family to the Bahamas to visit friends every two years and visit Mrs. Gibson up to the time of her death.

★★★

I credit Alfred and Agatha Bellot with introducing me into the upper middle-class social circles in Nassau. Genuinely interested in my future, Alfred convinced me that Canada was the place that I should go to continue my education. Alfred sold me on Nova Scotia, where he had gone to a technical college in Halifax and had qualified as a land surveyor. Seeing the high standard of living that land surveyors enjoyed in the Bahamas, I figured that I would be well served by pursuing that profession, plus it would bring me back to my beautiful Paula. Agatha, on the other hand, wanted me to go away and see more of the world and its possibilities before I settled for less than was achievable. She knew that I was mad about Paula, and with the intuition of the female, she wanted to shield me from making decisions that I might later regret. My friend of blessed memory, Ivern Davis, who by this time had returned from Canada as a civil engineer, also inspired me to go to Canada and continue my education.

I was on the horns of a dilemma. I loved Paula, wanted to marry her and create the pretext to never leave, but I thirsted for the discipline of higher education as well. Paula put self-interest aside and helped me make the decision, tearfully convincing me that I had much further to go in life than to just settle for an existence in the Bahamas. I simply had to go to the developed world and study. She, for her part, was willing to take the chance of losing me to make me a better man. *She could never really lose me, for there are secret corners in our hearts that are especially ours. We have something everlasting.*

Nothing now remained but for me to play out the last year of my contract with the Bahamas Police. I had associates who had buddies in the hotel trade, and we would go to the Out Islands some weekends. Some of them were quite close to some of the local fishermen and would go off on jaunts with them while others of us enjoyed the beaches, the booze and fun. I noticed that one guy, in particular, would return with neat weatherproofed bags of something, but I did not want to admit to what I was seeing. I had made earlier note in my mind that this gentle young man dressed in a much more expensive manner than his earnings as a hotel clerk should manage. After I left the Bahamas I learned of his early death, and later in life when I became Chairman of the Airports Authority of Jamaica and aware of drug smuggling techniques, it dawned on me that I had been a witness to the early development of the illicit drug trade in the Caribbean and one of the conduits of drugs through the islands into the United States.

My time to leave the Bahamas seemed to be divinely ordained. I believe that I would have had the strength of character to resist the temptations presented by my newly formed relationships, but avoidance is often better than the test. After four years of learning and growing, of partying and drinking, of lovemaking and improving my social graces, of making a lot of friends and few recognizable enemies, I was on my very first commercial airplane trip, first to Jamaica and then on to Barbados. The BOAC liner was a most luxurious craft, and the flight to Jamaica was heavenly. In those days, before deregulation and the proletarianization of air travel, they fed you on airplanes, and we were beautifully taken care of.

The Bahamas Government surprised me and the other returnee to our homeland, my friend Doc Straughn, by giving us first-class tickets. We got smoked salmon to start our meal, champagne, and – what was this? – a white man serving us! I was being introduced to a whole new world, leaving one existence where I had to salute white men daily or face a charge if I didn't, and within a few hours, I was being served lunch by a white servant. What was this, Lord? There were white men on horseback when I was a boy in rural Barbados, white merchants and property owners in Bridgetown, white officers in the Bahamas Police, and now white stewards on BOAC calling me sir. *Enjoy it boy, and go get yourself ready to take command in this changing world.*

The first thing I noticed in Jamaica was the difference in the quality of the water. We had arranged to stop over for three days to explore Kingston and learn something about our big island neighbor. My first shower there remains etched in my mind. The water was so soft and refreshing that I recall getting lathered up so easily, and felt so clean and invigorated afterward that it was hard to believe. While the water in Jamaica is beautiful and soft, the whole thing was exaggerated by the memory of the hard limestone water that I'd known in Nassau. It was so difficult to work up a lather in the shower there.

Kingston was the largest city that I had seen up to that time. It was also the dirtiest, but it had a vigor and an essence that remains unmatched in my memory, and with all those black people ... where in hell did all those people looking like me ever come from? Working men and women had a pointed dignity about them, in so many shades of black, so many ethnic types, so many beautiful nymphs, barefoot and shod, all gliding with equal ease and so many uptown houses with swimming pools, many of them with black women sitting on their verandas, and their black children playing in the yard. And a university too, up at Mona in the foothills of the Blue Mountains, with many black professors, some of them from my home island, with Hugh Springer – the distinguished scholar and respected nation builder that every scholarly Barbadian of my era used as a standard – as chancellor. *I must get back to Jamaica*, I dreamed.

In April of 1959, I was back in Barbados. I spent one month in my beautiful home island before setting out for Canada. Many things had changed in my family and politically in Barbados during the exactly four years (April 1955 to April 1959) that I had spent in Nassau. In 1957, my mother had been able, with help from the money that I sent her out of my earnings, to finally acquire her own home in Bridgetown. It was a modest three-bedroom cottage in Station Hill behind District A Police Station, near Glendairy Prison. The lot was leased, a normal occurrence for residential areas in the less pretentious parts of Bridgetown. By this time, our old family home in Cane Garden, St. Andrew had been abandoned.

Fertile land all over the country was now being thrown up as Barbadians migrated to the city or emigrated to England. The island had started to import basic foodstuff and was gradually acquiring a fondness for imported cornflakes and scotch whiskey. The ubiquitous rum and ginger was gradually giving way to a scotch and soda, and that old beautiful way that men knocked back a shot of white rum straight and chased it with a mouthful of water was hardly the practice anymore. I suppose that many of the old rum drinkers who frequented the rum shops and played their dominoes in the yards, street corners and beaches were dying out. The culture was changing. Interestingly enough, I did not see any of the old African *warri* game (an ancient numbers board game) being played, another sign of the times.

My sister Thelma was back home from Trinidad and mom had her family back in place for a full month. Uncle Hugh, he of the infamous bicycle, had suggested that sister Thelma was too underexposed in Barbados, and would become more outgoing and engaging if she finished her secretarial studies in Trinidad. I was able to help mom support Thelma for two years in Trinidad while she studied there and lived in San Juan with Uncle Lloyd and his wife Lee. Uncle Hugh was surely on to something, for within a year after Thelma returned from Trinidad, she became a full-time secretary in the Barbados civil service. The young men were paying attention to her, and she was now responding positively to their overtures. Within two years of her return, she was married.

When I left Barbados in 1955 for Nassau, the Barbados Labor Party was in power. Grantley Adams was premier in the first ministerial form of government ever formed in Barbados. Sir Grantley had won the first elections ever held under Adult Suffrage in 1951, and his party held sway. In 1955, Errol Barrow formed the Democratic Labor Party in opposition to Adams' Barbados Labor Party. The BLP again won the general elections in 1956, but Barrow was coming on strong, and by 1959 when I returned to Barbados, Barrow was on everybody's lips. Even my mother, a longtime Grantley Adams supporter, was for Errol Barrow. My father, however, remained wholeheartedly in the Adams camp and Mom conceded that, although Adams had brought her the vote, Barrow knew better what to do with the country.

A few things began to fall into place for me regarding the political moves being made. In late 1953 when I was in the original sixth form at Modern High School, Cameron Tudor was our teacher in a course called British Constitution. I was aware that Mr. Tudor, Sleepy Smith and Errol Barrow along with others, used to meet at Tudor's sister's home on Fontabelle Road for political discussions. I also knew that they were trying to get my headmaster to join them. Mr. Lynch did not join the group, for he was at heart a conservative businessman with his own political agenda. He was not a party man, and certainly not one to be sensitive to Labor Party politics. It was out of these meetings that began the process through which Errol Barrow split from Adams, crossed the floor, and established the Democratic Labor Party that emerged in 1955.

When Adams moved on to head the West Indies Federation in 1958, he left the door wide open for a man of Errol Barrow's acumen to walk in. I in no way mean to demean or disparage his foresight, political skills or bravery, and having met and entertained him in my home in Jamaica much later in life, I have tactile experience of the man, his style, and his strength of character. By 1961, the Democratic Labor Party had won the general elections, and he became premier, then the country's first Prime Minister when Barbados became an independent nation in 1966.

The month in my homeland in early 1959 wasn't spent just visiting relatives and catching up on political developments. I was also reassessing my plans for advanced education and checking out the local fun spots and playgirls. Remember, I was twenty-two years old and had retired from my first career, four years as a Bahamas police officer. I was as fit as a fiddle, considered by friends to be a good dresser, a smooth dancer, a man who could hold his liquor, and someone who was fun to be around. It didn't take me long to find Alice.

She was a very good friend of one of my colleagues in Nassau. He asked me to look her up and say hello, so I did. Alice was just a few years older than I was, perhaps about twenty-five to my twenty-two. She was a schoolteacher, single, well-groomed, from an upper-middle-class family, nicely educated, a great conversationalist, and a looker. When she crossed a room, she displayed the feline grace of the hunter, not the domestic cat. Alice offered one a challenge, at least in the way I read it: "If you think you can catch and handle me, try nuh!" Alice entertained me with tea, homemade cookies and conversation while we both assessed each other. I knew that this would be more than a lay, but that lay would not be easy. After meeting her, I spent the first night thinking about her and planning strategy. I had only two weeks left on the island, so whatever I wanted to achieve in this early phase had to be done quickly, but could not seem to be in a rush.

When I went back to visit a couple of days later, I turned up in a rented car and we went riding about the island, visiting some of her friends and exploring the beaches and points of interest. Alice knew the island extremely well and introduced me to unfamiliar places of historical interest. We soon reached a point where I could sense that the jungle feline was beginning to purr and I started to pet her, gently and tentatively. I was fearful, not of harm, but of making this primal creature run away. It turned out that I was both wrong and right. Our kisses began as gentle pecks, checking the terrain for danger spots, gradually growing more confident and probing, then moving to an exploration of each other's bodies. I started to mash the accelerator, to show Alice my *savoir-faire*, and some of the moves I was bringing from Nassau, but she was way ahead of me. She found erotic areas of my body that had never been pinpointed, but I kept striving to be in command, for this cat had to know that she had at least met her match. I still had my best card to play in this game before the game. I turned to the clitoris. I gave it undivided treatment, and soon Alice was pleading, "Fuck me, you son of a bitch, fuck me!"

We were on her bed and so locked in that we fell to the ground still hitched just like dogs, even when chased away. We continued on the floor, and I knew that to hold this thoroughbred I had to make her come before I did, so it was game-on. Soon Alice started to moan. She was coming, but she did not come and stop, she came in series, several times in a row. Even then, it was not over for her. Her vagina started to contract and squeeze my penis in pulses like one does when milking a cow, and I certainly came like I'd been milked. Alice held me in her arms and boldly said, "You are the first man who ever satisfied me".

I was still naïve enough to be shocked at her openness. Of course, I had no experience of Barbadian women and very little experience of women in general. I did not even realize that what I had just found was a rare thing over which men can lose their minds. I spent every remaining day of my stay in Barbados with Alice. It was heavenly. My mother loved her and told me that she would make me a good wife. I did not argue with mom. After all, I'd be gone in a few days, and I believed in the future. I had places to go and things to do before I slept. In the meantime, I would only snooze and learn.

A few things happened while I was on vacation in Barbados in

April and May 1959 which led to a change in my plans for Canada. During discussions with my former headmaster and employer at Modern High School, Mr. Lynch, I learned that a few of my schoolmates were already out in Western Canada. Lynch had succeeded in placing them at an institution in Moose Jaw, the Saskatchewan Provincial Training School, which was established by the Provincial Government in 1955 to house and train the mentally retarded (as they were called at that time) in the hope that the more trainable among them could be taught viable skills. The school also had a registered nurse training program where they paid student workers while they were on their way to becoming psychiatric nurses. Mr. Lynch suggested that I consider joining my colleagues in Moose Jaw where I would be paid while I studied, rather than going to Halifax, Nova Scotia where I would have to pay to qualify in land surveying. At twenty-two, I was young enough to be open to this and other educational options that were bound to come at a later date.

Three of the smartest men in my high school graduating class were in the program at the Training School. Grant Proverbs, Ethelbert Thompson and Ken Waldron were better-prepared students than I was and were well ahead of me in Barbados. I started high school much later than they did, but because of the double promotions that I got each year, I caught them in the last two terms of fifth form and we all graduated together. I remembered Grant as the best-prepared student; Ethelbert was the smartest and Ken, the most disciplined. Ethelbert went on to earn a Ph.D. in psychology and had an excellent practice as a clinical psychologist before his death at an early age. Ken Waldron became a medical doctor but chose to teach English at a university in South Korea before his retirement in northern Alberta. Grant Proverbs drowned in the Saskatchewan River one year after we reconnected in Moose Jaw, a few months before he was due to enter the University of Saskatchewan in Saskatoon to study engineering. Reports said that he had gone swimming in the late spring runoff and got into difficulty after suffering cramps.

Within a couple of weeks, arrangements were made for me to go to the Training School. I already had a student's visa to enter Canada, so there was no problem there, and my colleagues in Saskatchewan spoke on my behalf before the Principal and staff at the school. My colleagues were doing so well and had established such an enviable reputation that it was relatively easy for the administration to accept another young man of their caliber and the same school that they had attended.

11. NEVER SAY GOODBYE

I left Barbados for Canada in the middle of May 1959 with great expectations and no special agenda. I was open to experience and anxious to see where this ride would take me. With the princely sum of one thousand United States dollars, I carried all my belongings in a regular-sized grip: one pair of black oxfords, a pair of brown shoes, a blue blazer, a grey suit (all summer weight), a white shirt, a blue one, and a pair of brown slacks. I also had a couple pairs of socks, maybe two changes of underwear, two polo shirts, three ties and some toiletries to complete my possessions.

The flight to Toronto's Malton Airport was uneventful except for the mild snowstorm that greeted us. An immigration officer cordially greeted me and joked that Canada had reserved this snowstorm for me as a special honor, seeing as I had brought no topcoat. I joked that my blazer would have to do. I was now in Canada and could go wherever I chose, but I was not willing to venture out of that airport until my flight was called. In the meantime, I walked around and studied the local culture as seen from an airport terminal.

The enormity of Malton Airport was the first thing that struck me. Our Caribbean airports were so small by comparison and this one had moveable ramps that jutted out from the terminal into the exit door of the aircraft, allowing passengers to exit into the terminal building without having to brave the elements. How civilized! There was nothing so sophisticated in the islands that I had seen so far. Back in the Caribbean the halt, the blind, and sometimes the lame had to walk from the tarmac to the terminal building. This sometimes became an ordeal depending on where the aircraft came to a stop.

I was only accustomed to seeing a few white people in any setting in the West Indies, but here in the Toronto airport, everybody was white. As far as I could see, I was the only black man around. It felt so strange, as if I had gone to a different planet where everything was so clean, like a hospital. And what is this? White men picking up the trash, cleaning floors, driving taxis and buses. I had had a slight glimpse of my new world four or five weeks before with the white steward on a BOAC airplane, but I was not culturally prepared for this bigger shock. Colonialism had acculturated me into expecting white people to do only cushy jobs, and with jolting haste, the unfair game within the colonial structure continued to unfold before me – and my feet were barely on the threshold of the real world.

After two hours in Toronto, I flew on to Winnipeg, Manitoba. There was nothing to see but snow. It was particularly cold for May, and for the first time, I began to wonder why I would want to leave the tropics to submit myself to the weather in this enormous country. Personal growth and achievement is the quest. Forget about the weather. It's already May, think of what you have to look forward to in January and February, and contrast that with the hot summers and beautiful Septembers that you hear about.

After a short stay in Winnipeg, we flew to Regina, Saskatchewan, where there was much more snow on the ground, and then boarded a bus for the short ride to Moose Jaw. We had spent about four hours of travel time getting from Toronto to Regina, and yet the clocks in Regina showed that we had only used up two hours. I had traveled two time zones west of Toronto without knowing what a time zone was, and I was now in a country that had five of them. Just imagine the insularity of the city folk in my home country who had the effrontery to call my people country bumpkins, yet we lived only ten miles from Bridgetown on an island that was just twenty-one miles long and fourteen miles wide.

Four Modern High School boys were together again after four years of separation and growth. Ethelbert was still the funny one, Grant was still the most serious, but his jokes were always biting, and Ken remained the most reticent. After greeting each other with bear hugs and back-slapping, the guys invited me back to their digs to meet their landlord and plan my moving in with them since the Training School did not provide living quarters.

It was fine with me. On reflecting now on this event, I recognize an interesting personal trait, and that is that I have never been too concerned about where I might live or find a place to sleep. There is a bit of the nomad in me, which might be attributable to my African roots, or my Boy Scout camping experiences, or indeed to my elementary understanding of my Biblical readings. Somehow, I believed and knew that the Lord looked after all His children, and reminded us that even the birds have nests but the Son of Man had nowhere to lay his head. Like Him, I thought, I would always find a place. To their credit, my comrades wanted to spare me the embarrassment they had faced in finding digs in this lily-white underexposed town.

I went along with the guys to see where we would live, landlord permitting. My colleagues were living in the attic of this small two-bedroom, one-bathroom house. The landlord and his wife and young baby occupied the main floor. The bathroom only had a tub, no shower. At least I would have the experience of bathing in a tub since my indoor plumbing experiences so far had been limited to showers. There were two beds in the attic and a hot plate for cooking. The bathroom was downstairs.

Our landlord Dick and his wife were a young couple of maybe thirty years of age to our twenty-two and twenty-three and were quite happy to earn the extra rent money that I would bring to the pool. They indicated that their only concern was that we observe the morning bathroom arrangements and that we leave the bathroom clean after each use. These conditions offered no hardships to us, for we were all disciplined young men being trained as psychiatric nurses.

I agreed to stay with my colleagues. I was a little concerned about sleeping with three others in a small attic room with only a hot plate and no room to scratch or fart, even though the guys assured me that the meals I would get at the Training School made cooking at home unnecessary. That first night in Moose Jaw in May 1959 was so cold that I was glad to be among friends and colleagues who could warm each other with conversation and jokes. The landlord controlled the temperature from his quarters downstairs and was not going to change his routine to accommodate young men from the tropics. Six o'clock came quickly and by 7:00 a.m. we were dressed and gone to meet the bus that picked up staff and students from various points around town.

Gene the bus driver was a Hungarian refugee. This was my first encounter with the large number of European refugees and immigrants in Saskatchewan and Alberta. Gene kept up a monologue all the way to the Training School campus, but he did not manage to prevent me from noticing that all the garbage truck operators and the waste collectors on the streets were white men. My new-world education was continuing through observation, personal analysis and interpretation.

It was beginning to look like a job was a job, with none reserved for any particular race. What one did was based on his level of preparation, the opportunities that were available to him to prepare, and his willingness to grasp those opportunities. In case you may think that my dwelling on this issue is pathological, I beg to remind you that the period is early 1959, that I was a very young man from the British colonies and that I had agonized over the unfairness of colonialism from my earliest years. Now I was in a society where my family's teachings about a fair and free society – and my uneducated instincts – were being confronted as Canadian life passed before me.

I was first directed to the chief instructor's office. Ms. Gabriel was as deceptively sweet as you can imagine. Her uniform, white from the bottom of her shoes to the top of her nurse's headdress, was as beautifully starched and ironed as was the uniforms of my former colleagues when we were rookies in the Bahamas Police. I kept thinking that to obtain such a result, the launderer must have had access to my grandmother's arrowroot starch, which she produced from her home garden. Villagers would buy grandmother's starch to prepare special shirts for their menfolk, the altar vestments at church, and to make diaper-rash powder for babies. I was the one who planted and maintained the arrowroot patch, so I knew its purposes well.

Ms. Gabriel proved to be a regular martinet in disguise. There were a few other young men and women who were part of my new class beginning that morning, and Ms. Gabriel turned us over to the principal, Dr. Armstrong, for our initial tour of the Training School. An English psychiatrist, Armstrong explained that the school was established by the provincial government to house, train and prepare students for gainful participation in the economy of the province, and at the same time free their parents, so that they could continue to perform in society, freed from the stress of looking after developmentally disabled children. Dr. Armstrong further explained that the school was divided into two distinct sections, a low-grade side and a high-grade side. The low-grade side housed inmates who were on the lower scale of intelligence ratings such as what were then called idiots, cretins, hydrocephalics, and so on. The high-grade side housed inmates of generally higher intelligence such as those whom the profession then regarded as morons and mongoloids.

Dr. Armstrong sobered us a bit by explaining that wherever possible, he liked to chat with parents upon their first time visiting their children. He stated that in the majority of cases, higher-achieving parents, especially those with demonstrably higher IQs, would be directed by him to the lower-grade side. Severe mental retardation more often occurs through chemical imbalances than through genetics, or so the thinking was sixty years ago. Morons, went the logic, were hardly ever expected to be produced by high-IQ parents.

Nothing I had ever encountered prepared me for the shock that overcame me on that initiation tour of the Training School. I got sick when I saw the physical specimens that nature can produce: cretins, idiots – and there were so many of them – contorted, bent, hydrocephalic, pin-headed, some with bedsores, all of them needing more prompt care and attention. This was partially why it was relatively easy for me to get here to be trained to look after these patients. It occurred to me that we must have had children born like this in our villages back home, but I had never heard of or seen any formed like these. Maybe the level of medical practice that made births like these possible was not available to the developing countries; maybe our midwives dispatched our deformed and stricken babies at birth, thus sparing parents and society the cost and anguish of looking after these products of human intercourse.

The high-grade side was much more pleasant but carried its own set of challenges. Many of the inmates looked normal but were only capable of functioning at a below-normal intelligence level. This presented its own special set of problems for us trainees. Indeed, we had to be trained to handle our behavior, especially as regards expectation of rationality from these normal-looking, abnormally-behaving adult children.

Lunch was a non-starter for me. The kitchen was massive, and it was completely open to the dining room. The ranges were huge, and ovens and grills took up a complete wall and everything was stainless steel, gleaming clean, and had post-modern lighting, sort of like sunlight indoors. There was so much food that it boggles the mind even now. I can understand what my colleagues meant by not having to cook at home since all the meals were free. Staff and ambulatory residents ate together in one dining hall. That first day was beef steak for lunch, and you should see the size of the steaks, at least sixteen ounces of sirloin broiled to perfection and presented like matching sisters competing for attention. They caught my attention all right, but only the visual, not gastronomic. No food in the world could enter my stomach after seeing what I saw that day. I kept fearing that I would not make it. Wouldn't I have been better off to have gone to land surveying school in Nova Scotia?

That first afternoon was spent in orientation and meeting other students and staff. The psychiatric nursing course was of three years' duration, so there were students representing each year. The guys from my high school were second-years. There were about eight or nine Barbadians, all placed by my former headmaster, but only five of us had been his students. The other three showed the generosity and public-spiritedness of Louis Lynch. He was showing us the importance of service to our communities. But maybe he had ulterior motives, judging by all the things he accomplished after we left school. He was a good man, there's no denying that.

There were several central Europeans in our courses and more general work areas. The Hungarian Revolution was only struck down two years earlier, so I met and later became friends with many men who had fled Hungary. The Slavs and the Croats were still trying to find common ground; Tito, who ethnically represented both sides, couldn't keep the lid on the unrest, so many Yugoslavians wound up in Moose Jaw. I struck up a strong friendship with a colleague, Peter Koritnik, a Croatian, from whom I got an education and a foretaste of what was to come thirty years later with the breakup of Yugoslavia and the atrocities that would take place in the Bosnian War.

Peter had been a third-year medical student when he got out of his country. He did not have a good enough command of English to pass the entry exams to Canadian medical schools – not to mention the money – so he found himself among us at the Training School. Then there was Jim Kojack, the school's podiatrist. Jim had been a practicing podiatrist in Hungary for many years before he had to flee his homeland. Jim showed me how to keep my feet in proper condition, the best kinds of footwear to use, and make walking and running a pleasurable pastime. And then there was Willie Shergul, a former lieutenant in the German Army during World War II. He was at the Training School for nine years by this time and had risen to the level of nurse supervisor. Shergul still seemed to think that he was an officer in Hitler's army, and tried to lord it over us blacks. That is, until two of us cornered him in the men's room one day and scared the hell out of him. He was very congenial after that.

I met many other staff members that afternoon. The recreation director mentioned that he would need help with summer camp which would open in a month; then there was the physiotherapist, a cute little redhead from Ontario, who looked like an interesting date. And then there was the occupational therapist, a very young, remarkably composed lady, with sparkling ocean-blue eyes and a prominent nose that made her otherwise non-remarkable face distinctly memorable. Never in my wildest dreams would I ever have imagined that this young professional would play such a powerful and influential role in my life.

I introduced myself to the recreation director and offered to assist him with summer camp. When he learned that I had been a Boy Scout and a member of the Church Lads Brigade in Barbados, had been to many camps, and moreover had earned a certificate in First Aid from St. John Ambulance while serving as a member of Her Majesty's police force in the Bahamas, I was a shoo-in for his team. His job was to convince the director of nursing to release me from her programs for two weeks in June. They worked it out. A certain amount of self-study was necessary while I was effectively out of the main training program so soon, and for two weeks at that. When I broke it down, working at a summer camp with mentally challenged children would provide excellent training for someone whose eventual job it would be to provide health care and guidance to the handicapped.

I was so happy and excited when we got home that evening that in spite of the cold, I decided that my colleagues and I should go out and have a drink. When I broached the idea to the boys, it was met with a high degree of apprehension. I couldn't understand it. I mean, where in the world could you find four healthy young men under twenty-four years of age, especially Caribbean Christian men, properly brought up and schooled, who would not want to go to a bar after work and knock back a few? Evidently in Moose Jaw, Saskatchewan, in May 1959. My fast-moving education curve was again in play.

The liquor laws in this town were primitive. To get any alcoholic drink other than beer, one had to have dinner in a restaurant, and if that person was a female, she could not have a drink without male company. Some parlors served beer only, with men on one side, and mixed couples and women on the other side of the separated hall. No one under twenty-one years of age could even take a message to the grounds of these drinking places. My colleagues swore that they would give up drink rather than submit themselves to such regulations. So why not buy a bottle at a liquor store and have a drink at home to celebrate my going off to camp then? This I learned was an equally demoralizing idea. The nearest liquor store was miles away on the edge of town, and no one had a car. What's more, the liquor stores were all government outlets, and the managers, by law, had to record purchasers' names, addresses, dates of birth, as well as the quantities and types of liquor purchased. No native people were allowed to buy any kind of alcohol, and our landlord did not allow alcoholic beverages in his house. So much for that.

What a hell hole this place was going to be! I had been given sips of alcoholic beverages before I could walk and had grown up in a society where everyone had a drink, and sharing a drink with a friend at home or in a public place, day or night, was the civilized thing to do. I could remember when my mother or father would put a finger in their drink and then put that finger in my mouth so that I would not be left out of the fellowship (and also to keep away worms, they told me). And now here I was at twenty-two years of age, hoping to survive at least three years in this medieval town. All this after leading men twice my age, arresting adults for all kinds of offenses, some quite serious, and being a known regular at several watering holes around Nassau, now I come to these kiss-me-ass backwoods, so cold and begging so hard to be warmed by a simple civilized drink. No wonder folks engaged in binge drinking when they got the opportunity.

One of the first truly outdoor activities I got engaged in was a local hunting trip. I was very excited when some of my caucasian colleagues asked me to join them in a hunt for rabbits and grouse in what was early spring. I was beginning to forget how much I used to enjoy the company of my male friends at cricket or soccer games in Nassau, plus the banter and wordplay that we engaged in and the simple camaraderie that bound men together at our police club. I had no gun, but that didn't matter since I only wanted to walk in the great Canadian outdoors on a lovely spring day. There were still patches of snow on the ground, and I was so fascinated by the large expanse of the landscape that I was not paying sufficient attention to the terrain that we were covering.

After a while, I could hear the ice crunching under my feet and before you could say "cat scratch yuh", the ice gave way and I was up to my ankles in ice-cold water. I was overcome by two emotions: on the one hand, I feared catching my death of cold, and on the other, my status as a man was now threatened in the presence of new guys. The fellows all tried to put me at ease and quickly allayed my fears of suffering any serious problems, assuring me that it was only a minor setback. We abandoned our hunt shortly after this incident, and rightly so, for what useful purpose would we make out of a skinny rabbit or a half-starved grouse especially considering the fleshy steaks and pork chops that were so generously served in the Training School cafeteria?

A few short weeks after my first foray into the open prairie country, we were off to summer camp with thirty boys and girls specially chosen from residents of the Training School. All those selected were what we called high-grade, mostly morons and mongoloids, with a few Attention Deficit Disorder students to provide an extra challenge. Saskatchewan is a large province, covering over 251,000 square miles, and the longest motor trip I had ever taken in my life so far were the trips from Moose Jaw to Regina, the capital, about fifty miles away. My colleagues and I would sometimes slip east to Regina on weekends for the occasional beer and more urbane activities. But this campsite was near Saskatoon and the University of Saskatchewan, approximately two hundred miles from Moose Jaw.

The bus ride to the campsite was memorable. We sang camp songs for much of the four or five-hour trip, and once I got the hang of the songs, I pitched right in and blended and bonded with the group. Many of the songs were universal camp songs that I already knew, but there was one French Canadian song "Alouette" which tickled my fancy, and when I finally got it my stock went up the charts. I had always fancied myself a singer and had grown from a boy tenor in elementary school to a budding adult baritone by this time. The fact that I was black did not hurt, for Billy Eckstine and Nat King Cole were in their heyday and folks expected that there were a lot of black men with equal talent.

I had anticipated that we would be pitching tents, cooking outdoors, and sleeping on groundsheets, or at most in sleeping bags. There was no such luck. The main cabin had sleeping rooms with males and females manageably separated, a cooking range in the kitchen, supervisor's quarters, a large dining room, and several project rooms. That first night and every night for the next week, we made a bonfire and sat around it roasting wieners and marshmallows and singing our hearts out.

Alouette, gentille alouette,
Alouette je te plumerai ...

Every lover instinctively knows when he or she has connected with a member of the opposite sex. Kim, the occupational therapist, and I connected that first evening over the bonfire. This is not an art form for which one can be trained. It's a matter of two kindred spirits recognizing each other. It then becomes a question of what they want to do about it. I slept peacefully that night, having had the presence of mind to travel with a sleeping bag. I was glad to climb into it and pull the bed covers over me. Late spring nights on the Canadian prairies are not designed for people of darker hues. Tomorrow would be soon enough to address the matter of Kim.

After breakfast the next day, she held occupational therapy classes in the day room. I volunteered to help as an assistant. I was impressed by her earnestness and her empathy with the students. She was able to establish rapport very quickly, and the students loved her. I noted quite early that these mentally or otherwise challenged youngsters trusted others very readily, and they were very quick to express their love and affection. They endeared themselves to you and consequently exposed themselves to abuse or mistreatment. I noted Kim's patience and recognized that she would be capable of teaching me a lot. My observations led to the recognition of the effectiveness of genuine humility. One of the life lessons that I had learned in the Bahamas police force was the ability to observe, and I had made effective use of my skill in this area while I was in Nassau. I would put this training into play again and possibly make my effectiveness felt at an early stage.

I checked our supplies and found some half-inch rope in a cupboard. After obtaining permission to use it, I invited a few seemingly bored students to sit with me at a table. I figured that I might amuse them and maybe gain their attention by teaching them how to tie knots that I had learned to use as a Boy Scout and member of the Boys' Brigade. The Anglican vicar of my parish taught us many useful things at this kind of camp when I was a youngster. To be sure, our camps were far more rustic and outdoorsy, but the idea was the same.

Quietly, I sat and started tying knots. I made half-hitches, clove-hitches, figures of eight, bowlines, reef knots, rolling hitches, sheet bends, round turns, two half-hitches and slip-me-nooses, and one that didn't have a name, one that I used the most as a country boy. We used it to temporarily restrain small stock when we had no swivels. This knot prevented the rope from tightening and strangling the animal as it grazed in the field. It's a very simple and effective tool which my father and I often used, especially when we bought small stock from neighboring villages and had to get them back to our home. My table became a big hit, and in a short time, I had youngsters filling every available seat, tying knots under my guidance.

Every student was now fully aware of my presence in camp and wanted to learn some of my skills. The supervisors too wanted to know more about me and engaged me as often as time permitted. It was all genuine and guileless, with no hint of condescension. It was an interest in the culture of others that Canadians naturally expressed, an aspect of the Canadian personality that I would find constantly as we engaged each other over the next ten years. These events gave me and Kim an early opportunity to exchange ideas.

We both began to talk on the second day of camp and sought to find out about each other's culture, exchanging ideas and finding commonality. It was like an interview, but not for a job, just a search for human identification. I learned that Kim was my age, twenty-two, almost twenty-three, and that she had graduated the previous year from McGill University in Montreal with a bachelor's degree in occupational therapy. She was a Saskatchewan girl from Prince Albert, and her parents still lived there. Her job at the Training School was her first, and I was impressed with the poise and assurance of this young and seemingly not very worldly white woman, and how she engaged me. I had built up a reputation among my colleagues in the Bahamas police, and civilian friends, as Mr. Cool, and so I was.

Kim and I kept the conversation around generalities. I knew that many Barbadians and people of color had attended McGill University over the years, and there were many West Indians in Montreal. Kim was sure to have met many people like me while at McGill, hence her ease of discourse. I was, however, unprepared for her command and natural leadership, and was highly impressed. I had been associated with bright females all my life, from my mother, other family members, high school classmates and lovers, but this was my first encounter with a white woman my age, who was also my boss, and with an education that I craved but as yet had no path to achieving. Regardless, I figured that I could learn from her. I also knew that I wanted to fuck her, but I would not be in a hurry. Education, an introduction to Canadian culture and my aspirations were at least as important.

★★★

Fascination with politics and the political process never left me from the very first time when my father took me to hear Grantley Adams speak on my village corner in Cane Garden, St. Andrew in 1944 when I was eight years old. Canadian politics, both Federal and Provincial in 1959 was captivating to a young and impressionable observer. John Diefenbaker, leader of the Progressive Conservative Party was Prime Minister of Canada, and Tommy Douglas of the CCF was premier of Saskatchewan. John Diefenbaker was a Prairie boy representing the Prince Albert Riding in Saskatchewan. I was in for a good dose of nationalism and western agrarianism.

I grew up thinking that only black people were exploited by whites under a system of European colonialism and that the colonists perpetuated the system through white managerial control in conjunction with voting restrictions for the local or indigenous people. I also knew that colonial power politics was led by conservatives and that it was usually some form of a Labor Party that tried to break the yoke of conservative power in the interest of popular local advancement. John Diefenbaker gave me a different perspective.

The man was a sort of evangelical political prairie leader who was completely home-bred. He took all three of his degrees from the University of Saskatchewan before establishing his law career in Saskatoon and his political career in North Battleford, not very far away. Diefenbaker was a conservative, but a strange one and his life-long battle was fought on at least four fronts: first, he had to defend and promote the interests of Western farmers against Eastern manufacturers' power; second, he had to defend Canada and Canadian natural resources against American exploitation and to disabuse the thoughts of those Eastern Canadian business people who seemed willing to accept American capital without national guidelines; third, he had to shield the nation from US cultural dominance, and fourth, he had to protect Canada from following blindly into US dalliances overseas.

This did not endear Diefenbaker to the hearts of Canadian conservatives, and so in spite of being in Federal politics since the 1920s, he did not become leader of the party and Prime Minister of Canada until 1957, and even then, by having to form a new party called the Progressive Conservative Party. None of this is meant to diminish the political astuteness of McKenzie King who was Prime Minister for all the years except for the last few during Diefenbaker's attempts to gain control of his party's leadership. The breadth of Diefenbaker's concerns was far greater than I could ever have imagined until I got a feel for the Canadian challenge, and moreover, here was a conservative sitting in a typical radical's saddle, with his nation against him most of the time. This was all pretty heady stuff for a young man from the colonies just starting his meaningful education. Diefenbaker also had British Commonwealth of Nations concerns to deal with, and he showed his genius as a diplomat when he proposed a condition for continued membership in the Commonwealth which South Africa was not willing to accept, leading them to resign and become a republic.

My colleagues were glad to welcome me back in Moose Jaw, and I was happy to be back in our attic digs. My training as a psychiatric nurse now took full flight. I began to carry a full program of work with the patient-students, as they were called, and carry a full classroom load during the week. I do not remember all the courses, but there were nursing practices such as making beds properly and administering medications; pharmacology, psychology; introduction to the different types of mental conditions, behaviors and needs of the handicapped and many others. It is worth noting that many of the things that I learned during the year that I spent in training there, I was able to use in later life. I can still make a bed as precisely and crisply as any chambermaid, and when the time came that we were able to have household help, I delighted in demonstrating to maids how the corners of any bed that I slept on had to be shaped.

Whenever my roommates and I found time to converse, the emphasis was on what were we going to make of ourselves now that higher education in this wonderful land of opportunity was available to us. All of them planned on spending two more years in the nursing program and gaining their psychiatric nursing certification before going on to the University of Saskatchewan. Grant planned on studying engineering, Ethelbert intended to study psychology, and Ken was set to study medicine. I planned to leave Saskatchewan after a year and head to Halifax, Nova Scotia to become a land surveyor like my friend Alfred Bellot, and then head back to Nassau, where the sun was warm, the beaches were beautiful, the girls were friendly, and the drums sometimes went all night.

Kim and I started to see each other regularly in the evenings. At first, we would just talk in her condo. Kim lived with two young roommates from Windsor Ontario in a two-bedroom unit. Her roommates were sisters; both worked at the Training School, one as physiotherapist and the other as a secretary. It was during my dates with Kim that I was introduced to two significant and life-changing concepts. The first was an assessment of my plans for advanced education, and the second was an introduction to the Baha'i Faith.

One evening out of the blue, Kim asked me if I had been exploring the possibilities of attending a Canadian university. My answer was that the thought had crossed my mind during wild speculations, but I could not see how I could afford it. Moreover, I had not finished sixth form, had not completed the sciences, and probably would not be accepted. Kim responded that she knew many university graduates who were not as well prepared after graduating from university, as I was in my present stage, and asked if I would mind exploring the possibilities of going to university. This young woman was getting into my mind, and constructively leading me away from the thoughts that burned my groin. I wanted to make love and she wanted to introduce me to higher education. After much discussion, I agreed to send my high school transcript to McGill and Alberta to ascertain my qualifications for entry.

It was now June 1959. The University of Alberta responded within two weeks. McGill responded in late 1960 when I was four months into my first year of studies at Alberta. The reply from Alberta had been that they would accept me if I could produce acceptable levels of passing the Province of Alberta's Grade 12 examinations in physics, botany or chemistry, and mathematics. I have always responded to a challenge. First, I had to complete my year in training at Moose Jaw. That would be satisfied by May 1960. A check with the Alberta Department of Education revealed that I could take only two subjects at summer school, but that correspondence courses were also available. I decided to take botany by correspondence starting September 1959 and to register for summer school for the six weeks of June to mid-July 1960 where I would take Grade 12 physics and mathematics. The die was cast.

I started to attend gatherings of the Baha'i faith. Moose Jaw's faithful were led by a charming elderly white lady named Anne. I remember her mostly for her openness, her sisterly trust and the full-length mink coat she wore in June. She always seemed so fragile, and maybe the mink coat was making more than a style statement since she wore pretty light blouses beneath that animal hide.

At my first meeting, Kim, who had started to study the faith, introduced me to a wide cross-section of people that I never would have imagined were in our little town. They were mostly young adults from all parts of the world, mostly Europeans, some Asians, one or two mixed couples, and a few older Canadians. The meeting was low-key. Anne invited newcomers to explore the faith and gave us a short introduction. She invited those of us who were interested to join the weekly study group. What I learned that evening was sufficiently interesting to make me want to go back.

I was not particularly interested in religion at this stage of my life. I had grown up in the Anglican Church at a time when my country was under total control of Britain. Everyone in a position of authority or control in any meaningful area of the island's existence was a white man. God himself was portrayed as an elderly white man with a long beard and an unsmiling visage. Jesus, his Palestinian son, came out of the middle eastern desert as a blue-eyed blond man in the image of our European masters, further confusing my impressionable mind. I gave up on religion as soon as I entered high school. I was not ready to go back to this charade, I thought, but this is where Kim was, and she was genuine and good and I wanted to spend as much time as I could with her. This exploration of a new faith is an additional facet of my education, I thought.

I attended many Baha'i meetings and grew to enjoy the atmosphere. Like so many major religious beliefs, the faith came out of the Middle East – Persia to be exact. A merchant known as the Bab was moved with compassion for the poor and recognized the oneness of humanity of all individuals, the oneness of all religions, the equality of women, the need for a spiritual and moral transformation, and the essential harmony of religion and science. This was heady stuff in Persia in the middle of the nineteenth century, and the Bab soon lost his head. It was left to Baha'u'llah, followed by his son Abdu'l-Baha to promote the faith.

In 1959 when I first encountered Baha'is, they had no church. Their tenets were quite appealing and I could easily have accepted their faith, but events were moving so fast that I had only one year to mark, learn, and inwardly digest all the ideas to which I was being subjected. As I record these thoughts nearly sixty years later, the Baha'i faith has grown all over the world, and most exposed people recognize the name, even though I suspect that not many can tell you anything about the faith itself. Kim and I found immense warmth and comfort, knowledge and growth among the Baha'is of Moose Jaw, and I will be forever thankful.

***

Now that I have a chance to reflect on that first year and to compare it with other single years in my life, I realize how much I learned from 1959 to 1960. I was carrying a full course load at the Training School, working eight hours a day, studying the Baha'i Faith, seeing Kim most evenings, and immersing myself in Canadian politics.

There were three very interesting men in Canadian politics when I started in Canada in May 1959. First, there was John Diefenbaker.

After many long years of struggle and disappointment, he finally got control of the leadership of his party and became Prime Minister of Canada in 1957 with a minority government. On the other hand, here was Tommy Douglas, a Saskatchewan man like Diefenbaker, premier of the Province. One was a conservative, the other a socialist, and supposedly in the middle was Lester Pearson, an Ontario Liberal, leader of the Federal Opposition. Theoretically, one would expect John Diefenbaker and Tommy Douglas to be miles apart philosophically, but to me they were not. Diefenbaker appeared to me like a colonial native leader fighting to preserve his country from the rapacious business activities of the imperialist master – in this case, the Americans. For much of the time, he was waging an equal battle with eastern business Interests who seemed not nearly as concerned over the Americans as Diefenbaker would have liked them to be.

Diefenbaker sought to impress on his fellow Canadians that they must not blindly follow US foreign policy and be taken for granted by American leaders. They could not without serious debate simply accept ballistic missiles on Canadian soil, or allow Americans to treat with Canadian water rights without restraint and negotiation; the extraction of minerals from Canadian soil and timber from Canadian forests ought to be agreed on with meaningful inputs from an independent Canada; Canadian waters could not be fished indiscriminately, Canada should trade more with Great Britain to offset the imbalance of trade with the USA, and most important of all, Canada had to guard its culture against the domination of its big brother to the south. "The Chief", as he became known, had few friends in his party and fewer among leaders in Ontario and Quebec, but his concerns were familiar to me for these were partly the things I grew up hearing Caribbean leaders Grantley Adams and Norman Manley, Marryshaw, Butler, Eric Williams, and Bustamante talking about. Diefenbaker managed to hold on as the Prime Minister of Canada until 1963, the year I graduated from the University of Alberta.

I never had the pleasure of meeting Diefenbaker, but I did meet Lester Pearson and Tommy Douglas. Let us talk about Tommy Douglas first. He was born in Scotland in 1904 and emigrated to Manitoba with his parents when he was six years old. After high school, he went on to the University of Manitoba and later to a Baptist seminary for a master of divinity degree. He was a Baptist pastor during the early years of the Depression but was convinced that he could do far more in politics to relieve the prolonged suffering of the farm families on the prairies than he could do as a minister. He became a member of the CCF, the Cooperative Commonwealth Federation which had been founded in 1932.

Tommy Douglas was elected to the Canadian House of Commons in 1935 but lost his seat after only a few years. He went back to Saskatchewan, became leader of the CCF there, and in 1944 led the party to victory, becoming premier of the province. Tommy Douglas and the CCF stood for such policies as a mixed economy through the nationalization of some key industries; a welfare state with portable universal pensions; a single-payer health insurance system; welfare payments to the needy; children's allowances; unemployment insurance and workers' compensation.

When I started in Moose Jaw in May 1959, he was premier of the province of Saskatchewan. I've maintained a love affair with radio since my boyhood days when every man in our village would assemble outside Albert Springer's window to hear broadcasts of Joe Louis' fights. He was the only man in our village who had a radio and for the entire week before a fight, we were reminding Springer to make sure that his old Model A Ford had a strong battery. There was no electricity in our village until after I grew up and went abroad, so Springer's car battery and shortwave radio were our only direct source of important news.

When I was a youngster in Barbados, my father took me everywhere. Fortunately, most places we went to were honorable, except for a few dice and rummy low-stakes games. And so, I would hang out among the men and listen to our hero Joe Louis slay whatever dragon he faced that night in the ring. We almost collapsed that night in 1944 when little Billy Conn gave Joe Louis a run for his money, running, bobbing and weaving, and hiding for thirteen rounds until he started to believe that he could beat Louis. Then, he stood still to exchange punches with Joe Lewis, and it was lights out for Mr. Conn.

It was over the radio that I first heard Tommy Douglas speak. He was completely captivating. He was talking about all the things that I thought a leader should be thinking of putting in place for his people. I was twenty-three years old by this time and knew enough about the nuances of politics to know instinctively what underprivileged people needed. I just did not expect to hear these things in the white world, and Tommy Douglas could tell jokes, sir! Every joke cemented his argument. He could hold you in his hand and entertain you until he educated you on your need and how his government would put the legislation in place to satisfy that need.

The CCF led by Douglas became the first socialist government of any major state or province in North America. He remained premier of Saskatchewan until 1962 when he retired from provincial politics to lead the newly formed New Democratic Party (NDP) at the Federal level.

I met Tommy Douglas in 1962 during my junior year at the University of Alberta. By this time, I had become the leader of the NDP on campus and led the party to win the second-largest percentage of votes for Model Parliament and became the leader of the opposition. Tommy Douglas had come to Alberta to campaign for the NDP in the coming Federal elections. He gave a major speech to about fifteen hundred people at the Campus Auditorium where he invited a heckler to "sit down and keep your brains warm".

I had the honor of moving the vote of thanks to the speaker that evening, thus addressing the largest live audience that I have ever faced. I believe I was the only black man in the auditorium that evening, and when I concluded by looking Tommy Douglas in the eye and quoting Paul Lawrence Dunbar I said:

Go on and up
Our eyes shall watch thy continuous climb
Our ears shall list thy praise

I felt empowered to write and tell my mother that I was cut out to be in politics and that I would seek a career in the field of elective politics. Her answer was short and emphatic. "Politicians are whores," she said. "They will sacrifice you when it suits their purpose. I do not recommend any dependence on political colleagues." Uh-oh! Re-analysis and realignment?

Tommy Douglas was so moved by my remarks before the largest crowd that I have ever addressed, that when I was finished, he hugged me and tried to lift me off my feet. The crowd roared to see this little five-foot-three 135-pound man trying to lift a 190-pound six-footer. Tommy won his seat in the Federal Parliament, but his party never won enough seats in the House of Commons at any time to make him prime minister. Every one of the NDP policies, however, has become a part of the fabric of Canada's existence. Either the Liberals or the Conservatives have adopted and passed into legislation policies that the NDP first stood for and to which they objected. It was only fitting that in 2017, Tommy Douglas was deemed the most influential Canadian of the twentieth century.

Throughout the summer and fall of 1959, my relationship with Kim continued to grow. I continued attending Baha'i programs and studying the Baha'i faith under her encouragement and Anne's tutelage. I also started my correspondence course in Botany with the Province of Alberta Department of Education. Interestingly, my instructor's name was Miss Weekes. My superstitious people back in Barbados would have considered this a good omen; after all, what would be the probability of traveling almost five thousand miles from home to find a correspondence schoolteacher with the same surname as mine?

Miss Weekes didn't cut me any slack, though. She made sure that I understood what I was supposed to be learning, and her notes and comments were very instructive. I passed the Alberta Grade 12 Botany exam with flying colors in the spring of 1960, and almost simultaneously was accepted into summer school in Red Deer, Alberta to take Grade 12 physics and mathematics.

Evenings with Kim warmed my heart, soul and body. Our relationship warmed with the weather and was at boiling point by the end of that first summer. I will admit to growing frustrated at times though. It seemed as though all these Canadian young women could do was neck and peck, and this one was driving me crazy. We would reach heights of ecstasy in our necking and pecking, and when I thought that surely this was the point when the fort would be breached, the gates were bolted. The drawbridge would go up, and I would cross the moat and head to my digs cussing that rass white girl who was fixing to kill me by turning me back into a teenager. Me, a former man about town, now in this town without a bar, where the beer parlor closed at nine o'clock, and there were no known houses for fun and relief. But there was a charm and a beguiling innocence and truth in those blue eyes, and an assurance that made Kim's presence a continuing draw.

I met Lester Pearson – Mike, as he was popularly called, during my final year in 1963, at the University of Alberta in Edmonton. He was on a western tour of the country while I was the leader of the New Democratic Party Youth on the Alberta campus. Pearson assured me that my country would be glad to have me back, a sentiment that I never got the opportunity to test. I had been reading about Mike Pearson for years and felt as though I knew him, but I did not physically meet him until he came to our campus.

Pearson came to politics late. He was an athlete, scholar, and professor, but finding the salary of a professor hard to live on, he joined the Canadian civil service in the Foreign Service Department. He served in Britain in the 1930s, eventually becoming Ambassador to the USA in the 1940s and took part in the formation of the United Nations. Mackenzie King brought Pearson home in 1948 and made him minister of external affairs, effectively allowing him to enter politics at the top. A safe seat was found to get him elected to the House of Commons. In 1957, Pearson won the Nobel Peace Prize, a reward for designing the 1956 strategy that facilitated the exit of Britain and France from the Suez, bringing that war to an end. When the St. Laurent government lost to Diefenbaker in 1957, St. Laurent resigned as party leader. Pearson became the leader of the Liberal Party as it went into the opposition.

I entered Canada shortly after this and started following Mike Pearson's career and reading about Canadian politics. Pearson the novice was mismatched against the veteran Diefenbaker who carved him up and kept him in the opposition until 1963 when the Liberals finally were able to form a government. Pearson served as Canadian Prime Minister until 1968. His critics say that it is hard to find any meaningful mark left by Lester Pearson on Canadian politics, but he did preside over the adoption of a new flag, the establishment of bilingualism, a universal health care system and a Canadian pension plan. Ironically, these are all the very things that non-Canadians know about Canada.

All the foregoing policies were planks in the New Democratic Party's platform for many years previous. As NDP youth leader at the University of Alberta during the early 1960s, I took the affirmative on these issues in continuing debates with my Conservative and Liberal fellow students. The messengers were denied but the messages were heard. Tommy Douglas' legacies by any name are in the books in Canada.

In the fall of 1959, I went to Regina to meet my high school sweetheart Beverly, who had gone to England in 1955 immediately after graduating from St. Michael's Girls High School in Bridgetown to study nursing. I went to the Bahamas at the same time. I first met Beverly on one of her visits to her grandmother's at Mansion Road, just up the street from my home at Powder Road and Hinesbury Road, and my friend Ronald's house was immediately beside Beverly's grandmother's. I seemed to know when Beverly would be visiting, so I soon found a way to meet her. She lived with her parents and siblings about two miles away in the Pine subdivision off Government Hill Road. It would have been less than honorable for a Boy Scout to allow a young lady to take on that journey alone, so on my honor, I started walking her home. It mattered not that I had to walk back to where I lived. Beverly and I enjoyed our long chats. I can't remember what we talked about, but we enjoyed each other's company. I had just completed the fifth form and "O" Levels, and she was starting fifth form. I think we may have reached the stage where we exchanged a quick kiss before Beverly took off and ran the last thirty yards to her house alone. God forbid that her parents should see her being escorted home by a young man. Barbados was like that during the early 1950s. In less than a year, we were both off to prepare for a future in different countries.

When I met Beverly after four and a half years, my heart skipped several beats. The blossoming girl that I last saw had grown into a polished and accomplished lady and a fully registered nurse-midwife at that. She had come to Canada to take a position at the hospital in Humboldt, Saskatchewan. I thought that we enjoyed a pleasant evening on that occasion in Regina back in 1959, but we did not meet again for fifty-seven years when we were in Atlanta for a celebration of Barbados. I invited her home to meet my family and they all fell in love, they with her, and she with them. Beverly was now a retired professor and a balanced and lovely woman. It was on this occasion that I learned that my behavior towards her so long ago had been atrocious. No pleading on my part could make her divulge the nature of what I had done. I honestly can't identify what it was, but I do confess that in my younger days I had always tried to open the door to an unattached and free woman's bed, no matter where the room was, especially if she was captivating. Was that unmanly?

★★★

Christmas of 1959 was a memorable one for that was when Kim took me to visit her parents. Kim's parents lived in Prince Albert, two hundred and twenty-seven miles straight north from Moose Jaw by way of Saskatoon. It took us three and a half hours to get there. It was cold with no snow and the roads were beautiful. The drive through Saskatoon was exhilarating. Kim had a beautiful 1958 DKW two-seater motor car and it held the road nicely. The DKW was the precursor of the Audi and Kim's was a three-liter two-stroke vehicle, more like what one would expect in a motorcycle than a car.

I believe it was I who drove all the way up. This was the first time that I had the opportunity to drive on the open highway in Canada, and I reveled in the moments. Kim's was the first German car that I had had a chance to be familiar with, for before that the only cars that I thought of were English or American. Little did I know that I would be preparing myself for a love affair with Mercedes and BMWs as I matured as a manager, senior executive and business owner in later years. Interestingly, I never saw another DKW after I left Moose Jaw in 1960.

Kim's parents, Joseph and Anne, received me very graciously. They lived in a comfortable but unpretentious apartment in the city of Prince Albert. In those days there were only towns, or farms, in rural northern Saskatchewan – no suburbs. At tea that first afternoon, Joseph and I talked while Kim and her mother went to visit friends. Joseph was an Englishman who had emigrated to Canada after World War II and found a good job with the public works department in Prince Albert. He and Anne had only one child. We had no difficulty finding common ground, Joseph and I, but I had difficulty calling him by his first name. After all, I was a strange young man brought home by his daughter, and it was only natural that I should feel like I was being interviewed by a senior director for a very important post. Joe was a cool pro and he made me feel at ease very quickly. I had dealt with Englishmen pretty much all my life, but never with one like Joseph. He was not a representative of the Colonial Office in London sent out to the West Indies to promote imperial interests. He was interested in me as a person and in my educational plans. I was still only twenty-three.

Cricket was the first mutual wicket for Joseph and me. We talked first about England's test players: Len Hutton as an opening batsman, Alec Bedster as a medium pace bowler, Jack Ikin as a wicketkeeper, Fred Truman as a fast bowler, Dennis Compton and Joe Hardstaff as solid middle-order men, and Locke and Laker, the spin bowlers. Joseph was impressed that I had watched these players in Test matches in my native Barbados. We went on to talk about West Indies cricketers of the 1950s, since he had left England before their ascendancy. I was only too pleased to tell him of Jeff Stollmeyer's command of the leg side as an opening batsman, the beauty of a Frank Worrell "on drive", the power of Everton Weekes going through the covers, and the emerging genius of Garfield Sobers. We were off to a good start.

Dinner that first evening did not start well for me. I was Sidney Poitier in "Guess Who's Coming to Dinner" before the movie was made. I had no idea how Kim had prepared her parents for my introduction. What did she tell them? Was I a friend? Was I just an international student that she found interesting? Was I someone with whom she planned to explore a serious relationship? Kim and I had no game plan, no previous rehearsal that I can recall. I knew that Kim's parents loved her and trusted her judgment, but they must have had some concerns about the nature of our relationship. Kim and I had made no declarations to each other. We really liked each other, but In a sense, we too were like fencers feeling each other out, not in search of vulnerabilities in this case, but in search of viable and enduring terrain.

This family was so comfortable in their skin that it was enthralling. They invited one of their friends who happened to suffer from multiple sclerosis to join us for dinner, and I recall that the conversation flowed easily. The Canadian penchant for simple and good food was very much adhered to in a dinner of roast beef, mashed potatoes and gravy, carrots and green beans, washed down with red wine. It was a very formally set table, strengthening my belief that Kim had told her parents that I leaned towards English formality.

My mother had taught my sister and me very well in the area of etiquette. She always served us a sit-down dinner with a knife and fork and insisted that we use the tools properly. In contrast, my mother ate her dinner out of a bowl using her fingers, while sitting on her favorite chair near the stove, near my sister and me, counseling and coaching. Even after our people were three hundred years out of West Africa, my mother maintained the eating habits of her roots. I was thirty-two years old before I met anyone other than my mother who ate with her fingers, and that was an Indian lady from Bihar State, India, with whom my wife and I dined in New York City. It's a beautiful but virtually lost art in the West. I feel like food always tastes so much better when you eat out of your hand. How else do you handle fried chicken, or lemon chicken wings, or a bone in a well-seasoned lamb or pork chop, or the last part of a steamed amberjack head, a Julie mango, or a cashew bobba? I know how I handle them all, every time, and anywhere, with my fingers.

The next morning was greeted with great anticipation. We were going to the family cabin at Christopher Lake, about an hour to the north, and we planned on staying there overnight. I was looking forward to this new adventure. Mind you, it was now late December, and we were way up north. The temperature was way below freezing, and we were heading to a cabin in the woods. I am not sanguine about it, but Kim was there, and I had my love to keep me warm, so the four of us, Kim, her parents and I loaded up the family station wagon and headed to the lake, where it was beautiful. Here was this large body of pristine water, frozen over for as far as I could see, smack in the middle of nowhere. Joe's cabin was the only one in sight, and the lake shore seemed to stretch for miles. This all had to be beautiful in the summer months but in December? I'll wait and see what surprises the day brings, I thought.

After unloading the station wagon, Kim and I went walking and exploring the lake shore while her parents set up camp. I still remember after all these years, the one kiss that Kim and I shared on that walk fifty-nine years ago. Our lips were so cold from exposure to the elements that they almost stuck together. That was the end of kissing on this trip, for thereafter we were mostly in the presence of Kim's parents, and our intimacy was conveyed through eye contact. I don't mean to infer that we were restrained in any way, but we were both in a sense very private and decorous people.

Kim and I returned from our walk to an extremely warm and inviting cabin. Joe and Anne had transformed the place into a homey den and there was a good fire going in the fireplace. We all pitched in to make and set up lunch. While all of this was going on I was reconnoitering the place, and I noted that there was no bedroom. It was a one-room cabin with an outhouse. Of course, I wondered about sleeping arrangements. These folks were fine and generous people, but I was not disposed to us all bedding down in this single room. Then too, there was the question of my stomach's reaction to all this good Canadian food. I have been known not to be able to discretely manage the build-up of gases in my intestines, which often caused noxious emissions in the dead of night. I would often blame my roommates, but how could I blame my generous hosts in this case?

As if by telepathy, Joe invited me to walk outside with him and have a look at the facilities. After showing me the location of the outhouse, we repaired to the woodshed, where we spent the next few hours demonstrating our individual skills with the ax. We split several cords of wood, probably enough to have Kim's family remember me for a long, long time. Concern about my sleeping quarters was now far from my thoughts, but that would return later. With a vengeance. It turned out that the girls, Kim and her mother, would sleep in the cabin. Joe and I would be sleeping in the car-top carrier out in the yard. I had never heard of this kind of contraption, so Joe took it on himself to introduce me to this modern lifestyle improvement. Joe had built a rectangular structure about eight feet high set on 4x4s. It was the length and width of an F150 pick-up truck bed. The floor was made of 2"x12" pine set on 2"x6" joists. The structure was covered by the bubble top of an F150 pick-up truck. When the time came for us to retire that evening, Joe and I climbed up a ladder and crawled through the only window into our cubby hole and entered our sleeping bags, fully clothed. I had been wondering how we would stay warm and not freeze to death, but we managed. In fact, we both slept very well. The next morning Joe and I climbed down to earth like brothers who had found each other after a long separation.

I learned a lot during those couple of days Kim and I spent with her parents. I was the only boy in my own immediate family, so I was not accustomed to sleeping with a man beside me. Furthermore, I had grown accustomed to the joys of sleeping with women, and never imagined that there was a warmth, though completely different, from sleeping near a male friend. Perhaps in this case of Joe and me, our mutual survival depended on our shared warmth. Just in case any reader sees homosexual musings, be assured that it was Joe's daughter that I wanted to fuck, and that thought never left my mind. The maturity and graciousness of Kim's parents never left my mind either. Even today, fifty-nine years later, I do not see myself as sufficiently evolved to take a young man that my daughter brought home for the first time, away for a weekend to my cabin on the lake, and feel comfortable enough to sleep with him despite the separate sleeping bags, in a car-top camper, deep in the woods. Sorry.

At the start of the drive back to Moose Jaw, Kim gave me a gift that I still turn to today, any time that I feel low. *Songs Of A Sourdough*, a book of poems by Robert Service, published by the Ryerson Press of Toronto, Canada, and copyrighted in 1907 by Robert W. Service. My copy is the reprint of 1959. We took turns reading to each other as we shared the drive back. I fell in love with Service's *The Cremation Of Sam McGee*. I identified with McGee, who was from Plumtree, Tennessee, USA. I came from Cane Garden in Barbados, about as far from Tennessee to the Dawson Trail in North Western Canada, as it is from Barbados to Prince Albert in Northern Saskatchewan. We had both traveled equally far from home to tackle our quest. Sam was following the Gold Rush at the turn of the twentieth century in the Northwestern Territories, and I was following the education rush of West Indian immigrants in the post-World War II mid-twentieth-century period. Neither of us liked the extreme cold of Canada, and both of us enjoyed the beauty and spaciousness of the vast land.

Service tells the story of mushing his way with Sam McGee as his companion along the Dawson Trail during a very cold Christmas. Sam got so cold that he felt that he would surely die, and he begged the poet to cremate his remains so that they would not have to forever face the deathly cold of the exacting North. It's truly a fun poem:

There are strange things done in the midnight sun
By the men who moil for gold;
The Arctic trails have their secret tales
That would make your blood run cold;
The Northern Lights have seen queer sights,
But the queerest they ever did see
Was that night on the marge of Lake Lebarge
I cremated Sam McGee.

Back in Moose Jaw, I settled back into my coursework at the Training School and completion of my Grade 12 correspondence course in botany. By March 1960, I passed the examination and in April, I completed my first year in my psychiatric nursing program. I did well in both endeavors, excellent performance in psychology and pharmacology, but poor in nursing care. Not wanting to violate my student visa stipulations, I was very painstaking about informing the Training School about my change in study programs. They were not enthusiastic about seeing me go but still offered their best wishes. My buddies, who were all in their second year, opted to finish their third and qualify as psychiatric nurses. Ethelbert and Ken did but never worked in the field professionally. Ethelbert went on to the University of Saskatchewan where he studied psychology, eventually gaining a Ph.D. Strangely, Ken came to the University of Alberta, but never declared himself to me. His excuse sometime later was that I was too busy with my politics to have time for him. After Alberta, he went to medical school in the Dominican Republic, completed his degree, but chose to become a professor of English in South Korea rather than practice medicine.

But the fair Guerdon when we hope to find
And think to burst out into sudden blaze
Comes the blind Fury with the abhorred shears
And slits the thin spun life. But not the praise.

It was a full three months after Grant Proverbs' death that I got to reading John Milton in my first-year English 200 class at the University of Alberta. The foregoing passage from Milton's Ode to Lycidas sums it all up for me. Like Lycidas, Grant was a young scholar, the brightest of all of us. As close as Lycidas was to Milton, so was Grant to Ethelbert, Ken, and me. As Lycidas died by drowning in his passage from Chester on the Irish sea, so did Grant die in the Saskatchewan River. I never got to go to Grant's funeral because the tragedy occurred on the day that I had to drive out of Moose Jaw for summer school in Red Deer, Alberta, to complete my requirements for acceptance into the University of Alberta. Milton continues:

Lycidas is dead,
Dead ere his prime, young Lycidas,
And hath not left his peer.

Kim and I were back on the road, heading North through Regina to Saskatoon, then straight northwest to Edmonton, Alberta. I guarantee that you have never seen so much land in your life, so much open country, so many grain fields, so few people. In Edmonton, Kim took me directly to the home of Frank and Daisy Garrod, longtime family friends where we spent the night. The Garrods had married late in life and had no children together, but Mr. Garrod had a daughter from an earlier marriage. They grew to play a very important role in my life. I loved them dearly, to the point where I called Frank Garrod "Papa". Mrs. Garrod was a retired schoolteacher, and Papa was a plumber – no retirement for him. He had a garden out in the back of the house where he grew all the potatoes and vegetables needed to take them through an entire winter. Mrs. Garrod must have been the greatest canner in the world, for her basement, except for my bed, desk, and bathroom was stacked floor to ceiling with every canned vegetable or preserve that their back yard and the nearby countryside could produce.

The Garrods loved Kim like a daughter, and from that first evening, I was like a son. Kim's judgment was unquestioned by everyone. That first evening, I met Papa's daughter and her husband Jacques. Jacques was a Frenchman and a veteran of the French-Vietnamese war. We talked about Ho Chi Minh, General Giap and French colonial politics in Indochina. I had to explain that during my high school years, I was a regular listener to the BBC Radio overseas broadcasts, and I was aware of the fact that French soldiers went straight from fighting World War II to a war in Vietnam. The British commentators seemed to exult in the successful exploits and stratagems of Ho Chi Minh and Giap, and my high school mates and I thought of Giap as the Scarlet Pimpernel, the dangerous man that the French couldn't find.

The French eventually were defeated by Ho, Giap and the Vietnamese, and six years after my encounter with Jacques, fully a third of my graduate school class at the University of British Columbia were American white men running away from the draft as the US fought their own futile version of war in Viet Nam.

The next morning, after a solid Canadian breakfast of poached eggs, back bacon, toast, homemade preserves and coffee, Kim and I were back in the DKW heading south to Red Deer where I would attend summer school. Red Deer was about one hundred miles south of Edmonton, and about eighty miles north of Calgary. The plan was for Kim to drop me off at the College in Red Deer and continue south to Calgary, then east to Saskatoon and south again to Moose Jaw.

After a brief stop in Ponoka, a little town sixty miles south of Edmonton to say hello to Hal and Eudene, high school classmates of mine, we continued to Red Deer. After high school in Barbados, Eudene went to England to become a nurse-midwife, and Hal went to Alberta. They got together and married in Ponoka and stayed to raise a family in the idyllic countryside. Eudene has now passed over to the other side, and Hal still lives in Ponoka. One of their three children, Verhomme, is my godson, and the family is scattered all over northern Alberta.

Kim and I parted in Red Deer without ceremony or emotional demonstration. She just dropped me off, stated that she knew I would do well, and left. I had no problem with that, for in my family we never said goodbye anyway. Maybe Kim instinctively knew that it was the end of a beautiful romance. I have heard only slim reports of Kim since that day in June 1960. She went south and east, and I was heading north and west, in a country that spanned 3.875 million square miles, the second-largest country in the world.

This photograph of Broad Street, the busiest part of Bridgetown, Barbados, was taken in the spring of 1955 when I left the island on my grand life's adventure.

The Fray Bentos corned beef can was a major component in homemade children's toys during the war years. The author often asked neighbors to save theirs for him to use.

A familar sight around the Bridgetown docks, a mauby (local homemade drink) seller fills a customer's glass from the canister on her head, c.1950.

Men playing *warri*, an ancient African game, in Bridgetown, 1955. By the time the author returned in 1959, the game was fading from the culture.

The graduating class at Modern High School in 1953. A new school compared to Harrison and others in Barbados, it had had less than ten classes graduate by this time. The author is fifth from the left in the back row.

An exterior view of Modern High School, Barbados in 1959. There, as always was the shiny sedan belonging to the founder and principal, Louis Lynch.

Athlete, teacher, sports administrator, mentor and the founder of Modern High, Louis Lynch (1916-1969) was the quintessental black Bajan.

The author in Barbados at age 17 in 1954. A young high school teacher, he was teaching while learning.

A fine example of Barbados Black-Belly sheep, a variety that originated on the island and was raised by the Weekes family.

An aerial view of the Pine housing scheme. The author walked his teenage sweetheart all the way out here without a thought about how he would get back home.

Irvine Weekes' mother Leslyn in 1958. She was still quite a young woman at 40.

the author's sister Thelma, the second of his mother's children, pictured at age 18 in Barbados, 1956.

The author's father, Carlton 'Pretty', in 1958. He was a country-man with two suits: one for weddings and another for funerals.

A 'force-ripe' man at 19, the author marks his first Christmas in Nassau, Bahamas, 1955.

A year into his deployment in the Bahamas police, the author was showing interest in bodybuilding.

Constable Weekes on patrol in Nassau, 1956.

The author in the summer uniform of the Royal Bahamas Police Force, 1957.

On duty at Cable Beach Police Station, Nassau in 1957 with a fellow peace officer. The author is the constable on the left. At that time the Cable Beach area was exclusively white residential and luxury hotels.

The twenty-one members of the riot squad, Nassau, Bahamas in 1958, trained by Captain Granger (seated at center), who had them ready in a hurry. The author is fourth from left in the back row.

Bay Street, Nassau, the center of life in the Bahamas. Looking west with the British Colonial Hotel in the background, c. 1956.

The author in his first white dinner jacket on the night he saw Roy Hamilton, 1956.

A Bahamas police guard of honor for the opening sessions of the supreme court. The author was a member of every guard of honor during the four years he served on the force.

Dr. Paula Newbold, Irvine's dearest Bahamian friend, 1958.

The author as a 21-year-old island cool cat in Nassau, 1958.

Timothy Gibson, the writer/composer of the national anthem of the Bahamas. He and his wife greatly inspired the author.

Agatha and Alfred Bellot, dear friends who helped along the way in Nassau, c.1975.

Later renamed the Valley View Center, the Saskatchewan Provincial Training School in Moose Jaw, for youth with intellectual disabilities, was established at the urging of provincial premier Tommy Douglas in 1955. Shelving his plans to become a land surveyor, the author began training here as a psychiatric nurse and had to adapt to working with the developmentally disabled. (Inset: Kim, the occupational therapist at the facility and a great friend of the author).

1960 summer school class in Red Deer, Alberta in Canada. The author needed to prepare for the Province of Alberta's Grade 12 examinations in physics and mathematics in support of his application for studies at the University of Alberta. He is in the photograph, third from left, third row.

The University of Alberta was a hotbed of debate in the Canadian political sphere. The author, a prominent Socialist Party leader in the early 1960s, is seated at right.

A beaming Irvine Weekes in his bachelor's official photo at the University of Alberta, 1963. He was the only black student in the graduating class.

Mrs. Leslyn Weekes in 1964. She was proud that her son could write 'B.A.' after his name.

Façade of Queen Elizabeth Hospital, Bridgetown. The author's father died here, the first time he ever slept outside of Cane Garden.

The author stands proudly with his first new car, the two-door tan 1965 Chevy Malibu V8. He picked up Vilma on their first date in March, 1965 on the first day he drove the car. The young Jamaican woman was not at all impressed by the automobile, but they continued courting and he shed all his other involvements. Five months after their first date, the pair were married.

Miss Vilma Nesbitt in Vancouver, Canada in the spring of 1965.

The Weekeses, newly married in Canada.

Vilma and Irvine Weekes on their wedding day in August 1965 in Surrey, British Columbia.

The author as he and his wife set out on their honeymoon in 1965.

Vilma and Irvine visit a greenhouse in Stanley Park, Vancouver, Canada, 1965.

The Watts Riots in Los Angeles from August 11-16, 1965 prevented the couple from touring California on the route they had planned. This picture of Fisherman's Wharf, San Francisco, is from their second honeymoon in 1966.

Looking down Nob Hill towards the Golden Gate Bridge, San Francisco, 1966.

The couple returns to Vancouver, 1967.

The author at Banff in the Canadian Rockies, 1967.

Irvine, Vilma and our friend Ivern Davis of Nassau, Bahamas on the Columbia Ice Fields in the Canadian Rockies, 1967.

The author at left, with University of British Columbia classmates after completing his MBA in 1968. He was the only black business school graduate that year.

Master's candidates graduate at the University of British Columbia, 1968.

The author and his wife Vilma on graduation day, University of British Columbia, 1968.

Stepping out on the town at Christmas in New York City, 1968.

Mrs. Weekes takes Irvine's second cousins siteseeing in New York, 1969.

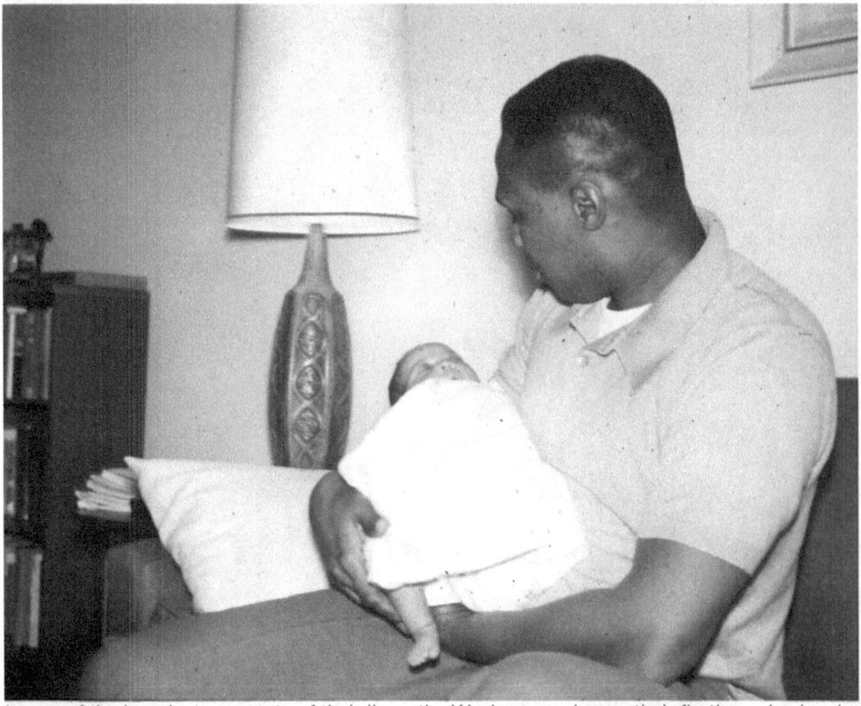

In one of the happiest moments of their lives, the Weekeses welcome their firstborn, Leslyn, in New York City, April 1969.

The family grows up in Jamaica, clockwise from left: Mr. and Mrs. Weekes flank three of Vilma's sisters with their children Paul and Dionne in front; Irvine and a visiting friend, Vilma, and the Weekes children, Melanie, 6, Scott, 8, and Leslyn, 9, on the front lawn in Spanish Town, 1978; the author with daughter Lesyn celebrating her Sweet Sixteen in the living room at Spanish Town family home, 1985; the next generation, the Weekes kids and their cousins, get together for a party in Kingston, 1978.

The Weekes family made its first foray into the lucrative Jamaican tourist industry with the acquisition of Villa Carmel in Runaway Bay. Even the Beatles stayed here, but the investment would eventually become a financial millstone around their necks.

Irvine Weekes as a young Citibank executive in Kingston, 1971. His arrival from New York ushered in the era of new banking products such as term loans, replacing overdraft culture.

The author in 1974. Developing a reputation for innovaton and problem-solving, he led Jamaican industrial giant Thermo Plastics out of receivership and back on sound financial footing.

The Hon. G. Arthur Brown, Governor of the Bank of Jamaica (right, head of table), addresses participants in a banking course at the Courtleigh Manor Hotel on February 20, 1971. Others at the head of the table are Mr. Irvine Weekes, assistant manager Citibank King Street (left) and Mr. Bill Rhodes, the bank's resident vice president.

Friends, mentors and collaborators, clockwise from left: Tomas Désulmé, O.J., founding director of Thermo Plastics Jamaica and the author's closest confidante; Errol Barrow, regional integrationist, founder of Barbados' Democratic Labor Party and first Barbados prime minister was often a guest in the Weekes home; Eric Bell was a Jamaican solicitor, mayor of Kingston, minister of finance and a frequent visitor of Weekes' at Citibank and would talk about political philosophy for hours; Robert Lightbourne, O.J., shaped Jamaica's early industrial infrastructure and co-created the country's national anthem.

Home in the USA (clockwise from top left): The Weekeses relax at home in Stone Mountain, GA; Irvine enyoys his first grandchild, Christopher, 1994; Vilma and Jamaican friend Pansy Jackson as volunteer drivers at the 1996 Summer Olympics in Atlanta; Irvine with college classmates Judge Ernie Marshall and Dr. Gladys Marshall at the 2001 World Athletic Games in Edmonton, Alberta, Canada.

Leslyn graduates college, 1992

Leslyn and Melanie with Vilma and Irvine at Christmas dinner in Stone Mountain, 1994.

L-R: Son Scott, sister Thelma, and niece Michel with Irvine at Scott's wedding in Grenada, 2002.

The first granddaughter, Taylor, graduates high school, 2019.

Granddaughter Alexandria, 2017

Grandson Christopher, 2017

Mr. and Mrs. Weekes, from their church directory, 2016

12. BACK IN THE BOOKS

It was a total commitment for the sixty of us who were there for summer school in 1960. I got to know only one of my fellow students, a young man by the name of John Barr. John and I went through the University of Alberta together and shared many political science courses. The one we enjoyed most was Professor Mardiros' Social Philosophy 350. I understand that John became a respected journalist with the *Edmonton Journal*, and continued his right-wing views well into his mature years.

I was compelled to qualify at Alberta Grade 12 level in math and physics in six weeks of study. I did. The teachers, particularly my physics teacher, were fantastic. They made what had hitherto been difficult concepts extremely easy to understand. I believed that I had had good teachers throughout my school days in Barbados, but they never approached the level of capability of relaying a concept that my Alberta summer school teachers did. There is no doubt that my Barbadian teachers had as vested an interest in seeing us succeed as my Canadian teachers did, maybe even more so, but none of my early teachers had gone to a teacher's college, and none of them even had a first degree. My summer school teachers in Canada all had formal training with at least an undergraduate degree in their subject area and a further degree in education from a teacher's college. By the time I entered the University of Alberta in September, I was as enamored with math and physics as I had been with economics and political science.

Two minor shocks greeted me on that first morning at U of A. The first was a letter from the Canadian Department of Citizenship & Immigration advising me that I was not allowed to work in the country and that upon graduation I would have to leave Canada. Thankfully, the letter did not state that I had to show proof of my ability to meet my expected expenses, or I would have had a serious challenge because I had the princely sum of one thousand dollars to my name. Fees were $450 per year. Books were yet of unknown cost, and the school year stretched from September to May. I could not even imagine staying in a university dorm, for the fees were not only higher than tuition but had to be paid upfront. I was not too put off by this, however, for I had spent four years of my young adulthood living in military barracks in the Bahamas and was in no hurry to resume that lifestyle.

The second surprise occurred when I was at the course selection table. I was directed to a seemingly disengaged Professor Grant Davies.

"What do you want to study?" came his first question.

"Political economy, sir," I replied.

"There is no such thing," he retorted flatly, "and you don't have to call me sir."

I became more assured and explained that I wanted to read for a degree in both economics and political science and asked if he would help me to select courses that would get me there. Davies explained that I had to make one of the areas my major and the other my minor. I chose to read for a degree in economics with political science as my minor, with as much French, English and philosophy as I could get in among the compulsory core courses. All courses started at the 200 level and I would have to complete fifteen courses in three years, each one of seven and a half months' duration. The first course Professor Davies selected for me was his own Political Science 200.

We became great friends. In my second year, he went off on a study program at Harvard University and came back with a very bright man that he met there. That young assistant professor's name was Neville Linton, and it turned out that Cameron Tudor, my fellow Barbadian, who taught me British Constitution at Modern High School in Barbados, had earlier taught Neville Linton at Queen's Royal College in Guyana. Linton taught me political theory, then known as Political Science 300.

I believe that on my very first day at U of A I met Ernie Marshall and Tom Tait, fellow students. Tom and I went all the way through together, but Ernie would finish his degree at the University of Saskatchewan, where he also completed a law degree before practicing law in Peace River, Alberta. Ernie retired as a high court judge in Edmonton a few years ago. Ernie and Gladys, who completed her medical degree at the U. of A., and is now also retired, introduced me to the InterVarsity Christian Fellowship, where I found lots of fun and fellowship. Ernie and Gladys have remained very close friends with my family for fifty-nine years. They have visited us in Vancouver, Spanish Town, Jamaica and Atlanta, and we visited them during the 2001 IAAF World Championships in Athletics in Edmonton, with side trips to Jasper, Banff, Lake Louise and the Columbia Icefield in the Canadian Rockies.

I lost track of Tom Tait after we graduated, but I never will forget him. Tom introduced me to the game of golf in 1960 and gave me my first set of clubs, an old bag that had originally belonged to his grandfather. Tom's game by then had moved beyond them; the five iron was not an iron at all, but a spoon with a wooden shaft. I developed a love and efficiency with that club that was weird. Whenever and wherever I found myself in difficulty on a golf course, I would pull that old baby out of my bag, and she would bring me out of trouble. I played with that partial set of golf clubs that only comprised a driver and a three wood, odd-numbered irons from one to nine, a pitching wedge and a putter. I stopped playing golf 1972 after twelve years because I felt that I could use five hours on a Saturday morning in more useful pursuits than selfishly wasting them on personal gratification. My golf buddies felt differently. A few have openly expressed the thought that the game ran me off. They may be right, for I never did master it in any appreciable way after all those years of trying and wasting money.

The first digs that I entered was a basement room at Mrs. Miller's on a side street about fifteen minutes' walk from campus. It was a reasonably clean-looking place, with breakfast and dinner provided. I had walked around the campus for most of a day trying to find some landlady on the prescribed list who had a vacant space and was glad when Mrs. Miller opened her basement to me.

Black people were a rarity in Edmonton in 1960, and many residents of the city had never met or seen a black person close up. I, of course, was too naïve to recognize rejection and overlooked things like that. People were strangely constructed, I thought. To worry about their foibles was to take on insoluble problems that one did not need.

It turned out that I was the only black undergraduate at U of A in 1960. Lionel Jones was another black man, but he was in the law school. There were also three black graduate students, two from Jamaica and one from the USA, all pursuing their PhDs. I later learned from Ted King, a friend and colleague that I met in Vancouver when we were both officers of the British Columbia NAACP, that his sister Thelma had earned a degree from U of A in the 1950s before leading the Girl Guides Association.

I spent one day at Mrs. Miller's house. Earlier that evening, she served fish for dinner. When I stuck my fork into the fish, the darn thing bled. "What in the hell is this?" I asked myself aloud. It was Johnny Saunders and Nassau all over again; bloody-fish meals were destined to follow me everywhere. I immediately called Mr. Garrod, Papa, Kim's parents' friend and told him what happened. He asked for the address of my digs and told me not to worry that he was on the way to get me. Within the hour I was out of that place. I didn't even ask for my money back.

The Garrods lived on the north side of town on the other side of the Saskatchewan River from the university, so getting to classes posed a time problem. I had to take buses, plural, to get across town. By now it was getting to the end of September and starting to get cold. Within a couple of weeks, I met Robin Hunter who lived north of the Garrods, and I rode with him in his car in the mornings during my first year. When we met, Robin was about eighteen or nineteen years old and in his first year of the political science program, so we shared many classes over our undergraduate years. He introduced me to many of his friends, most of whom were young socialists.

The political left was my natural bent, stemming particularly from my colonial experiences. Grant Notley was the leader of our group. He was then in his final year of school with classmate Joe Clark, later a prime minister of Canada. Grant would become a member of the Alberta Provincial Legislature, but his career was cut off very early when he died in a plane crash in Northern Alberta. Grant's daughter became premier of the Province of Alberta, leading a government formed by the New Democratic Party, the NDP. Back in 1960, one would be hard-pressed to believe that the NDP could ever form a government in Alberta. This was potentially the richest province in Canada, a prospect now realized, and Ernest Manning and his Social Credit Party was the most right-wing of them all. Alberta was so independent and far-right that under Mr. William Aberhart, the founder of the Social Credit Party, the provincial government printed its own money in the 1930's, giving $25.00 to everyone in the province to help them through the Depression. The currency became funny money and fell on its own weight.

★★★

Social life during my first year in Edmonton was very constrained. Every Saturday night, I played bridge with Mr. and Mrs. Garrod and their sister Constance who lived nearby. At first, I didn't know anything about bridge, so Daisy and Papa Garrod taught me the game. I knew how to play whist, so that helped. I was also not unfamiliar with cards since I had sat or squatted at my father's side during many gambling sessions when I was a small boy. I caught on very quickly, and Papa was pleased to have me help him take on the girls at bridge on Saturday nights. The winter weekends of 1960 were more tolerable because of our bridge games, except for that Saturday night when my partner Papa opened the bidding with "two no trump". When my turn came to bid I passed. Papa hit the roof. He was livid. I was supposed to show him my longest and strongest suit by bidding at least 'three' of that suit, throwing the game back to him, to play it however he wanted. I had failed my first real test, but I learned a great bridge lesson. A "two no-trump" bid from your partner is a demand bid. One simply must not pass.

The very first paper I submitted in University was in English 200. There were fifty of us in the class. When Professor Sutherland returned our graded work one week later, I was extremely elated when I saw 'A+' in the top right-hand corner of the cover page, giving me the feeling that I was where I always belonged, at the top of the class. In after-class discussions with my fellow students, I discovered that twenty of us got A+ for our work. This was a new world for me. The bright ones were meeting in this place. No longer could one be singled out as the best student, since there would be many at the top. The truly smart ones would have to find the vehicle for separating themselves from the other bright students. I had a jolly good time reading the early English poets, particularly Chaucer, Milton and Pope. My professor was very disappointed that I would not be reading for a true arts degree, and only had room for one English course. Why, he wondered, would I want to do something as pedestrian as economics?

The course that I enjoyed most in my first year was French 200. It may have been my attraction to the professor, Ms. Coulter. She was a very young woman from Montreal, quietly attractive, with a Gallic flair that was so different from the English-cum-Scottish style that Canadians of that era assumed. I had fallen in love with French during my high school days and had even done oral French in my matriculation exams, but Ms. Coulter made the French culture come alive for me in a more fulsome way. She took me from *Les Chansons de Roland*, through Rabelais, Moliere, Voltaire, Francois Villon, Baudelaire, Rimbaud, Antoine de Saint Exupery, and Guy de Maupassant to Sartre and Camus. I loved French a lot and did the advanced French 350 course in my junior year. I even wrote a one-act play in French, dedicating it to my Ms. Coulter. We read it in class; I don't have a copy. A few years ago, I finally threw out all my university writings. There was mostly juvenile stuff in there, I thought, stuff that even my sixteen-year-old granddaughters would find pretty maudlin.

Towards the end of my first year at Alberta, I discovered that discussions with my fellow students were as enlightening as going to lectures, so I started to regularly hang out in the cafeteria nursing my single cup of coffee and mostly listening to my senior fellow students discuss politics, philosophy and economics. I would first determine the references that a particular professor was using to strengthen his arguments, and I would read those writers' work myself, in addition to studying the assigned text. I would then cut many of the classes and spend time with the amateur intellectuals, like Dan de Vlieger, Bob Gordon, Grant Notley, Robin Hunter, and a smart young honors economics student named Adolf. This group stimulated me into joining the NDP, the center-left party on campus. Grant Notley was the leader, and I was made president when Grant graduated that following spring.

Throughout my sojourn at U of A, no-one ever singled me out for unusual treatment. My professors mostly showed me the same disregard that they did the other undergraduates. If one wanted to consult them, one referred to their hours that were posted in the office. You selected a time, you got the guidance. Otherwise, you knew from the outset what the subject matter was; it was your duty to do the work, no mollycoddling. There are teachers that I will never forget, like Dr. Winch, a young Englishman who taught Economics 300 – Microeconomics. This was the toughest course I encountered in my entire university exposure, undergraduate or graduate. He could tell you all about marginal cost curves that were exogenously determined with passion and without taking a breath between sentences, for five minutes while you sat spellbound and understood nothing – and this was a key course in my degree field. The only other person I have ever met who could talk like that was the Honorable Michael Manley, prime minister of Jamaica. I became Michael's bank manager in 1970 while he was Leader of the Opposition in Jamaica and I was a young manager with Citibank of New York. Michael would sit at my desk and try out his verbal perorations on me as a prelude to his deliveries on the stump. Maybe it was the water that one drank at the London School of Economics, that famous institution from which both men came.

Professor Mardiros was an unforgettable teacher. I took his Social Philosophy 380 course. Here, I read Karl Popper and listened to many lectures on the Open Society and Its Enemies. We discussed Hegel's

Dialectic, Engel's early theories, Karl Marx's transpositions of these early philosophical expositions on the social order, as well as Lenin's interpretations leading to the Bolshevik Revolution, the formation of the Soviet Union, and the beginning of the supposed quest for the disappearance of the state. Professor Mardiros' course was jam-packed, and you had to arrive early to get a seat.

All the young intellectuals were there, along with the plants from the Royal Canadian Mounted Police (RCMP), the FBI, and one student who was thought to be an informant for the local authorities. Remember, this was 1961, at the height of the Cold War and the infancy of movements among students for Black Power, women's rights and other causes of the time. The Cuban Missile Crisis was a Damocles Sword hanging over our heads; Nikita Khrushchev was beating his badly-made shoe on the desk at the United Nations; Red China was demanding to be returned to its rightful seat at the UN, and communists were supposedly hiding under every rock in North America. Professor Mardiros was fearless, the university supported him fully, in this, the most right-wing province in Canada, we listened to his booming Australian voice for three hours every week for seven months. I did well in the course.

Daisy Garrod, my landlady, was concerned that I was not meeting any black people, whether townspeople or students. She knew of a black family who lived on the north side of Edmonton, not far from her home at 11321 101st Street. She hadn't met them, but their son John Utendale had been an extremely popular youth hockey player. Everyone in Edmonton felt that Johnny deserved a call-up by the National Hockey League, but he didn't get one because he was black. Mrs. Garrod swore that Johnny was the greatest skater since Gordie Howe, her idol, and that it was too bad that Gordie played for Detroit and not her favorite Toronto Maple Leafs. She taught me the rudiments of ice hockey, and after our Saturday night bridge games, we would settle down to watch Frank Mahovlich of the Toronto Maple Leafs take on the Montreal Canadiens. Montreal had the better team, however, and with Jacque Plante in goal, Bernie "Boom Boom" Geoffrion, Jean Belliveau and Henri "Pocket Rocket" Richard as forwards, it was almost always Montreal that won.

Mrs. Garrod called and arranged for me to go over and meet the Utendale family. That was the beginning of a beautiful relationship. During my three years in Edmonton, I spent many evenings of food and fellowship with the Utendales: Mr. and Mrs., one brother, two sons – one older than I was, the other, the famous Johnny, my age – one daughter Susan, and her small daughter. Mrs. Utendale was a beautiful matron of Caucasian and Australian Aboriginal descent.

Mr. Utendale's father hailed from Guyana in South America, a neighboring country to my Barbados, and a fellow British colony. The senior Utendale, a man of African and Dutch descent, had emigrated to Britain in the late 1800s. He married an Englishwoman before the turn of the twentieth century and emigrated with his young sons and wife to Canada where he acquired a homestead of one section of land (640 acres) in Northern Saskatchewan. The young Utendale brothers were trained as auto mechanics in Edmonton, and after World War II worked for the GM Dealership there. The Utendale men knew very little about colonial life. Their hardships were different but were hardships nevertheless. They engaged me in deep conversation, and as I expounded on topics like slavery, colonialism, and our steps towards self-governance, they began to get a feel for some of the things that their father had talked to them about with no understanding on their part.

All of this was going on over rye and water – and my strategizing on how to get to Susan. About twenty-six or twenty-seven years old at this time, she was arguably one of the most beautiful women in Edmonton. She cultivated a natural outdoorsy kind of look: little or no make-up, boyish western clothes, jeans and boots. She was luscious, a black woman of no describable color, ready for adventure. *How would I, a virtual carpetbagger, a student just passing through town, being befriended by her parents, frolic with this nymph and keep my character viable?* The day would come. I would be patient.

Towards the end of my first year at U of A, I won the presidency of the New Democratic Party on campus and thus became the leader of the young socialists in Alberta. I had so many things going on, carrying a full load of five courses, working in the library ten hours a week for a dollar an hour and occasionally modeling for two hours a week in front of noncredit-students, mostly older matrons. Mrs. Garrod was one of the art students. The ebony shades that these students saw in me was amazing. My sittings were mostly only semi-nude, thank heavens, for I am too sensitive a man to fully expose myself to more than one woman at a time. I got five dollars an hour for modeling. These sums may seem paltry today, but at that time, a full meal of meat, potatoes, a green and a red vegetable in the cafeteria on campus cost only a dollar. Dessert was an extra fifteen cents, and coffee was just ten cents. A dollar went a long way.

Before classes broke up that first Christmas, the undergraduates put on a variety show, with foreign students required to do something representative of their culture. My colleagues insisted that I present something. After all, I was the only black undergraduate on campus, an automatic draw, and since the elections for Model Parliament would be coming up early in the new year, my NDP supporters wanted to put their leader in the spotlight. Only I knew the quandary I was in.

Up to the time I left my native country in 1955, Barbados did not fully celebrate or embrace indigenous culture, especially if your family thought of itself as above the "third class". My village in St. Andrew was one of the true harbingers of African culture, but my grandmother wouldn't allow anything that was not a religious song or something of European or white American origin to air in her house. We had the finest drummers, tuk band musicians (playing a two-headed bass drum, triangle, flute, traditional fiddle and a snare drum), mask makers, tin-whistle makers and players, and proponents of African dance in our village, but as much as I wanted to learn from them and participate, I was not allowed to join the fun. My sergeant-major grandmother was sure that this would be a sure way to hell at worst or to become a good-for-nothing man at best.

For most parts of my island home, this was the prevailing sentiment. As a consequence, the celebration of Barbadian culture became *au courant* after I had graduated from high school and moved on to the Bahamas. It was there in Nassau that I fully encountered the panorama of black Caribbean culture. I was now living among Haitians, Trinidadians, Guianese, Bahamians, and Jamaicans, all of whom were able to celebrate distinct aspects of their culture, while my Bajan colleagues and I tried to form the supporting cast. Among the usual revelers in the Bahamas were top civil servants, professionals, internationally known exponents on drums, like "Peanuts" Taylor, Paul Meres on native dancing, and others like my friend Larry Davis who earned a Ph.D. in engineering physics, and Lynden Pindling who became prime minister of the Bahamas.

But one must never underestimate one's creativity. I love to dance; indeed, I have won a few prizes for my dance performances over the years, the latest being in my sixty-fifth year. I decided to select some of my male and female classmates, teach them the Cha Cha Cha, and choreograph a dance for us. You would have been proud of us on the night of the show because we were a smash hit. Twelve young fresh eighteen and nineteen-year-old white kids, all dressed in white slacks, red shirts, red-and-white headdress, black cummerbunds and black shoes, away from their mostly farm homes and villages for the first time, were behaving like Cubans in gay abandon, doing a wicked Latin thing, with their black leader up front. All undergraduates should go away to university, but not necessarily 5000 miles away.

That night, I made a connection which made an expectedly cold Christmas very warm. It came in the form of a voluptuous Ukrainian older student, Nina. She was one of the few older students on campus, in her thirties, and she had come back to university to complete her professional degree in social work. I was twenty-four years old by this time. We had dinner together, a treat for me since my expenditures were always shaped by future daily constraints. Nina invited me to spend Christmas with her and her family at their dairy farm in southern Alberta. I may have been a trophy, but this trophy would have to be well earned.

What really struck me was the liberated women that I was encountering increasingly on campus. Canadian university women in 1960 were stepping out boldly and doing whatever they wanted to do that was within the bounds of reasonable behavior, without fear of judgment from their male colleagues, their parents, or society. This was all new territory for me.

Do not think that I spent all my time thinking of women and sex. Not all of it, anyway, but an effective part. I promise to share only a part of these experiences with you. This I believe will keep me credible on the one hand and preserve my goodwill with you on the other. I have always been able to compartmentalize things, and so I maintained good grades while engaging in extracurricular activities on campus.

Nina's parents were very welcoming to their guest. I noted that Nina had not placed my stuff in any room but had left it in the hallway. That little old valise occupied my mind all through dinner. I was aware that she and I would spend time in the same room that night and during succeeding nights, but imagine my astonishment when Nina announced shortly after coffee that we were both tired and wanted to excuse ourselves and repair to bed. We then left the dinner table as Nina picked up my bag, grabbed my hand and led me to our lair. I may have been a trophy, but this one was going be the live, fucking variety. Or so I thought.

Nina's bedroom was gorgeous, fit for a princess who was now almost the age of a queen. I saw that she had put out silk sheets, my very own dressing gown and pajamas – not bad for a guy who hadn't owned or slept in pajamas so far in his life. I never had any need for them as a boy in the tropics or as an adult sleeping in my bed. I didn't think I'd need them in this bed. We had barely climbed under the sheets before we went after each other like animals who had not eaten for a long time, biting and chewing and swallowing and tasting, all at the same time, just like dogs. As only humans can, we sometimes paused to caress each other. It was during one of the caressing periods that we decided to change gears. Nina opened up herself willingly, and like a stallion, I jammed Peter in, stiff, hard and strong. And just like a stud I went off in one bang! The breeder could collect his fee, and the mare could go back to her stall, but not only did I have to face and sleep with a disappointed woman, but I had my self-esteem to manage. I had fooled myself into thinking that I was a great lover, maybe on the beaches in the moonlight, but these downy sheets and lilac pillows must have intoxicated me too much. My apologies and tears got me reprieve and a show of understanding from Nina, whose caresses were so warm and tender that I fell asleep in her arms.

I awoke before the rooster crowed. I had to redeem myself after my undignified efforts over the past evening, so I tentatively reached over and started a finger game with Nina's body. I was very slow and deliberate, ensuring that I played only with the most innocent parts. I soon found that spot that makes every woman feel alive and wanted, the place that seems so different on each one. My lady came alive and rolled closer to me. I gradually shifted my fingers over to her mound and continued the play, hearing her groan as I searched for her clitoris. I kept the game going as if I had no interest in entering her. My honor was at stake. *I simply must do it right this time,* I vowed. I kept that clitoris between my fingers, and the higher our desires rose, the more concentrated was my attention. Nina was more than ready.

This time I was no stallion. Once I gently entered her, like a lover should, the real dance began. It was a slow and deliberate grind. The lady kept trying to push me out of the center and into corners as I plunged forward. I countered her moves and kept her centered while we rode. This was going to be good. Nina drew me in as close to her as possible and took my lips with cool fire. She was telling me that I had to finish it, for only I could finish it. She did not have the words of command like I had experienced with my island lovers, but we knew what she wanted, so I went into fifth gear and drove until we came home, together. She slept hard afterward.

I got out of bed, dressed warmly and went out to the barn to help her dad do the milking. Poppa was reluctant at first to entrust such an important job to me, for little did he know how adept I was at playing with nipples. He didn't know that I started life on a farm, and had been milking cows, goats and sometimes sheep since I was a lad. At breakfast later that morning, he related how good I was at milking, and I could see a satisfactory smile on Nina's lips as she knowingly concurred.

★★★

In the new year of 1961, I committed to go for an honors degree in economics. This required a greater academic effort on my part. The textbook that was assigned was a new text called *Economics in a Canadian Setting*. I did not find it nor the professor particularly enlightening, so I got an old Paul Samuelson text and guided myself through economics. I don't know why the university chose to discontinue the Samuelson text since it was generally considered the clearest exposition on the subject ever written for freshmen. Samuelson reportedly made a fortune out of the book he simply called *Economics*, and the university may have been subtly trying to encourage a Canadian textbook author, but Inman was too turgid and hard to follow. I believe that the university switched back to Samuelson the following year, thus making further contributions to the American Nobel Prize winner's financial fortune and the understanding of economics by first-year students.

The year progressed with my entry into debates and building a campus following in social and philosophical theories, while I familiarized myself with (and educated my fellow students in) the policies of the New Democratic Party. For me, the biggest event that year was Model United Nations, staged every year at the University of Alberta. Naturally, all the budding politicians vied for selection to represent their favorite countries. The opportunity to represent a country was not limited to any particular discipline, and so we had students of varying persuasions participating. One had to display familiarity and confidence in presenting the views and policies that their 'country' espoused. There was no qualifying examination. The acid test was one's ability to earn the acknowledgment and coffee-shop favorable gossip from the student body which was duly noted in the campus newspaper.

In 1961 there were only four black countries that were members of the United Nations. Those black countries were Haiti, Ethiopia, Nigeria and Ghana. Being a Caribbean country, Cuba held strong appeal. I suppose I could have tried to represent a white nation, but that was not my first choice. I chose to represent Cuba and won approval. But first of all, I had to overcome my sensitivity about the entire English-speaking Caribbean being under colonial rule, and except for a few countries, all of Africa was under colonial rule as well. Nothing focuses the mind more than the realization that one is not equal among his peers in any endeavor, particularly in situations where one is competing for prestige and power. Being second class can be a severe handicap, and my mind harked back to the problems that the colonized faced in most life experiences with power groups, and also with their people in getting them to appreciate the importance of being sovereign nations, as well as their viability as leaders with whom to be reckoned.

The topic chosen for debate in 1961 was "Should Red China Be Seated At The UN?" There was an opening ceremony, where members were introduced and the protocol established. The topic would be discussed over three nights with a wind-up on the fourth. Discussion times were to follow strict timelines. At that time, the Cuban Revolution led by Fidel Castro was only two years old. Cuba had not yet declared that it would adopt a Communist system, and Castro was generally loved by the entire world, except for the United States, where opinion was divided. On the one hand, there was love for Castro and exultation over the overthrow of Batista, and on the other, there was deep concern over the confiscation of private property by state fiat. John F. Kennedy had just been inaugurated, and the United States was generally being showered with goodwill.

But can a country lose its seat in the General Assembly of the United Nations by a change of government?

After a prolonged and bloody civil war, the Chinese communists under the leadership of Mao Zedong defeated the nationalists led by Chiang Kai-shek. Chiang continued his government on the island of Taiwan and with the support of the United States and its allies retained the Chinese seat at the UN, along with China's permanent membership on the Security Council.

My delegation's position was that the nationalists had to cede the seat to Communist mainland China because they were the true representatives of the Chinese government. For us as students it was a moral question, and I, as leader of the Cuban delegation was able to present a very plausible case for my country, it being not only the expected position of a revolutionary country of socialist-communist leanings, but also buoyed by the strength of moralistic certainty of my young and innocent colleagues. The resolution to seat Red China was won by the affirmative and my stock soared on campus, catapulting me into a very strong position to attain the largest percentage of the votes in Model Parliament the following year. It would, however, take ten more years for Red China to be seated in 1971 with full representational honors as the official member of the United Nations representing China.

The second half of the university year began in January. Final exams would come at the end of April, so it was truly time to get to work and bring those grades up. I have mentioned before that our courses lasted a full seven months. I was enjoying campus politics immensely and had no intention of reducing my commitment in this area, so I learned effective time management very quickly. I also developed a respectable body of friends, most of whom were females, and I found their company and ideas most intriguing. Perhaps I should interject here that not all my female friendships and relations were carnal. I have neither slept with nor sexually pursued a significant number of my female friends – only a few. The males were my competitors, colleagues who sharpened their swords in combative clashes. Whether it was political posturing, debating the economic policies of the Diefenbaker government or exploring Liberalism or Marxism, we tried to gain yardage on each other. I sought solace among my female friends. There were young ladies from India, a local Japanese, some from Grand Prairie and Cold Lake in Northern Alberta, from Lethbridge and Calgary to the south, from Edmonton itself, from Saskatoon, and French speakers from Quebec city.

I would not be true to this task if I failed to mention a very special sweetheart from the Punjab. She knew what true suffering was, but she was too soft and gentle to be bitter. Her family had been caught in the internecine warfare that engulfed India and Pakistan in 1947 when the British granted Independence. We had much to talk about, since my native land was still a British colony, though with far fewer resources than hers, and not shackled with the twin sins of religious dogma and contrived tribalism. Her gossamer clothing and kisses were the softest I had encountered up to that point in my life. She was cool fire in contrast to the scorching kind with which her male homeboys threatened me.

I finished the academic year with good enough grades to be accepted into the honors program in economics for the ensuing year. I was now out of funds. Then, the dreaded Damoclesian letter from the Canadian Department of Citizenship & Immigration arrived, reminding me that I had to leave the country as soon as I graduated – a consistent threat. My dear friend Ernie Marshall tried to get me a job with the construction crew that he worked with every summer, but his boss would not hire me. I could not stay at the Garrods without money and a job, so I packed my grip and hitchhiked the sixty miles south to Ponoka where my high school mates Hal and Eudene lived. Hal was a psychiatric nurse at the mental hospital in Ponoka. The following morning, I rode with him up to the institution, went to the office, and filled out a job application. When they saw that I had been a police officer and had finished a year's training in psychiatric nursing, and my first year at the University of Alberta, they hired me on the spot. For the next four and a half months, I worked as many hours as I possibly could, just leaving recreation time for one hour of tennis, two hours of golf and seven hours of sleep and reading. The rest of my time was spent working. I lived at the institution and got free meals.

In the middle of September, I left Ponoka for Edmonton with three things: enough money to pay for my second year at U of A, (I would still have to work ten hours a week in the library), a new blue blazer, and a good haircut. As far back as I can remember, I have always taken great care of my body and my appearance. My associations made proper grooming second nature. From Cub Scouts to Boy Scouts, to the Church Lads Brigade, to standing before a classroom, to the colonial police, to the Training School in Moose Jaw, I always had neat haircuts, provided by my father, professional barbers, or competent colleagues. Sadly, I could find no barber in Edmonton who could cut a black man's hair. There was even one who asked me pointedly when I first went to his shop, "What do you expect me to do with your head, sir?"

Fortunately, afros were just becoming the fashion, so for most of my undergraduate days, I was bushy-headed and bearded. I found a French-Canadian barber in Ponoka who could cut my hair, and from thence whenever I could afford the time, I would hitchhike sixty miles down the road ostensibly to visit Hal and Eudene, but assuredly to get that sweet haircut.

In the second year of my studies at U of A, I found digs at the home of a Mrs. Hunter, within walking distance of my classes. The half an hour walk was thrilling that September, but as the winter lengthened, that half an hour became a frozen hell. I became convinced that no one had ever had to undergo harsher conditions to get a university education. First, there was the dress. After getting fully dressed in long woolen underwear, there was flannel trousers, shirt and tie, sweater, sport jacket, scarf, earmuffs, hat, gloves and mittens. Then there were woolen socks, properly fitted walking shoes, and galoshes or toe rubbers in light snow.

To Mrs. Hunter's credit all six of us, her tenants, got solid Canadian breakfasts, usually consisting of thick porridge, scalded eggs, and thick slices of heavy bread. There were four engineering students, one guy Herb in education (who I remember because he was so big and tall), and me in economics. We all occupied Mrs. Hunter's basement during that period from 1961 to 1962. It was a large basement, where everyone could find a desk to work at, and everyone could find the one bathroom to perform his ablutions. We all had beds to sleep on, with memorable mattresses, although mine was under the stairwell. I remember that bed even today as the only bed I've ever seen which enveloped its occupant. No lover had ever caressed and wrapped itself around its love like that mattress folded itself around me. I didn't get out of bed like others on mornings, I uncoiled like I was coming out of a quilted wrap. That old mattress must have come out of Mrs. Hunter's mother's house, and Mrs. Hunter was a least seventy years old at the time.

It was there that I first started to appreciate what engineers have to go through to become degreed: study from seven to midnight every evening, attend classes from eight to one during the day and do labs every afternoon. No hanging out in the cafeteria, no debates, philosophical or otherwise were allowed. In economics or the arts in general, we were real students, enjoying our university years, but these Engineers were overworked technicians, being fed a steady diet of physics and thermodynamics only to become the first to be laid off whenever the economy shivered.

Mrs. Hunter was kindhearted and motherly and did her best to make us feel at home. Once, when she sensed that I might have grown a bit tired of the usual sausage and mash with the ubiquitous hole in the center to trap the gravy, she enquired what my favorite native meal was, and tried to treat me to one. The split peas and rice came out like her Scottish porridge, and instead of pork chops that could not be accommodated within her budget, she served pork sausage of questionable age. Poor Mrs. Hunter; I was reminded of my headmaster who had told me he was giving us a little something to encourage us to travel and study. Now Mrs. Hunter was giving us a little something to encourage us to speed up our studies and get the heck out of town.

I had excellent professors that year and grew increasingly impressed with their grasp of the subjects, but I knew that I was not working hard enough. I was spending more time getting my party ready for the ensuing elections for Model Parliament than I was in preparing my classwork. I felt that I had a good shot at creating campus history by forming the first socialist government in Model Parliament in the history of the University of Alberta. A miss is as good as a mile, but I almost did form the government. When the elections were concluded the Liberals had won the largest percentage of the votes cast. My NDP was second, and the conservatives were third. My party formed the official opposition, and I was its leader.

The debate that year reflected national concerns: the adoption of a new Canadian flag, bilingualism, (the notion that Canada should officially speak both French and English), a national pension plan, and universal health care. These were all policies that my party, the NDP had spent years trying to advance in the national debate, and we had finally succeeded in having them aired openly. It took another ten years to have all of them become the national policy of Canada, but I am pleased to have played a part in the student debates of the early 1960's.

I had some tough but very interesting courses in that particular year. Soviet government was informative, and Lenin has to be one of the most tough-minded and brave politicians of all time when looked at objectively and without prejudice. Political theory was a philosophical endeavor exposing us to the art of the possible and awareness of the use or misuse of trust, as well as the effectiveness of compromise. Microeconomics, the theory of the firm, was the hardest course that I took in my entire seven years of advanced studies. Dr. Winch, he who could talk for five minutes without taking a breath, was very credible in this Economics 300 course, but those marginal cost curves, whether endogenously or exogenously determined, are still incomprehensible to me after almost sixty years. Dr. Gainer in macroeconomics was as dour as Dr. Winch was flashy, but thank heavens for diversity and Dr. Gainer, I have been able to carve out a good living through my general understanding of economics, particularly government and private financial issues.

I did not get an honors degree, but I was getting excellent life lessons.

During final exams in early May 1962, just like clockwork, my greetings arrived from the Canadian Department of Citizenship and Immigration.

"Dear Mr. Weekes," the letter read, "this is to remind you that you are expected to leave Canada upon graduation, and the terms of your student visa do not permit you to work in Canada."

I do not remember which was worse; harassment from Canadian Immigration, no money, or limited sex. I decided to concentrate on passing my exams first and dealing with other matters later. I did get through my exams handily, and as soon as I could, I went across town to visit the Garrods and the Utendales. They were very happy to see me, for I was too busy over the last school year to get across town to visit them. They did manage to see me the one time that I was interviewed on Edmonton local television and ribbed me about my local celebrity.

The Utendales treated me royally. Lots of good food and drink flowed, and I exulted in Sue's presence. Sue was still one of the most beautiful women I had met to date, and I basked in the light of her presence. I tread carefully for I was not yet even near the capability of the man that this woman deserved – and her parents were my friends. I had this Victorian sense of honor. Was I softening up, or was I growing smarter?

Back at Mrs. Hunter's, I packed my little grip, went out on the Calgary Trail and hitch-hiked south. After leaving my things in Ponoka at my friends Hal and Eudene, I continued to Calgary to party with friends. I then hitchhiked to Banff and Lake Louise, stayed in a youth hostel, made it to the Columbia Icefields, and hitchhiked back to Ponoka. I must have eaten, though I don't remember any meal in particular. My children and grandchildren marvel at my temerity and the cavalier nature of my expectations. To think that a young black man of twenty-four or twenty-five years would fearlessly hitch rides all over Northern Alberta and the Canadian Rockies in the early 1960's and receive nothing but goodwill is quite stunning to them.

I have fond recollections of some of the characters I rode with on my hikes. There was one in particular who fed his dog grapes as we rode from Banff to Jasper. He did not offer me any, thank goodness, for I feared that the old dog would consider me a rival and go for my head. We were pretty close together in the front seat of that old pickup truck, too. As my circumstances and my pocket improved over the years, I have been to Banff, Jasper, Lake Louise, the Columbia Icefields and Calgary on three subsequent occasions, some of them with warm and willing bedmates, but no return had the same sense of adventure from my penurious hitchhiking days.

Let the immigration department write its letters. They had their work to do, and I had mine. I went back to my old summer job at the mental hospital in Ponoka, and I resumed my summer tennis games and my golf. I was becoming quite good at tennis, but golf, the great leveler, remained as mysterious as ever.

My home during the third and final year at the University of Alberta was my best digs to date. Fittingly so, for by now Edmonton, at least the university area, was very familiar ground and I had become a genuine burgher. Through my old friend Ernie Marshall, who was now in law school at the University of Saskatchewan, I was introduced to Vernon Gleddie at the InterVarsity Christian Fellowship, and along with six other students we took over the vacant Methodist minister's official home near the campus. We called it "the Villa"; here were four bedrooms and a full basement. Vernon had the basement, and I had a single room. The other three bedrooms were double occupancy. Eight of us lived in this gorgeous house. We prepared our own meals, mostly breakfast, and took care of ourselves.

Vernon was the coolest cat you'll ever meet. Vern was studying for a degree in Agriculture and was the only man in the Villa who seemed unconcerned about getting his degree, and about what the future held in store for him. He was a strong member of the student Christian movement, and his religious faith may have had something to do with his ease, and perhaps his family background led to his nonchalance. I learned that Vern's family were cattle and sheep ranchers on one hundred sections of land in Southern Alberta. This alone was impetus enough to try to conquer the world. I understand that Vern later became a member of the Legislative Assembly of Alberta, along with my friend and early mentor, and university mate, Grant Notley (whose daughter was premier of the Province of Alberta).

The first snowfall came early that October of 1962, and four of us roommates set off one Friday with borrowed rifles to hunt moose near Jasper National Park. That Friday night we were like boy scouts huddled into our sleeping bags on the cabin floor telling jokes most of the night for we had no camp leader to order lights out. Very early the next morning, we started on our hunt for moose. We walked for several hours along the power company's easements, hoping that a moose would appear. What a strange way to hunt, I thought, but since this was my Canadian colleagues' territory, I said nothing, even though I knew they didn't know what the dickens they were doing. I simply made sure that I stayed out of anyone's line of fire. We tramped around those woods until about noon, and the only game we glimpsed was a half-starved rabbit. Before one could blink, David Owen had blown it to shreds with a shot from his .303 hunting rifle. We were so disappointed that we wended our way back to our cabin and left that same Saturday afternoon for Edmonton, where we knocked back a few Molson beers and contemplated how we would concoct our moose-hunt lies in future years.

That winter of '62-'63 was bitterly cold, but there was an extremely plentiful carrot harvest that fall, and one of our housemates brought back several tins of homemade carrot cake, along with frozen cuts of moose meat when he went home that Christmas. We stored them under the snow in the backyard and feasted on them for several weeks that winter. The weather remained below zero degrees Fahrenheit for most of the time between December and May. We'd got our moose after all.

I was left all alone to look after the villa when my housemates went home for the Christmas holidays, but I was not alone for long. My female friend from across town passed by to check on me and assist me if I needed help. What thoughtfulness! I was pleased and expressed my gratitude. After visiting with each other in the comfort of the living room, we decided to go for a walk around the campus and then enjoy hot chocolate at the tuck shop. We had never really had the opportunity to talk seriously with each other before, and we welcomed the chance. One of the wonderful things about young people is that they can spend hours talking and dreaming idly over a cup of coffee or any beverage without noticing how the time flies by. Before long, day had turned to evening and night approached fast, as darkness does in Edmonton winters. My friend called home and told her parents that she was with me and that there was no need to worry.

We walked back to our warm and empty villa. The situation was tailor-made for young healthy lovers. The kisses were teasing at first, flirtatious, then probing, testing to see if what we knew was about to happen was fully expected on both sides. I have never forced myself on a lover, and this one was a kindred soul. She, too, was making sure that she was not trying to take me where I did not want to go. This young Canadian woman seemed so mature as we went to my bedroom with alacrity and were out of our clothes before a sprinter could leave the blocks. Our sex was very traditional at the outset, and then in a quick wrestling move, my lover tossed me over and was on top. She rode me like I was her favorite horse, and she my Pocahontas, riding bareback and hanging close, then keeping me pinned between her knees as she came out to the head of my doggy and spun circles punctuated by plunges, driving me mad with pleasure and helplessness. This was truly different.

As quickly as before, my lover relinquished control and knelt on the bed before me, presenting her nubile ass. I became her dog and she my willing bitch. I went at it with slow careful strokes as the fire in us raged to match the intensity of the snowfall outside until like the canines I saw in my backyard as a boy, we became motionless and spent – but not stuck together. My friend then turned around to face me and we kissed and hugged, returning to that frontal gesture reserved for humans.

I cooked the only steaks I found in the fridge before we ate and fell asleep. The next day I took her home to her parents, who were glad to see me. My education was growing broader every day. Oh Edmonton, my nurturing city!

The new year was going to be my last as an undergraduate, and I wanted to make it my best. I believe my courses were foreign trade, comparative economics, Soviet government, philosophy and international relations. In the meantime, politicians were visiting our campus regularly. Ernest Manning and his Social Credit Party were immovable in rich Alberta, and the Federal Conservatives were losing ground in Ottawa. Every politician was smelling blood in the water, and they were in and out of Edmonton every week. Davy Fulton, the Federal Minister of Justice from Kamloops, British Columbia, came through, and Lester Pearson, leader of the National Liberal Party visited, as did Tommy Douglas, former premier of Saskatchewan and now Federal Leader of the New Democratic Party. I got to meet them all and to converse with them.

I will never forget the impression that Lester Pearson made on me. "Mike" Pearson's visage shone with an honesty and openness that I have not seen on anyone before or later. I liked and trusted him immediately, inspired. This was not easy for me, an NDP leader, but such is the nature of politics.

As my final year at Alberta progressed, my thoughts became more concentrated on my future. I considered going to law school somewhere in Canada but ruled that out since a law degree from a Canadian University was only practical for Canada, and I did not want to practice law in Canada. I toyed with the idea of preparing myself for the diplomatic service, especially since the West Indies Federation was just being established. I contacted the *École des Haute Etudes Internationales et Politiques* in Paris, a school famous for the study of international law, and was told that they would be happy to accept me, but I needed the sponsorship of my country. I wrote to the department of government in Barbados that I thought would be responsible for such matters but never received a response.

Spring came, and the importance of getting my degree superseded everything else. As we approached final exams at the end of April 1963 I couldn't sleep and grew very agitated. I was five thousand miles away from home, about to become the first person in my family to gain a degree from a university, and the enormity of my preparation and situation suddenly overtook me. The doctor prescribed a mild sleeping pill and I was able to sleep and relax sufficiently well to write and pass my exams. Thank heavens for the work I had done during the year, for the finals counted for only a minor percentage of the necessary grades.

Just as suddenly as the storm had set in, the gloom cleared. I received my accustomed letter from Canadian Immigration. I knew what it was going to say, but I was back to my old self, fearing nothing and no man. I opened the letter. "Dear Mr. Weekes," it said, "We think that you would make an excellent citizen of Canada, and we hope that you will consider staying. We invite you to apply ...."

You could have flattened me with a puff of air. The university year was now over and my undergraduate days were done. I had no job, no offers, no money, no home once I graduated in two weeks, and no plans for graduate studies. In stark contrast, all my economics classmates already had job offers.

My macroeconomics Professor Dr. Gainer had always struck me as a humane realist. He did not have the flash and the glibness of the academic stars on campus, but there was a homespun awareness and practicality about the man. He was as dull as a potato in a meal, offset by its ability to deliver expected satisfaction. I went to see Dr. Gainer and told him about my plight. I needed a job. Dr. Gainer remembered that one of his colleagues, Dr. Gordon Goundrey, had a consultancy practice, and might be able to help. Dr. Gainer called Goundrey on the spot, was told that he had a client in Vancouver, Rip Robinson, president of British Columbia Central Credit Union, who might be interested in talking with me. Right there and then, Goundrey called Rip, who told us that he had to travel East to Toronto in a few days, and he would adjust his schedule to stop over in Edmonton and interview me before going on to Toronto.

I met Rip Robinson (no-one dared call him Mr. Robinson) at the local downtown hotel at nine o'clock the following Monday morning for what was supposed to be a short interview, half an hour at most. We talked for two hours and became so engaged that we both got hungry, and I was rewarded with a delicious Canadian lunch of steak and baked potato, an Alberta specialty.

13. A REAL JOB

I was offered a job as a research economist for the British Columbia Central Credit Union, in Vancouver, at all of $5,400.00 per year starting the following Monday morning at 9.00 Pacific Standard Time. Not bad at all, considering that the 1964 Chevrolet Malibu due to come out that following September was priced at $ 2,800.00 and the Canadian dollar at that time was stronger than its US counterpart.

In Canada, credit unions were and still are very strong financial institutions, something akin to financial cooperatives. They are designed to serve the financial needs of their members, who all had a common bond, at least at that time in 1963. The Central Credit Union acts as a central bank for all the credit unions in a province, keeping their reserves, being overnight lenders to those in need, being the clearinghouse for all their checks, offering them economic or financial advice, and giving operational guidance. The Central Credit Union had no dealings with the general public. The job seemed tailor-made for me, a young theoretical economics graduate and idealistic socialist, heading into the Cooperative Field, albeit from the money side.

By Wednesday of that same week I had packed my lonesome grip, (Caesar's soldiers would have been ecstatic if their backpacks could have been as light as my bag), said goodbye to my few available friends, taken the train down to Calgary where I boarded the Canadian Pacific Railway for my trip west to the city of Vancouver on the pacific coast of Canada. The train ride was and still is, one of the most hoped-for tourist experiences in the world. The scenery from Calgary to Banff, past Lake Louise through the heart of the Canadian Rockies, down to Revelstoke, continuing through Kamloops, then through the coastal range and the Fraser Valley into Vancouver remains indelibly stamped on my mind.

I went straight to the YMCA and got a room. I lived at the Y for the remaining two weeks of May, then got an apartment at Oak Street and 12th Avenue when my first paycheck came at the end of the month. My rent was $65 a month for a one-bedroom apartment in a relatively nice area of town. Soon, I was able to afford to fly back to Edmonton for graduation. I stayed with my hockey player friend, Johnny Utendale.

Only one person, Mrs. Daisy Garrod, my first friend and bridge teacher, came to see me receive my bachelor's degree at the University of Alberta in May 1963. I think I was the only black person receiving a degree that day. It was very pleasing when six years later as a bank manager with Citibank in Jamaica, my wife and I were privileged to entertain Mrs. Garrod at lunch in Montego Bay, when she came to the island on a cruise, and to have her hold our first child in her arms. My beloved Papa Garrod was not there, unfortunately. He had passed on to higher ground by this time.

★★★

Rip Robinson, the president and Bob Wadsworth, CPA, the chief financial officer took me under their wings immediately and started to teach me what my job was supposed to be about. Rip's secretary, Connie, a most lovely lady, showed me how to treat and work with a secretary, and filled my day with jokes as they also introduced me to Vancouver and Canadian cultural activities. The chairman of the board, John Lucas, brought me into his family activities immediately. John had sons my age, and we all bonded well. Rip's son David was my exact contemporary, having just been an engineering graduate of the University of British Columbia.

David had a small Shark Class sailboat and we spent many afternoons sailing in English Bay. I enjoyed the experience of learning to handle a sailboat, even though the water in English Bay was never warm, and one can't truly put a Shark Class boat through its paces without getting wet. David was a cadet officer in the Royal Canadian Navy, and we spent many hours exploring naval lore at the Vancouver training facilities. On Saturday mornings we would hike in Squamish and sometimes in the snow at Whistler, and then go sailing in English Bay in the afternoons, even in winter. I had walked into two families who loved and respected me. I even had one date with Rip and Connie's daughter, Diane, when she came home from her Paris sojourn, but it was tepid.

During my first year with BC Central, I presented many reports on the economic activity in the country, to credit unions all over the province of British Columbia, especially as they related to credit unions in general. I also did one major operational analysis of the New Westminster Credit Union just outside Vancouver. My main research during that first year, however, was to study and make a report to the board of directors on the composition and performance of the organization's bond portfolio. As mentioned before, credit unions like commercial banks were by law required to keep a percentage of their customers' savings and deposits as reserves with their Central Credit Union, which in turn had to maintain reserves sufficient to cover any demands made upon it by its members. These reserves were maintained in government bonds, and cash deposits with the regular commercial banks. Earnings from this reserve portfolio were extremely important to the Central Credit Union, since its only other sources of income were interest from deposits with commercial banks and overnight charges to member credit Unions.

I believe that when John Diefenbaker became Prime Minister of Canada in 1957, he found that Canada had a large number of Federal bond issues outstanding, many of them issued at various times during the war, as it progressed, to finance obligations during the conflict. The management of obligations under these bonds was very cumbersome, so Diefenbaker made a grand consolidation of many Federal Instruments into one big issue known in the trade as the 4½s (four halves of '83), a long-term bond. I believe the issue was offered at par. BC Central had taken on a large portion of these bonds relatively, and by 1963 when I joined the organization, the market yields for Federal Government long-term bonds were more than what the four halves of '83 were earning. The 83's naturally declined in price. This potentially was a problem, so in walked this young economics graduate, with a first degree to boot, who had only two years of related courses: macroeconomics, government finance, and money & banking – why not throw him the problem, and get him to do a study?

I had never considered the ramifications of a bond portfolio before I came to this, my first real professional job. I never considered that bonds were traded with a critical income-earning objective. As far as I was concerned, people and institutions bought bonds, threw them into a safe, and clipped coupons every six months, exchanging these coupons for cash until the bonds matured when they would exchange them for cash. My research led me to maturity in a hurry. I spent hours in the Vancouver financial district talking to and studying the techniques and practices of bond traders in particular, but also stock traders with an eye on the salesmen. I not only learned about some of the practical rudiments of financial economics, but I made some long-lasting friends, like Phil Perceval who later became best man at my wedding; Colin Oliphant; traders and salesmen at Wood Gundy & Company; McLeod Young Weir; Jack Smart of Pemberton

Securities, and Michael Brown of Brown & Brown. Michael and his father Tom were both Rhodes Scholars.

The directors and management of BC Central liked my study and presentation and within a year of joining the organization, I was made an investments manager. *Now, how do I convince Rip, my boss, to take judicious capital losses and go for yield to become current with market yields and within a planned period outperform other bond portfolios?* We went ahead and sold the low-yielding bonds, took the loss, and made up for it with higher-yielding ones.

★★★

It was not all work without play. In the early 1960s, Vancouver was an emerging and swinging city. There were traditional swingers, and there was a large hippie population. I have always been traditional; I love to dance and sing and in those days, I drank moderately. To date, I have never had any form of narcotic, and have never knowingly been associated with anyone who used illegal drugs.

There was a beautiful young Australian woman named Linda in our office and she became my friend from my first day at BC Central. When I learned that she was from Perth in Western Australia, I figured that she must know something about cricket, and she did. My West Indies cricket team had engaged in many test battles with Australia over the years, including matches at Perth, and so Linda and I bonded over the sport. She did chafe a little when I recalled the third Test at Perth in the late 1950s when West Indies opening batsman Roy Fredericks scored one hundred and fifty-one runs before lunch, mostly off Thompson, the terrible Thomo, that destructive Australian fast bowler, and then rubbed salt into the wound by declaring, "He had it coming".

Linda introduced me to the Australia New Zealand Association (ANZA) Club of Vancouver, strictly a fun and sports club. We had parties just about every Friday night and played tennis every evening and on Saturday mornings. It's amazing how much like West Indians Australians are; I suppose it's our common renegade British heritage. On many a Friday night, Linda and I would turn the other dancers into spectators as they moved to the sidelines to watch us jitterbug. Please do not think that I had suddenly turned into a monk. Linda was my buddy. It was Pam, another Australian, that I was after. Pam was from Sydney and had been sent to British Columbia to study credit unions by her home Central Credit Union. She was a lovely person who succeeded in diverting me into a friend and not a lover. I was not a happy camper. Here were all these beautiful young women in Vancouver and I, this supposed swinger, couldn't get one for myself.

In the fall of 1963, I bought my very first car. I paid $600.00 for a 1957 four-door chocolate brown Chevy sedan with three standard forward gears on the steering column. It had been extremely well maintained. I drove that car for a year and a half and never had to touch it up to the time I sold it in the spring of 1965.

I was living in Vancouver for over a year before I got to meet another black person. I knew of Willie Fleming, the star halfback for the BC Lions, but did not meet him until late in 1964. I figured that there must have been other black people in this beautiful city, and eventually, I would find some of them. In the fall of 1964, I met Bill and Rose Mary Brown and their family. Bill was from Macon, Georgia, and Rose Mary was from Jamaica. They were both graduates of McGill University and Sir George William University in Montreal. Bill was a professor of psychiatry at UBC and also had a flourishing private practice in psychiatry in Vancouver. Rose Mary was a home-maker and amateur politician like I was. They threw wonderful parties at their home, where I met several other blacks.

There is a most interesting story surrounding Bill's personal Canadian journey. My understanding is that he went there to avoid the Korean draft. When he finished his first degree in chemistry, the U.S. Army called him up, so he got an exemption to go to graduate school. He was called up again upon obtaining his masters in biochemistry, so he went to medical school. He kept getting the call until he became a psychiatrist, and the US authorities figured that he was by now as crazy as his patients and was best left to the Canadians. Rose Mary became a member of the New Democratic Party of Canada, my old party, and went on to become a member of the Canadian House of Commons. She came to visit my family while we were in Jamaica years later, but unfortunately, I was away in Europe negotiating a deal for one of the corporate boards on which I sat. My wife was able to entertain her however, and to reminisce on our early experiences. Rose Mary has gone on to higher service with her maker.

Bill and Rose Mary led me to the British Columbia Association for the Advancement of Colored People, the BCAACP. It was here that I met pretty much all of the fewer than fifty black local Vancouver families. Within three months of joining, I was made vice president of the organization, and I took it upon myself to revive and restore their newspaper. The BCAACP had a paper in earlier years but it died for lack of an editor. I became the editor of what we called The BCAACP Gazette. I think we put out an edition every three months. I had a glorious time writing all the articles, collecting all the background information, being the only reporter, deciding on the format, making up the masthead, even writing all the editorials. I was enjoying myself thoroughly. This assignment brought me in very close touch with the local black community, and I found two competent ladies who helped me type, cut the stencils and run off copies of our publications on the Gestetner machine. The technology of the early 1960's was very primitive compared to twenty-first-century standards. We spilled ink all over the place.

Our little community was very imaginative. We had a vibrant Little Theater and staged many plays during the two years that I spent with the organization. All of the member families originated in the United States, and their ancestors had managed to find their way to Canada before, during and after the American Civil War; there was no-one of West Indian or African nationality among the members. The waves of the great West Indian migration had not yet reached Canada, and certainly not the west coast of the country. In that time, one could move around Vancouver for days and not encounter a black person. Maybe if you hung out around the railway station, you might be lucky enough to encounter a black porter when the Canadian National Railway or the Canadian Pacific Railway came in from the east.

I recall heading out of my office one early summer evening, and while waiting for the green light to cross the street, I saw a very familiar young black man, like myself well dressed, waiting to cross from the other side. It was none other than Harry Belafonte. We stopped in the middle of the street, shook hands and greeted each other. I truly felt transported. Here were two brothers bent on making our stamp on the fair city of Vancouver. Perhaps the sociologists will find it noteworthy that I found no local black people between ages twenty and thirty in Vancouver during the early 1960s. I theorize that they left Vancouver right after high school to find better job opportunities.

Simultaneous with these extracurricular activities I maintained a keen interest in economics, both macro and micro, especially as regards monetary economics. I continued to do operational studies on credit unions in the province of British Columbia, and to make reports and give advice to managers and directors all around the province. My work took me to places like Kamloops and Revelstoke, into the Rogers Pass, Prince George, Penticton, the Okanagan Valley (great apples and wine), Victoria, the west coast of Vancouver Island, Nanaimo, Burnaby, Coquitlam, the East Kootenays. I believe I have visited every area in the province of British Columbia and have made a speech in all of them. Credit union people are marvelous folks, and those in British Columbia in the early 1960s were the greatest.

★★★

I must relate two experiences that stand out above all my travels in British Columbia. I had to make a study and report to the board of the credit union in the East Kootenays and I became so enamored with the area that I spent ten days there on vacation. The town was located in a valley and glacial peaks could be seen pretty much all around. I was in the heart of the Canadian Rockies where eastern British Columbia abuts and bounds Alberta, on the Continental Divide. Here, rivers flowing west went to the Pacific, and those flowing east went to the Atlantic. I made great friends in the East Kootenays and enjoyed relaxing in hot-water sulfur holes in the afternoons and for dinner in the evenings, eating pierogies. These are tiny turnovers filled with a vegetable, like beets or cabbage or potatoes, or with meat, then folded and steamed, before typically being served with drawn butter poured over them. Every culture makes use of flour in its diet, but these things were marvelous – and not good for the waistline.

In the Kootenays, I got to know many members of a sect called the Sons of Freedom, the Doukhobors. These were nihilists who did not believe in any form of government and refused to pay taxes. They were severely disciplined by the Czars in Russia during the nineteenth century, and it was generally believed that the writer Leo Tolstoy persuaded Queen Victoria to grant them refuge in western Canada during the late 1800s. Doukhobors, in general, were not extremists, but members of the Sons of Freedom were. Their calling card was to blow up railway tracks and to have their females walk naked in the streets when they became especially pissed. There were public protests by the group in British Columbia when I was there, but I never witnessed any. It was only their old fat ladies that were sent out on nude parade anyway; they never offered their young sweet ones for public view. I failed to connect with any young Doukhobor woman during my unaccompanied vacation in the East Kootenays in the early 1960s.

I had a harrowing experience on one of my trips to northwestern British Columbia one year. I had done some work for the credit union in Kitimat that fall and was returning early in the winter to deliver my report when the event occurred. I left Vancouver at about 1:00 p.m. on a planned two-hour flight to Kitimat. We took off fine, but as soon as we got over Puget Sound and turned north, the pilot announced that the cover to the oil cup had blown off, and he would have to head back to the Vancouver airport to have the problem fixed before resuming the flight north. But first, he would have to circle Puget Sound and dump gas to make the aircraft lighter for landing. He said that he would be dumping enough gas to fuel anyone's car for at least a year.

It was three o'clock in the afternoon before we got our problems straightened out and were once again airborne to Kitimat. By the time we got over Kitimat, a whiteout had set in and we could not land. We pushed on northward, hoping to land at Terrace, but there was a whiteout there also, and so we found no joy there either. We went all the way up to Prince Rupert, hoping to find clear enough conditions up there to land, but there was a whiteout in that area as well. This was getting to be serious stuff. Prince George and Edmonton Alberta were now in play, but by now we were pretty far north and had jumped around so much that fuel was getting low.

The pilot announced that there was a good possibility of clear skies over Digby Island to the southwest. He came back down the road as economically as he could and was able to land at a military airbase on the island. We then had to find a Ferry to take us from Digby Island to Terrace on the mainland, and then drive about one hundred miles by bus south to Kitimat. I reached my hotel at 1:00 the next morning. Two hours had become twelve; it was about thirteen total hours for me. Unruffled at all times during that ordeal, I delivered my report at 10:00 that same morning as scheduled. At twenty-eight years of age, I welcomed adventure, and even though I hardly ever thought of God at that time, I was under the protection and guidance of the Holy Spirit. I left Kitimat that same afternoon on the flight back to Vancouver, my mission accomplished.

The Vancouver experience was flourishing on several fronts. I continued to grow in my job at BC Central Credit Union and was given several new and challenging assignments. I was also developing respect on the investment street in the city and familiarity and expected appearances at the business and university luncheon clubs and restaurants in the city of Vancouver. My associates were mostly older men who marveled at my ability to put away the largest of beef steaks, fat and all, washed down with excellent red wines. I needed to eat well, for I was jogging every day, playing tennis and golf, sailing, and hiking on weekends. What's more, I had found the ladies finally, or maybe they had found me. During that period in 1964, I was dating seven women, three of them from different Caribbean islands and the others from different parts of the world. I had numerous other friends by now, but my main outlet of emotions and camaraderie came from my Friday night flings with my fellow ANZA Club members. Little did I know that one day I would have lived long enough to have to pass up on the steaks for just Dover sole off the bone – and no wine, please.

One evening as I walked along Broadway, I stopped at a simple tailor shop, just to kill time, and met Amos the owner. We chatted and discussed the weights of fabrics and their suitability for Vancouver's weather and seasons. Amos, who had been a tailor in Poland, wanted to know how it was that I was so aware of fabrics and their applicability. I explained that my aunt's husband was a master tailor and he worked out of my grandmother's house, so from my earliest days I knew fabric. I explained further that during my youth all of our clothes were made by either dressmakers or tailors in the village, for the stores did not carry readymade clothes. Amos and I became friends after that visit, and he started to cut and make my suits. We had long and enlightening discussions of life in Warsaw and Eastern Europe before World War II, the pogroms, and the development and functioning of Ghetto economies, and the arts, and the ability of the Jewish people to survive and thrive.

Amos did good work, but he was not as good as Victor Wilson, my Jamaican bespoke tailor who would outfit me five years later. Wilson was trained on Savile Row in London and took the time to hand-stitch the finish on suits for those who cared about those things. After more than forty years I still make a quality sartorial statement when I wear suits made by Wilson.

Among my young male friends in Vancouver in 1964 were Michael Brown of Brown & Brown (a brokerage house), Haig Ferris, a young lawyer, (Ferris & Ferris), Jonathan Baker, a young American lawyer and clarinetist with the Chicago Symphony, (the Vietnam war may have brought him to Canada), and Haile Debass, a young Ethiopian surgeon in residence at the Vancouver General Hospital. Twelve of us got together and formed an association called "The Gentlemen". We met for dinner once a month, and at each gathering, one of us delivered a paper on a supposedly interesting topic of his choosing. We had a lot of fun with that, even including wives at dinner once a year. I left the group of gentlemen when I went off to graduate school in 1966.

The brokerage houses in Vancouver in 1964 not only traded stocks and bonds, but they also bought and sold short-term money market notes. Additionally, they underwrote these notes. Companies that were flush with funds for periods of ten days up to 180 days, or sometimes longer, found it advantageous to buy short-term notes of acceptable businesses or institutions. For an institution to issue such notes in British Columbia, it had to meet certain tests set by the provincial government. This process was called "blue-skying". I introduced the idea to my boss, Rip, as a method of raising short-term funds to accommodate requests for back-up loans from credit unions when statutory reserves were close to the margin.

I felt that BC Central would not only qualify under the Blue Sky Laws of the province but that the Vancouver market would be willing to buy its paper. Rip Robinson and Bob, our CPA, agreed to take the matter to the board of directors. John Lucas, our chairman, came on board. We got board approval, and I was given the job of writing the prospectus and working with legal counsel to get our money market paper blue-skyed. Within six months BC Central had its first short-term note on the street. I believe that it was a 180-day $150,000.00 promissory note, and it was placed with McMillan Blodell and Powell River through McLeod Young Weir and Co. I was by this time two years out of university with a weak first degree in economics, and basically creating an underwriting department and teaching myself the rudiments of merchant banking as I went along.

In the middle of December 1964, I left Vancouver to spend Christmas with my parents in Barbados, and to reconnect with old friends, family and neighbors. I was thrilled to revisit old roots. My parents were extremely proud of me, especially since I was the first one in our family to have gained a university degree. My old high school principal Louis Lynch was ecstatic. His comment was "You have shown that it can be done", referring to the fact that I had left Barbados in 1959 with only a thousand dollars and a half-formed notion of advanced education, and by 1963, four years later, I had earned a degree in economics from one of the best universities in Canada. Within a year and a half of graduation, I was now a research economist and investment manager of one of the leading central credit unions in Canada. The promoter in Louis Lynch saw to it that the local newspaper got the story and published it.

14. THIS CHANGES EVERYTHING

There were dramatic life changes waiting for me on my return to Vancouver in January 1965. I gave up my apartment at 12th and Oak when I left in December for Barbados and arranged to rent a fourth-floor apartment in a new high-rise that was being constructed in Vancouver's west end district on Robson Street overlooking Stanley Park. I moved into my new one-bedroom dream apartment on my return to Vancouver. The living was good. We had underground parking, a heated indoor swimming pool and a sauna bath. I had the pick of apartments since I was one of the earliest tenants to sign up, and my balcony overlooked the Vancouver harbor and Stanley Park, with West Vancouver and North Vancouver in the distance. I was able to walk to Stanley Park, and to work, for my office was now on Granville Street in the heart of the city.

Later that January of 1965, I got to know a few Trinidadians who were studying at the University of British Columbia, and we decided to form a West Indian Association. I am attracted to organizations like a labrador to water, so I naturally became a participant. Our second meeting was the following month, February 1965. Our meeting was held in one of the public rooms at UBC. The steering committee was seated on a slightly raised platform, and as a member of this committee, I was able to see everyone in the audience from my elevated position and noticed this extremely attractive young woman. She seemed genuinely interested in what we were saying, and egotistically I thought that she was paying more attention to me than to any of the fine young prospective doctors, business leaders, and prime ministers on the platform. Instinctively, I wanted to know who she was.

I decided to focus more on other members of the small audience, but every time I stole a look in this lady's direction our eyes met. Later during the social mingling, we met and chatted briefly. I learned that she was Jamaican and that her name was Vilma Nesbitt, a recent émigré to Canada. The moment we exchanged phone numbers, my life changed dramatically and irrevocably. I learned that a couple of the other young men were also struck by the charm and composure of Miss Nesbitt, so I resolved to plan my approach carefully. The competition was going to be fierce.

I had to wait two weeks for a date with her and felt like I stayed home the whole time. I theorized that if the lady had to clear her calendar over two weeks to squeeze me in, then I should purge myself and make myself pure for this new test, as some of my friends and I called a challenging woman in those days. To digress a bit, when I was a boy in the country, in Barbados, we would separate the chicken planned for Sunday dinner one week in advance and purge it with vinegar and water and select green grasses to clean it up before slaughter. Little did I know that I was preparing myself for a whole new life. Like a born-again Christian, I would die to one and rise to the other.

Way back in October 1964, I had placed an order with one of the local Chevrolet dealers for the new 1965 two-door tan V8 Malibu. That car was something else: a two-door hardtop, 283 V8 automatic transmission, the first automatic I would ever drive, Sierra Tan in color, but it had no air conditioning, which was not yet in vogue on the west coast of Canada. I paid $2800 for it, with $1,000 down and the balance financed by my credit union.

The wait time was six months. As fate would have it, at noon on the day of my first date with Miss Nesbitt, the dealer called and told me to pick up my new car. And thus I arrived to pick her up, driving my very first new car. That Malibu Chevelle was so pretty that it should have stayed in the showroom and remained perfect. It smelled newer than any new car before or since. I opened the passenger door, let the good lady in and closed it with flair and pride. I then got into the driver's seat and headed for the coffee shop in the Kitsilano neighborhood of Vancouver, all the while listening out for a congratulatory expression about the car, or at least some enquiry or the smallest comment. We had coffee and chit-chatted genially for about an hour, and then I drove her back to her apartment, still hearing no comment on the car.

The lady couldn't have cared less about the car. She was engaging though, asking me lots of questions about myself and my family, life in my native Barbados, and my education and job. This was certainly a different experience for me. An attractive lady who showed no interest in material things, but expressed interest in my family, my upbringing, my culture, my education, and my job, on our first casual date. *I shall have to take this lady seriously,* I thought hard and long.

Vilma was the first woman that romantically held my interest and about whom sex was not my first thought. *Did she have the discipline and the self-assurance to take a chance on me as a life partner, and would I have the discipline and maturity to love, respect and protect her?* I had great expectations for my future, and I had to have the right mate. But most pressing was the present. Would I be prepared to give up all my lovers for this one new lady? Believe me, I was well covered and could do without seeing most of the women I knew, but ah, my prairie girl with flaming red hair, and my virginal Pole who gave me a single flower at the start and numerous bouquets thereafter – forgetting these latter two would present gut-wrenching pain.

I went underground, instructing the telephone operator at the office not to put through any calls from women, and I quit answering my phone at the apartment. I stopped going to my favorite bars, restaurants and all my regular Vancouver haunts. I was preparing the way for a smooth relationship. On our very first real date, I took Vilma to a performance of the Vancouver Symphony. The major presentation that evening was Rimsky-Korsakov's *Scheherazade*. We were treated to a most beautiful orchestral presentation of ancient storytelling, with Rimsky-Korsakov's interpretation of Sinbad and Aladdin as told by the Arabs of antiquity and Scheherazade, the heroine, keeping the prince fascinated over one thousand and one nights.

I bought the LP the following day, and I have played it a thousand nights since our first date. The music and the story are like our love and our life, soaring and swelling, expressing despair and joy, achievement and disappointment, transporting me to such giddy heights that I have joined in telling the tales like a true convert.

I introduced Vilma to my friends as quickly as I could. Phil, my closest friend and Irene, his wife, absolutely adored her. The man who would become best man at our wedding was an Irishman from County Sligo whose family had been given their estate by Oliver Cromwell. We never discussed what exactly his people had done for the Lord Protector to earn the land, but in spite of going to private school in England, there was enough Irish left in Phil to remind me that our suffering at the hands of the English was neither as great nor as prolonged as theirs, for the English practiced on the Irish before they got to us. We drank lots of Guinness Light Ale on his balcony in Surrey, British Columbia, watching the sun set over Puget Sound and the U.S. border.

My chairman and his family loved my Vilma; my president and his family and everyone in my office loved her, and wherever we went, this regal young lady captivated the folks with her beauty and charm. I remember us going to a Bill Cosby concert in 1965 and we were the last couple to walk down the aisle. As we made our way down, Cosby started composing a poem, Shakespeare-style, to my lady. On another occasion in Vancouver, we went to a club where the famous Duke Ellington was in concert, and as we walked towards the bandstand, the Duke broke away seamlessly from the song he was playing into an inspiring rendition of "Sophisticated Lady". His eyes lit up over my girl. Ellington was a serious lover so I couldn't help quietly miming, "This one is mine, sucker," in his direction. Of course, the word was now out around Vancouver that I was running unchallenged for the fair one, so I upped the ante and Vilma and I got engaged three months after we met. Things went so swimmingly that we got married two months after our engagement.

My friend Frank Gilliam, a former wide receiver for the Winnipeg Blue Bombers under coach Bud Grant and now a high school teacher in West Vancouver picked me up early on the morning of Saturday August 28th and drove me to our wedding, which took place in a beautiful Methodist Church out in the woods in Surrey BC, about twenty miles from Vancouver, very near the U.S. border. We called it "The Church in The Wild Wood". We had twenty-four guests, no relatives, all friends since our families were six thousand miles away in the Caribbean. We had no-one to interfere or cause trouble, giving us time and space to work out our problems and challenges. We treated our guests to a beautiful champagne lunch, with a tossed salad, roast sirloin of beef, baked potatoes, carrots and green beans. It was typically Irish food, served outside at our friends Phil and Irene's home. It was a beautiful late August day with just a hint of freshness in the air.

We left our guests about 1:00 p.m., jumped into our Malibu, drove to West Vancouver and took the Ferry to Nanaimo on Vancouver Island for our honeymoon. We had originally planned to go to San Francisco and then continue down the coast to Mexico, but the Watts Riots intervened so we settled for Vancouver Island instead. From Nanaimo, we drove across the island and down to Wikannish Inn on the west coast of Vancouver Island. The hotel was pure rustic beauty, the food was great, and the beach was enticing. The sand was so firm that cars could drive on it, but the water was too cold for swimming.

We were at the most south-westerly point in Canada and the very western tip of the Trans-Canada Highway at that time. Everything had gone well thus far but after five days, we longed for brighter lights and drove back across the island to Victoria, the capital. Afternoon tea at the Imperial Hotel was a treat, but the great attraction had to be the magnificent Butchart Gardens. Our visit there, featuring lunch overlooking the Italian garden, still ranks near the top of our western travel experiences.

From our high in Victoria, we were rudely welcomed back to reality in Vancouver. Mornings, I would walk to work from Robson Street just outside of Stanley Park down to the financial district. It was a beautiful stroll, past all the little boutiques, tea and coffee stores, candy, meat, pastry and cake shops and their mid-European ambiance. There was even one tea shop that would keep a family's preferred tea blend on file for years.

On this particular morning, I chose to take the bus. On boarding, I noted one vacant seat beside a woman. I took the seat. Before the driver could get going, she jumped up and shouted, "You're not sitting beside me!" A silence, more consuming than that normally observed by early morning commuters, gripped the bus. The poor driver tried to speak but couldn't get a word out, as the unfortunate woman flounced off down the aisle. I called the local *Vancouver Sun* city affairs columnist Jack Wasserman, whose column next morning had a field day describing how this handsome young negro business executive encountered a white female bigot on a local bus; the woman chose to leave her seat and eventually rode standing up rather than sitting beside the young man.

Wasserman, who was known for his writing on nightlife and celebrity happenings, went as far as to describe the tailor-made suit I was wearing. Of course, he had asked me lots of personal questions to set me at ease, and I was too innocent at that stage to be overly modest. This all took place at the height of the Civil Rights crisis gripping our neighbors to the south, and it was newsworthy to find a mentionable connection in Vancouver. During my almost ten years in Canada, this incident was the only occasion of open bigotry that I experienced. The other passengers on the bus were visibly embarrassed. I was not hurt or particularly concerned. My style had been to disregard slights that did not threaten me physically, and to do nothing that would transfer sympathies that naturally fell my way, to my attacker or opponent.

We started our married life very modestly but comfortably. We bought a new bed and bedroom furniture, but most of our other stuff was inherited from friends and admirers. After more than fifty years, we still have serviceable stuff that families who had lost loved ones had given us to set up house. These things range from an old outdoors coffee pot to special knives, pieces of china, vases, crystal, living room decorations, bedspreads, and a copy of the *Good Housekeeping Cookbook*. I learned to cook simple presentable meals by using that old volume, and so did my wife.

We enjoyed our jobs during the workweek, but every weekend we were off exploring wonderful British Columbia. Some weekends we would visit Phil and Irene in Surrey, and sometimes we visited three Utendale Sisters at their lovely home in Burnaby. Most times we were gone for the weekend, sometimes exploring the Fraser Valley, often visiting old Pete, an Irish dairy farmer who had a Holstein herd up the valley, and sometimes we would be at the warm sulfur springs further up the road. Our favorite spots were Penticton and Kelowna, a city on Okanagan Lake. Penticton grew the most delicious McIntosh apples, and Kelowna was becoming famous for its wine and grapes, apart from being the home of Herb Capozzi, general manager of the then-dominant football team in the Canadian league, the BC Lions.

One night at a nightclub in Salmon Arm, I felt brave enough and sufficiently far from sophisticated society to join the band on stage and sing a number, Sinatra's "Fly Me To The Moon". The folks loved it; even my bride was tickled, reminding me however that it was not reason enough to think of quitting my day job.

That Sinatra song and the idea of actually changing my job seemed to have struck a harmonious chord with my Vilma, for she brought it up again a few weeks later. I had to make presentations to credit unions in Kamloops and Revelstoke, so naturally, my young wife accompanied me. We got into a serious discussion of the course we wanted our lives to take. Vilma thought that she would like to finish a degree and that I should think of advanced studies or a professional degree. She argued that in 1965 a first degree was not enough to match the coming competition and that I needed to go to graduate school first. I disagreed, and as I did so I realized the weakness of my argument, but I was not easily persuaded to give up the comfort of my existence to take on the rigors and deprivations of graduate school.

The seed was planted, but first, we had to spend the next three or four days exploring Revelstoke and the surrounding Canadian Rockies. Pristine Lake Louise was a joy, and the luxury of a night in the Banff Springs Hotel with my wife of a few months is an indelible memory. Our trip to the Columbia Icefields was awe-inspiring, especially our observation of a crevasse in the ice, and later the profusion of wildlife, some of it not at all perturbed by the closeness of intruding humans.

Back in Vancouver, serious planning began. First, we would start saving more money. We continued to explore and enjoy all of British Columbia, and the following year, 1966, we would drive down the Pacific Coast to Mexico, via San Francisco and Los Angeles, and then back to Vancouver via Las Vegas and Reno, treating ourselves to the honeymoon spots that the Watts Riots had denied us. Then In the fall of 1966, I would go to graduate school at the University of British Columbia.

During the latter half of 1965 and early months of 1966, we explored the islands off the coast of Vancouver Island in the Strait of Georgia from Nanaimo, south through Puget Sound and down to Seattle. We had great friends, the Hollamans who lived on Gabriola Island northeast of Nanaimo, and we spent enjoyable times with them. Mr. Hollamans was a black American gentleman of about eighty years of age, and his wife was an equally mature black Canadian. They had retired on this island and would sometimes come to Vancouver to meet city folk and enjoy evenings at the Vancouver Hotel or take in local theater.

It was Hollamans who introduced me to the comfort and beauty of Bally shoes, and the attraction of his 1962 two-tone convertible Thunderbird motor car. The man had style and class; he was a retired life insurance salesman from Tennessee, and it was a long time before I fully understood what he meant when he would tell me that if he had been a white man in his native USA, he would have been a multi-millionaire. He still managed to do well, even though he worked in the days when he had to go door to door and collect premiums in cash every week selling retail life insurance. As for me, the world was open in front of me, and at twenty-nine, I was heading out there to get my pearls.

After agreeing that I would go to graduate school at the University of British Columbia in the fall of 1966 to do either an MBA or enter Law School, we decided that we would spend as much time as we could before then exploring British Columbia and the west coast of the USA.

Vilma had a girlfriend who married a man from Prince George in the northern interior of British Columbia on the Fraser River. We took a week off and went to visit them. It was an exciting trip. We put snow tires on the car and left Vancouver in September 1965 to follow the mighty Fraser north. Our first stop was Aldergrove, a small urban community in the Fraser Valley about forty-five minutes from Vancouver, then we continued to Hope, a town at the eastern end of the valley and the lower mainland region at the southern end of the Fraser Canyon. From there, we continued upriver to Cache Creek, a historic transportation junction 220 miles north and east of Vancouver. Then we went on to 100 Mile House, a residential district of seven hundred homes in the South Cariboo region of British Columbia.

This was where the Cariboo Gold Rush began in the 1860's. The homes were beautifully preserved and set around pristine lakes and parklands. We overnighted here and toured the area after a grand Canadian breakfast the next morning. We then moved on to Williams Lake, the largest city in the central interior of British Columbia, another beneficiary of the Gold Rush and the largest urban center between Kamloops and Prince George. Continuing north, we stopped in the town of Quesnel at the confluence of the Quesnel and the Fraser rivers, an area well known for its production of National Hockey League players, and its great hunting, fishing and canoeing.

We then went on to Prince George. Situated at the confluence of the Fraser and the Nechako rivers, it is the largest city in northern B.C. The city was developed as a trading post for the Hudson Bay Company and the North West Trading Company and benefitted greatly from the development of the Canadian National Railway in the early twentieth century. After visiting with Wilma's friend and relaxing in this interior city we headed southeast to Jasper, Alberta to see what that part of the wild was like, before heading northeast to Edmonton. There, we were able to visit my alma mater, the U of A, and also call on my old landlady, Mrs. Garrod. I was now on old familiar ground and took pride in showing it all off as we headed south through Ponoka and Red Deer into Calgary on the trail that I had so often hitchhiked during my undergraduate years. From Calgary, we went through Banff and Lake Louise once more, following the Trans-Canada Highway back to Vancouver via Golden, Revelstoke, Salmon Arm, Kamloops, then through the Okanagan Valley into Vancouver. *Oh, for the energy and adventurism of youth!* I loved motor trips and wilderness country and I was blessed to find a life partner with the same spirit.

For Vilma and me, 1966 was a great moving year. First, we gave up my luxury apartment on Robson Street and moved into more modest digs near the University of British Columbia. Next, Vilma got a drivers' license in preparation for our big motor trip down the west coast from Vancouver to Tijuana, Mexico, then the big move from being an executive swinger on the Vancouver scene to becoming a graduate student at UBC.

Vilma had developed a great friendship with a wonderful girl of Flemish origin when they worked at the main Ford parts distributorship in Vancouver in 1963. Marge and Gordy, whom she married in 1964, and Vilma and I became great friends. Gordy and I were both car enthusiasts; he loved Fords and I adored Chevrolets. When I got my Chevy, Gordy got a '65 V8 Ford Mustang. Marge and Gordy decided to join us on our trip down the west coast as far as San Francisco, where they would peel off for Lake Tahoe and Reno before heading back to Vancouver while we would continue down the coast. I think that it was August 1966 when we set out from Vancouver, communicating along the way via walkie talkie (the cell phone was not yet developed, though it may have been on some engineer's mind). We went through Richmond, Surrey and White Rock, entering the USA at Blaine, Washington, continuing south on Highway 5 to Bellingham. We had to make a stop there so that I could show Vilma the golf course that drew me out of bed at 4:30 on Sunday mornings so that my friend Cleve and I could be the first to tee off.

From Bellingham we went through Seattle, a city that I had never visited in spite of its proximity to Vancouver; I was just too busy exploring British Columbia, I guess. South of Seattle we drove through the Boeing aircraft plant, which stretched for several blocks on both sides of the road. I had never seen such a large enterprise before – totally understandable – and totally in keeping with the largest export manufacturer in the United States.

Onward we went through Tacoma, then stopped for lunch at the foot of Mount St. Helens before heading into Eugene, Oregon. From there we hit Highway 101 and followed the coastal route south into Redwood National State Park. The giant redwoods were an overwhelming sight, and we stood in awe as we studied them and contemplated the wonders of nature. Continuing down the coast, we frolicked in Eureka, California, after stopping at several small towns, passing Fort Bragg, still following highway 101 into San Francisco at last.

Marge and Gordy separated from us here and we found a hotel on Lombard Street. After touring the Nob Hill area, we rode a streetcar through the hilly parts of town, before spending the afternoon on

Fishermen's Wharf and touring Chinatown. The next day we lunched at a beautiful Japanese restaurant overlooking the Golden Gate Bridge and roamed around the city before having dinner at Virginia's Hickory Pit, a soul food restaurant in the black district. Soul food was emerging at that time as a great American delight. We found it interesting but too hot, spicy and overcooked. The ingredients were not unfamiliar to us but were presented a bit differently from what we were accustomed to as West Indians. We enjoyed the pork chops and the cornbread but would have given anything for the smell and flavor of Scotch Bonnet pepper instead of the hot yet flavorless peppers that were used. We enjoyed ourselves because we were bent on learning about the different aspects of American culture to which we were being exposed. Neither Vilma nor I had had any previous exposure to the USA in terms of visiting among the people. I had passed through New York on my way to Barbados two years earlier, but I spent all of my stay going from one relative's home to another's.

After dinner, we went to the roof of the Fairmont Hotel for drinks. This was like moving from one underprivileged country to a luxurious first-world country, all within fifteen minutes, on the same streets in the same city. In these early days, we drank either Stolichnaya vodka (what everyone called "Stoli") or Tanqueray gin martinis. After about three martinis, I noticed that I was seeing different parts of the city at different intervals and wondered if that was what it was like to be drunk before Vilma reminded me that we were in the famous rotating bar on top of the Fairmont Hotel in wonderful San Francisco! We had invited my Australian friend Linda from my ANZA Club days, who had moved to San Francisco to join us. Linda was marvelous company, and we all left the Fairmont in wonderful spirits. The next day, we crossed the Bay Bridge and headed into Oakland. We spent most of the day on the Berkley Campus of the University of California before heading back to our hotel so we could rest before our big night out.

On our last night in San Francisco we went to Finocchios, the place friends had told us was a must-see if we ever got to the city. We were not at all prepared for the spectacle and the marvelous entertainment that we shared with the overflow crowd. The club was a drag queen spot, where artistes presented dances from Broadway musicals. I kept looking for the drag queens to come on stage well into the evening before I realized that I had been watching them all along.

Next day, on the road again, we drove down to Palo Alta to tour the Stanford University campus and continue our amazement at the abundance of blessings that God had poured out onto the USA. From Stanford, we drove through the Carmel area, checked out Pebble Beach Golf Course, found a quaint little country store where we bought smoked red herring, crackers and soft drinks, and sat on the rocks overlooking the Pacific Ocean. We certainly reveled in our West Indian country-man's lunch. My dear wife was alarmed and embarrassed when I peed against a lonely tree overlooking the ocean and the golf course and questioned my manners. I told her that I was leaving my mark for posterity. She was not yet bold enough to call me a dog.

As we continued down the coast to Los Angeles, we stopped at every mission that the Spaniards had built along the way, marveling at the history of early European settlement in America, and the way the British had taught it. There had to be more to the story than the Pilgrims and the Mayflower. On we went through Big Sur with its large collection of interesting artifacts, mighty cliffs and inviting beaches down to San Simeon, where we toured the Hearst Castle and were overwhelmed by the opulence, extravagance and sometimes bad taste of the supremely wealthy. Even at this early stage in my development, I was becoming aware of nature's way of balancing immense financial success and personal power with great social, mental health, genetic, and personality problems, which the average person is often spared. We stayed as close to the ocean as we could until we reached Los Angeles.

Our friend Linda flew down from San Francisco and joined us for the weekend. Linda's husband Ross was working in Los Angeles and he too joined us. I had known Ross from my earliest days in Vancouver when we were members of the ANZA Club. The four of us went all over Los Angeles, from the Farmers Market to Hollywood, and from the most lavish districts, to Watts, which still had the scars of the riots that had delayed our visit by a year. We went to Disneyland on the weekend that "It's A Small World" opened, and we also toured Knotts Berry Farm.

The freeways around Los Angeles were the largest and fastest that we had experienced to date, and the drivers were the craziest. Before Los Angeles, we had seen four lanes in either direction, more often two, but here there were six lanes and sometimes more in one direction, with traffic moving at eighty miles an hour. Drivers changed lanes without signaling, and many seemed surprised when their exits suddenly popped up, giving them just enough time to cross diagonally across four lanes of traffic at eighty-five or ninety miles an hour with scarcely enough time to exit safely. It reminded me of the tense crescendo at the end of a symphony – without the crash of the cymbals. Vilma and I drove down to Tijuana after our enjoyable weekend in Los Angeles. San Diego was a lovely city, but Tijuana was a disappointment. It was simply a dirty border town with good Mexican beer and uninteresting Mexican food. Admittedly, we knew nothing about Mexican food, so we did not eat until we came back across the border and found standard American food in San Diego. At least we could say that we had been to Mexico. I felt that there had to be something deeper and more profound in the Mexican culture and people than what we experienced in Tijuana; it was not until seven years later, when I was on a two-week tour of southern states courtesy of the U.S. Department of Agriculture to study livestock feeding cultures, that I had the pleasure of meeting and spending two weeks with two other young agriculturalists from Mexico.

I had enough time then to get a better feel for Mexican culture. Through my new colleagues I learned about their history, their politics, their food, their education system, their sports, their music, their attempts to cope with the hegemony of a far more powerful neighbor to the north, their social problems, their challenges with corruption and crime, and their unwillingness to forget the loss of the southwestern territory to the United States. We bonded well, those two young Mexicans and I, as we studied livestock farms in Louisiana, Arkansas, and Mississippi. We even took out a one-day membership in a Jackson, Mississippi golf club, just to get a legal alcoholic drink. When it became time for us to part, I flew from Decatur, Arkansas, to Dallas with them to spend our last weekend together before we all headed to our respective homes. We had a boys' weekend of fun and games before I was loaded on the last Braniff Airlines flight to New York late one Sunday night, and then on to Jamaica the next day.

From San Diego, we drove North to Las Vegas, which was a quiet fun town back in 1966. Vilma hit the jackpot on a nickel slot machine and the pot of nickels spilled all over our beautiful Malibu. Weeks later, we were still finding nickels in the car's crevices. We toured the area around the Hoover Dam and Lake Mead but did not undertake the arduous drive to the Grand Canyon at that time. It took us forty-four years more before we got back to Las Vegas and finally made a side trip to see the canyon.

The highlight of our 1966 visit to Las Vegas was seeing Sammy Davis Jr. perform live. Lola Falana, a hot young dancer, warmed the audience up for the appearance of the great entertainer, and great he was. We had had the privilege of seeing other great entertainers in live performances before, like Duke Ellington, Harry Belafonte and Nat "King" Cole, whose presence brought the house to an electric silence and trembling warmth, but Sammy Davis' presence energized you, wowed you, lifted you out of your seat. He gave a one-man presentation of "The Music Man", with emphasis on Robert Preston's role, keeping us all spellbound for one and a half hours. There was pure love in that theater that night and being the only visible blacks in the audience we were the beneficiaries of much of it. Our reserve was penetrated by the outburst and we hugged others as much as they hugged us.

The next morning as I was coming out of a stall in the lobby restroom, a white guy walked in, and when he saw me he exclaimed, "Sheeeet, fucking niggers!" It didn't dawn on me what he had said until I was at the checkout desk. Maybe my thoughts were far away and on other things, not unusual for me, and maybe I had failed to recognize insults before, but this would have been the first racial slur that I encountered in the USA. It was water off a duck's back, but a call for keener observation. Vilma and I discussed it, and later told it as a joke to our beautiful white friends.

From Vegas, it was north for an entire day through the Mojave desert to Reno without air conditioning, which was not found in the average Canadian car at that time. We were happy when we found an oasis to rest and fill up, but when we got to Reno late that evening, we could not find a room at any hotel after dinner. We hung around gambling tables and slot machines until very late that night, a front desk clerk found us a little closet into which we could crawl after he had put a bed in there. Once inside, we could not turn around, but that was no problem for us newlyweds. We were friends and lovers, husband and wife – who just wanted to sleep.

We got out of Reno as fast as we could that morning and headed north for Oregon. In those days there was no speed limit in Nevada, so we opened up that sweet Malibu on all eight cylinders with the 283 displacement and headed into the back roads of Oregon at 95 and 100 miles an hour. Of course, there would be someone to overtake us. On a flat straight stretch of highway, I spotted a Chevrolet sedan closing the gap quickly between us. It was not a cop, so I put the pedal further to the metal. The Malibu responded, but I just didn't have enough horses. Two gentlemen went by me in a flash in a 1962 Impala, calmly conversing, and seeming not to even notice that I was on the highway. I was a bit embarrassed and promised myself that if I were going to drive American cars, then I would have to go for the big-block V8's. As fate would have it, my Malibu was the last American car that I would own or drive for the next nineteen years. Once I got into European stick shifts, the challenges and fun of mountain driving and vehicle control on narrow roads, American cars lost their appeal.

We took the opportunity to stop in Portland, Oregon on the way back to British Columbia, where this time we explored the interior of both Oregon and Washington State before returning to Vancouver.

In September 1966, I entered graduate school at the University of British Columbia to take on the rigors of the master's in business administration program. My first class was a graduate statistics class, and the first person I saw on entering was Ivern Davis, an old friend from my days in Nassau as a young policeman back in 1957. Ivern had come home after earning a degree in civil engineering from the University of Toronto, and he and his wife Elma were among the folks who befriended me and encouraged me to seek higher education. Ivern had been sent by his country to do a graduate degree in town planning before becoming head of the planning department when the Bahamas became a sovereign nation. I took Ivern home that afternoon to meet Vilma, and our families have bonded and remained friends through more than fifty years and four generations.

Ivern was a champion squash player, and when he could find no one on campus to play with, he invited me to become his student. There was a well-appointed squash court at the graduate center, and before long I developed a reasonable game. I preferred the English ball, which warmed up more slowly than the American one, thus giving the neophyte player more time to get ready for competition.

Ivern was from a large family, and he was expert in the art of sharing. My family was very small, one boy and one girl. After a vigorous game one evening, we came out of the showers to find that there was only one bath towel. For me, this was a problem. For Ivern it wasn't. He showed me how I could use one end of the towel and he would use the other, then gave me the honor of going first. Problem solved.

A few years earlier, statistics had been my nemesis as an undergraduate, but in the graduate course, I had little difficulty. I found it ironic that I was able to explain portions of the statistical analytical tools to my friend, a civil engineer. Ivern passed away in 2008, but our families visited with each other either in Jamaica, Nassau, Barbados or the United States every two years from 1968 until then.

Vancouver is one of the prettiest cities in North America, and the University of British Columbia campus was the gem in her crown. I believe that there were seventy-five students in my graduate class, and I was sure that my concentration would be finance. The program followed the Harvard Model closely, with case studies as teaching tools. We were all mature young men and women, many of whom were Americans, and a few of whom were sitting out the Vietnam War. Some of our professors were young men from US universities, and I particularly remember Dr. J.W. Sutherland, who had just earned a Ph.D. from Stanford and Dr. Whata Winiata, who had recently earned his Ph.D. from the University of Michigan. These two young academics brought a new style to UBC, adding fun to study and presentation.

Sutherland taught business policy. With him, we had our most enlightening subject-area discussions in the local pub. Sutherland got us to read books from different cultures, and to attempt to plan business strategies within those contexts and environments. For the first time in their lives, many of our fellow students who had come out of quantitative programs as undergraduates found themselves reading books for fun. Sutherland showed us how to talk fast and pack in the content.

Dr. Winiata had a different style, more cerebral and laid-back than most. His field was finance, corporate and government. He and I found many areas in which we could bond: first, he was a New Zealander, and not only knew the game of cricket but had seen the West Indies team play in his native country. Second, he was a chartered accountant-turned-financial specialist and found that many of my academic and business interests coincided with his. Dr. Winiata was impressed by the fact that I had been a bond portfolio manager, had written a prospectus and gotten a security issue blue skyed by the Government of British Columbia. Dr. Winiata was a full-blooded Maori, as was his wife, and they, I, and Dr. Leslie Wong were the only identifiable minorities in the entire business school at that time. Dr. Winiata's wife and my Jamaican wife Vilma looked like sisters. I have never had the opportunity to express my gratitude to him for the part he played in my early success after graduation from UBC.

My business school courses were all fun – even operations research, my nemesis. Would you believe that we were still using slide rules when I started, and it was late in my first year that we began using calculators like the early Texas Instruments models? Imagine doing linear programs with basic tools, and many statistical calculations, literally by hand. My industrial relations professor was perhaps my best lecturer, but I will never forget my managerial accounting professor. Accounting can be dull, but Professor E. C. Roper got us to understand the muscularity of accounting and our role as managers and executives. Our responsibility was not just to keep the books, but also to design systems that maximize shareholder interests, and directed the rewards to management.

Our final exam in managerial accounting came in the form of a one-act play. I don't think that any of us who wrote that exam will ever forget it, because it had to be the most entertaining and comprehensive that we had seen up to that time. The current securities licensing exams in the USA, like the Series 7, 63, and 65 are perhaps moreso, but there is no humor in them.

About fifteen minutes into the exam, every one of us broke out into laughter. Professor Roper had written a comedic play featuring every principle of managerial accounting that he had spent seven months teaching us. His characters took seemingly plausible positions on accounting, sometimes laughable ones and our challenge was to cogently demonstrate the fallaciousness, truth and effect of the different stances. He had included positions on LIFO, FIFO, depreciation, depletion allowances, forms of stock, company formation, privatization, cash vs. accrual forms of accounting, and many other concepts. The paper had only one question: "Discuss".

I had a lot of fun on that exam, and couldn't stop writing. Poor Dr. Roper had to beg me to hand in my paper. A thesis was required to be granted an MBA degree at U.B.C. in 1968. I had had experience as an issuer of paper for BC Central Credit Union in the Canadian short-term money market, so I chose a topic in this area, *The Collapse of Atlantic Acceptance Corporation and its Effect on the Canadian Short-Term Money Market.*

In 1965, the Atlantic Acceptance Corporation, a company operating out of Toronto, and a regular issuer of short-term paper, declared bankruptcy. This sent shockwaves through the Canadian short-term money market. I was responsible for presenting short-term paper to the Vancouver Market for my employer at that time, so I thought my topic would be easy. Professor Winiata was assigned as my advisor, and Kate Turabian's *A Manual For Writers of Research Papers, Theses and Dissertations* became my constant companion.

The writing imposed tremendous strictures on me. I have been forever grateful for the opportunity to undergo the exercise in 1967 as one of only six students in my class of seventy-five who finished the MBA degree in two years. Dr. Winiata had me fully ready for defense of my thesis when I faced the faculty of graduate studies' examiners before I could be accepted as a graduate of their illustrious faculty. I do not have a copy of my master's thesis in my home library. I could get one from the UBC Library, I suppose.

My graduation ceremony at UBC in the spring of 1968, with the campus in full bloom, and the professors, administrators and students in all their regalia, was a spectacular sight. Few campuses can match the beauty of UBC in Vancouver at that time of year when tree-lined streets sprout blossoms, and many flock there just to walk the many gardens. I had three guests; my wife Vilma, our friends, Fiona Bergstrom (who typed my thesis) and her husband Lars Bergstrom. This was better than when I had only my faithful first landlady Mrs. Daisy Garrod as a guest when I graduated from the University of Alberta in 1963.

15. THE WHEEL TURNS

I did not have a job when I came out of graduate school. I had not really sought to be employed. My wife wanted me to teach at the university level, and to keep her quiet I explored going to the Wharton School of Finance at the University of Pennsylvania, but my heart was not in it. Simon Frazer University had just opened in Burnaby, right next door to Vancouver, and they offered me a position, but I did not accept it. I desperately wanted to be in 'the street' with the financial boys, either Bay Street in Toronto or Wall Street in New York. In the interim, I started my own consulting company with BC Central Credit Union as my first client.

I also had my eye on a political career in British Columbia. I could feel the improving openness in the society, making it possible for a foreigner, a black man, to win a seat in a Canadian Legislature. I had not severed my ties with the New Democratic Party since my days as a student leader at the University of Alberta seven years earlier. Neither my wife nor my mother was enamored with the idea of me entering elective politics, at this or any time, and so I gave up the idea for good.

Over the summer of 1968, I grew dissatisfied with my progress in Vancouver, and Vilma and I agreed that we should head East to New York, Montreal and Toronto and study those markets. Even though I was an Atlantic man, all my education and business experience had been acquired in the west, mostly on the Pacific side of the continent. I agreed that I needed to see and develop a feel for what the boys did in the east. I shared my thoughts with Professor Winiata, and he gave me a letter of introduction to a colleague of his who was a vice president of Citibank in New York and asked me to be sure to look him up when I got there. Dr. Winiata had earlier suggested to me that I should go to the US and explore representing professional athletes and manage their funds. I felt that those guys would have been well represented, and there would be no place for me. He told me that I would be surprised at the possibilities, but I did not explore that direction.

We left Vancouver for New York in September 1968. Vilma's sister Joy was to be married later that month, and we wanted to be there. Our plan was to go from New York up to Montreal, call on associates in the financial industry there, look around Montreal, then go down to Ottawa, call on contacts in the Canadian capital, then wander on down to Toronto, where I knew several senior executives in financial firms such as Wood, Gundy and Associates; A.E. Ames & Co; McCloud Young Weir; Pemberton Securities, and the Ontario Central Credit Union.

We chose to drive across the country. It took us almost six days after we got into the car and headed south towards Seattle one beautiful September morning. It was a time when we expected to see better weather below the 48th parallel, so we decided to drive from the Pacific to the Atlantic on the US side of the continent. It was a long trip, but we thoroughly enjoyed it, and our car was a joy to drive. Vilma shared in the driving, and by the time we reached New York she was an accomplished driver. She was pregnant with our first child, Leslyn, but we did not know it when we set out.

From Seattle, we hit I-90 through central Washington State into the Cascades and the Snoqualmie Pass, through Yakima and entered North Dakota at Coeur d'Alene where we spent the night. Continuing on I-90 along the Idaho-Montana border we went through Missoula into Helena, Montana, then into a little town called Roundup, where we slept that night.

Vilma and I had a most interesting experience in Roundup. While sitting in this rustic western cabin masquerading as a restaurant waiting to place our dinner order, we noticed a bunch of country yokels sitting at a table across the room from us. They all wore red jackets and were enjoying their beers and their male camaraderie. I observed them very closely because one could not be sure of people's civility in those volatile days of 1968. One of the older men in the group came over to our table and asked,

"Are you eating alone?"

"We are," I replied.

"You sure as hell are not," came the rejoinder, "You're eating with us."

I looked at Vilma for concurrence, and she agreed, so we went over and joined their table. It turned out that they were from out of town on a hunting trip and had popped into this restaurant for a good steak. Vilma and I also ordered steaks; she had a small, I had a medium. There were only three sizes, small, medium or large, each served on a large aluminum platter. Vilma's covered the entire dish, and mine hung over the sides like an overloaded country bus In the Caribbean or Africa. They had to put the baked potato on a separate plate. The meat was great, the beer was too weak, but the company was very congenial.

Somewhere along this route, we found ourselves on a very high plateau where we could see the countryside for miles around. We headed through Billings, Montana, north and east through Minot, North Dakota, then on to Minneapolis-St. Paul at the head of the Mississippi, where we spent the night. Throughout our trip east, we drove from daybreak until the late afternoon, stopping at regular intervals to explore a park or an interesting landscape. We tried to locate our motel before nightfall and have a good meal and a restful night before setting out the next morning. We managed to cover an average of five hundred miles a day. I remember gasoline being less than fifty cents per gallon at that time.

Next, we drove on to Madison, Wisconsin. We found an interesting park there, and while strolling through to relax from the concentration on driving, we found ourselves amid a Scandinavian cultural happening. The group leaders insisted that we join them for lunch, so we joined right in. The smorgasbord was as interesting and delightful as the folks were. We pushed on from there to Chicago and spent the night in a little town on the outskirts called Elgin. Richard Nixon was campaigning in Chicago that weekend and there was a lot of excitement and evidence of protests taking place. As these events would bear out, Chicago was not the place to be a stranger in the fall of 1968.

The next day we set off on our leg to New York. It was a regular routine, with turnpikes and hard driving. We overnighted at a motel in New Jersey, fearing our readiness for the evening traffic of Brooklyn where we were headed. The next morning at breakfast, fireworks started. Vilma and I went into a restaurant across the street and ordered food. After an inordinately long time of waiting, we recognized that many customers who had ordered much later than we had, were well into their meal, so we called a passing waitress and asked her to summon our table server. "Oh," the waitress said, "she had trouble serving you and has gone home."

I was so mad that red shone under my ebon skin. I summoned the manager, and in full voice, at stretched height, I told him,

"Look here, stop the blasted nonsense and get our breakfast on our table immediately – or I'll break every damn chair and table in this blasted restaurant!" I bellowed angrily while other patrons began to turn in their chairs and take notice, "we've spent the last five and a half days driving across America, from Vancouver to New Jersey, and met with nothing but goodwill from the Americans that we ran into … I will not stand for you insulting my wife and me!"

There were scatterings of applause, and you never saw breakfast appear so fast. And therein lies one of the most recognizable dichotomies of the USA. The underexposed would hardly expect to find that kind of bigotry in the northeastern USA.

We had a grand time at my sister-in-law's wedding, and before setting out for Montreal, I decided to call on the vice president of Citibank to whom Professor Winiata had sent a recommendation on my behalf. The office was on the fifty-first floor at the corner of 53rd Street at 399 Park Avenue, New York City. I had never been on a street more impressive or in a building so high. I just acted as if all was normal.

Mr. Hunt received me very cordially, but with a banker's reserve. He read the letter of introduction and presented me to his closest workmates. In those 1968 days, bankers sat on an open platform with the most senior officers seated at the back. Hunt invited me to call on him the following day around eleven o'clock. When I arrived the following day, he introduced me to a wider group of executives and invited me to join them for lunch at the Harvard Club.

During the magnificent lunch, they learned that I was on my way to Montreal and Toronto to talk with Canadian colleagues in the financial industry, get ideas and observe behavioral practices. After lunch, I was invited to meet with some of the officers the following day and to bring my wife to lunch with them at the Princeton Club. What I didn't know at that time was that they were doing due diligence on me. This was 1968 and young, black articulate MBAs did not turn up in New York every Monday morning.

Once they met with my wife, Citibank showed their hand. Back then, banking in the Caribbean was dominated by British and Canadian banks. They wanted someone like me to join their overseas division, and to go to Jamaica and help them break into the banking market. They made me an offer; I told them that I wanted to go on up to Canada on my study, and we could talk later.

We drove up to Montreal, another beautiful Canadian city. While Vancouver and Victoria, British Columbia are beautiful, their charm has a distinctly British feel, whereas Montreal is Gallic, not quite as French as Quebec City, but French nevertheless. We were able to visit my boyhood friend Donald and his lovely wife Diane and to tour McGill University from where so many West Indians had graduated over the years. Leaving Montreal, we took the long trek down to Ottawa, the capital of Canada. The public buildings in Ottawa are impressively Gothic, sturdy-looking, and seem built to withstand attack. Every street in Canada, urban or rural was so clean and sculpted. Everything was so orderly and proper, so well maintained. By this time, I had spent only about two weeks in the USA and returning to Canada awakened my consciousness of the difference in the treatments of public places.

Pierre Trudeau was now Prime Minister. I had seen him on the stump in Vancouver but never had the opportunity to meet him. I liked his fire and his confidence, but I was never happy about the timidity of his Liberal Party, whose leadership style was to criticize the platform policies of my New Democratic Party, and then quietly pass many of these policies into legislation once they had taken hold of the Government. Canada has excellent social legislation, but very little of it made its first appearance on any governing party's political platform.

I cannot remember the drive from Ottawa to Toronto. We stayed with wonderful hosts, the Liverpools in Scarborough. Bill and Rose Mary Brown, our friends from Vancouver, introduced us to this highly successful family from St. Vincent. The family had done very well in Toronto and had members in several professions. Toronto itself is not very large, but it attracts several satellite municipalities, making for widely spread bedroom communities. It's beautiful along the Lake Ontario shore, around the university, in the financial district or anywhere you go. Downtown is vibrant with bars, restaurants, shops, hotels, homes, offices, museums, churches, art galleries, and people. You can walk to any activity you could want to pursue. This is so unlike the modern city where so much of life is in the suburbs. The markets and food courts offer gastronomic delights from every nationality.

The flavor of the city is international, just like the colors of face and clothing one encounters as one walks around. I spent most of my time in the financial district around Bloor Street as well as King and Broad Streets. Many of the men in the investment houses I had met before in Vancouver, and they all encouraged me to stay in Toronto. I received one job offer, to join the research department of Pemberton Securities. I had done business with them in Vancouver in my early days in that city and got to know Mr. Jack Smart, one of their principals, pretty well. Their offer was the same amount as Citibank's, but in Canadian dollars, ten thousand a year. I did not want to be in research and felt I was going to be hidden. I wanted to be out front and in the street, dealing with the public.

It was now time to call Citibank. Once I did, they told me to come on down and report to human affairs. I told them that I would sell my car, and spend a couple of days around Niagara Falls before I came in. That presented no problem.

16. NEW YORK, NEW WORK

We received an excellent price for the Malibu in Toronto, rented a '69 Chrysler Newport to be dropped off in New York City, and headed for Niagara Falls.

Life was still a ball. We had no children, no debts, a few thousand dollars in savings, a desirable education, a baby on the way, and leading firms in two of the world's great cities vying for my services. We reveled in it. I still had not identified what I wanted to be, what I really wanted to do with my life. I was not at loose ends, nor was I unproductive, far from it, I had too inquisitive a mind to decide on commitment to one single professional pursuit.

Niagara Falls was thrilling. Somehow, I have this memory of mist around the falls and the spray from the water thundering over and clouding up our windshield. We were not sufficiently adventurous to take the boat ride on the river, especially since we were now responsible for another life in addition to our own.

After doing the usual tourist things around both the Canadian and US sides of the falls, we set out for New York. Our Chrysler Newport was a monster of a car, as big as a house and just as comfortable. At first, it intimidated me, but after a while, I was thankful for it. This car was not as nimble as the Malibu, but those eight cylinders could create some furor going down the road. Thank heavens I enjoyed motor trips, and Vilma was now driving more and enjoying it.

Citibank set us up in a studio apartment somewhere on 2nd Avenue and 32nd Street. The bank had so many people coming and going in and out of the city that it either leased or owned several units around Manhattan within easy access of the head office on Park Avenue. The plan was to put me through a six-month training program there, and then send me to Jamaica to help establish Citibank's presence on the island. One facet of my training was a series of lectures and business procedural programs conducted by one Professor Zak Zwick at Columbia University – the same professor who borrowed my master's thesis and never returned it.

I also went to that illustrious institution every Sunday morning to play squash with my new-found friend Harry, an Indian national from Bihar State, who like myself had just joined the bank. Harry was a terrific squash player, who with my friend Ivern would have enjoyed playing each other, apart from the fact that they were both engineers. While the bank was busy arranging my visa, they assigned us a real estate agent to help us find an apartment in Manhattan. I particularly remember the agent trying to encourage Vilma and me to take a place near Central Park. The apartment was in what seemed to be a converted large dwelling house, and the elevator was the smallest unit imaginable. The agent wanted us to take this ancient little one-bedroom apartment overlooking a dirt backyard, with not a blade of grass, bush, hedge or tree in sight.

"This is a Central Park West address," she told me snootily. "Why, Franklin and Eleanor lived here."

"This place may have been good for Franklin and Eleanor," I shot back, "but we're from Vancouver where we're accustomed to inspiring surroundings. We didn't come to New York to live in a dump."

She eventually found us a lovely one-bedroom, sixth-floor apartment at 81st and 1st, close to New York Hospital. It even had a liveried doorman, Rudolph, a Jamaican who especially looked out for us.

The training at Citibank was immersive and broad. I was assigned to Larry, a vice president for credit in Latin America, Brazil and Argentina, who should have been a teacher by profession. There was another Canadian under Larry's guidance at that time, Jean Marie, a young Jewish banker from Montreal. He had some experience working for Citibank in Canada, so he was more at ease with the system than I was. Within two weeks, Larry had us assessing credits from the Caribbean, Central and South America, and Mexico. Only credit applications above the lending limit of the senior officer-in-the-field came to our attention.

In my earlier stint with B.C. Central Credit Union in Vancouver, I grew accustomed to having a secretary, but I would have no such luck at my level with this new big boy. I was obliged to record my correspondence from my desk into the typing pool and whoever was available would type my stuff and bring it to my desk in due course. I met a lot of the female staff that way. Can you imagine the retyping that took place? A Barbadian man with a bit of a Canadian accent, presenting stuff by Dictaphone to a young New York typist somewhere in the bowels of the institution. Imagine further that Citibank had trainees from all over the world, working in many other disciplines than credit, communicating to colleagues, mentors and clients similarly. Great fun.

After about three months, Larry, Jean Marie and I started teaching ourselves Fortran programming. Remember this was 1968, before desktops, laptops, cell phones, iPads, iPhones or anything of the kind.

A computer was a huge piece of machinery stationed in a special air-conditioned room in a remote corner of the building, fed by hand-delivered punch cards at night and retrieved the next working day. I never got the chance to touch a desktop computer until I came back to the USA in 1985.

One day right after lunch, as I stood before the mirror in this royally decked out men's room with its marble countertops, glistening floors, and blue monogrammed cotton hand towels, a colleague from my floor walked in. On seeing me, he exclaimed "Shit! Fucking niggers!" and walked out. I had seen this scene before – Las Vegas in 1966, two years earlier. That time, it was a young white guy in blue jeans, this time it was a young white guy in a Brooks Brothers suit. That very evening, Vilma came down from 81st Street to have dinner with me and some of my white colleagues at the Yale Club. Oh America, how my heart bleeds for you. How long can we stand this schizophrenia?

New York – what a wonderful city! I had never been in a place where there was so much excitement and activity before, and I was ready to make the most of it. Every workday morning, I walked up to Lexington and took the local subway downtown to my office at 53rd and Park, but in the evenings after work, I walked home. The distance between the streets was very short, so the walk up to 81st was not difficult. I thoroughly enjoyed exploring the small shops and boutiques, bars, restaurants, bakeries and candy stores in every nook and corner of my route. My neighborhood was called Yorkville, and it was a collection of Europeans who carved out this Upper East Side section for themselves, it seemed.

My forays led me to a friendship with two shopkeepers along the way. Most evenings, I rummaged through the basket of daily specials in my new friend Alex's wine shop on 79th Street and invariably found a good burgundy for just a dollar. Drinking wine was not yet out of bounds for pregnant women so Vilma, who was about four months pregnant by that November, enjoyed a glass with me most evenings. My other shopkeeper friend was Tibor, a Hungarian Jewish immigrant. His little place was called the Gentleman's Resale Shop. He got me a couple of nice suits at very reasonable prices, including my very first tuxedo that set me back nineteen dollars. I kept that tux until 1977, a stretch of nine years until I got a new one tailored when I became a member of the Masonic Lodge. Tibor and I would have a cognac in the back of the store whenever I dropped in.

Church basements were a great discovery for us in New York. Most Friday nights Vilma and I found some cultural event taking place in a church basement in Manhattan. We attended Jazz concerts, folk song recitals, plays being prepared for the professional theater, debates, fine arts displays and sundry presentations in church basements, all for free that winter of 1968-1969.

Going to the theater on Broadway was magical. The glitter and glamor were unbelievable. Vilma and I managed to see one Broadway play while we were in New York, "Man of La Mancha". We felt that we had the rare opportunity to live for six months in New York, so we tried to get out and sample cultural events as often as we could with Vilma advancing in her pregnancy. Museums were a special treat for us, and we visited the American Museum of Natural History, the Metropolitan Museum of Art, the Museum of Modern Art, the Museum of the City of New York, the Guggenheim Museum, and the Frick Collection. Before the snow came, we went down to Washington Square to sample the NYU's university culture, and we spent Sunday afternoons in Central Park. As winter deepened, we visited the skating rink in Rockefeller Center, watched the skaters enjoy themselves, consoled ourselves by shopping at Macy's and drooled over jewelry on 35th Street.

On New Year's Eve, we braved the cold and joined the crowd in Times Square to watch the ball drop. Later that week, my friend and colleague Harry invited us to dinner at his Manhattan apartment, where we shared a wonderful Indian meal with him and his wife. For me, the highlight of the evening was to observe the beauty and grace with which Harry's wife ate out of her hand. Watching her eat was like watching my mother eat using her fingers. The setting was a contrast from my earliest days, but the human experience was the same, India or Africa, one common humanity.

I was now on the continent of North America mostly studying for ten years, but I knew hardly anything about my race and our achievements in that part of the world. I was now seeing so many black people everywhere I went in New York that my ignorance had to be addressed. I was aware of our prowess in athletics and jazz, and our stature among popular musical performers both male and female, but my knowledge of our contribution to American culture, politics, and general development of the nation was very shallow. I became acutely aware of the fact that although I had been reading and studying economics for six years – and had two degrees from highly accredited universities to boot – I had never heard of a noted black economist, even though Sir Arthur Lewis, a fellow West Indian, was the leading developmental economist in the world at the time, and was doing wonderful work as principal of the University of the West Indies. True, I had read James Baldwin widely and had gone through a bit of Richard Wright, with the most significant book being Ralph Ellison's *Invisible Man*, but in essence, I knew very little about my people and the importance of blacks to the American experience.

I set out to educate myself about the black American culture. Every Saturday morning after my early squash game with Harry, I took the subway up to Harlem. I would exit at 125th Street and roam around. My haunts were barber shops, nail shops, mom and pop restaurants, the Harlem Public Library and the Schomburg Center for Research in Black Culture. During these forays, I got my first real introduction to Marcus Garvey and Garveyism, to the meaning of the Harlem Renaissance, to the work of Countee Cullen, Jean Toomer, Claude McKay, James Weldon Johnson, Alain LeRoy Locke, Eric Walrond and Langston Hughes. My education into the untold American story had begun, but the true joy came much later in life when I came to read black American female authors like Zora Neale Hurston, Alice Walker, Toni Morrison, Gwendolyn Brooks, Lorraine Hansberry, Audre Lorde, Maya Angelou and Jesmyn Ward.

I always rode the bus coming back downtown. In one of his books, James Baldwin describes the ride on the bus downtown from Harlem into lower Manhattan as crossing the border into a foreign country. One cannot fully appreciate what Baldwin means unless one takes that ride. My first bus ride from Harlem downtown was so educational that I repeated it on several Saturday mornings during that winter of 1968. I didn't notice anything out of the ordinary when I first boarded the bus at 125th Street.

Only a few passengers were coming down from the Bronx, but the bus started to fill up as we proceeded south. I began to notice that boarding passengers wore lighter and shabbier coats and that their shoes were cheaper and less well cut as we came down the road, and their fragrances were cheaper. This continued until we reached the nineties when the boarding passengers wore dressier cloth coats, better quality shoes and more expensive fragrances. I normally would have had to get off at 81st Street, since we lived at 81st and 1st, but on many occasions, I would continue my ride down to the Village to carry on with my observation.

From 80th Street and on down through the sixties, the ladies boarding the bus wore fur coats, Gucci shoes and handbags, and very high-end perfumes. The men wore top quality oxfords or wingtips, expensive suits or sports coats topped with London Fog and Aquascutum overcoats. When we got past 42nd Street, the dress became mod, nondescript – "anything goes", I called it. In this manner, we rode into Washington Square and the campus of New York University where amateur performers displayed their skills on the streets. Baldwin mentions one border into another country, but I saw several borders into the same country.

During my New York education, Vilma's delivery time grew closer. When the weather was fair, we took walks along 1st Avenue down to the United Nations building, and sometimes we familiarized ourselves with the way to New York Hospital where the baby would be born. Leslyn finally came – two weeks late – with long fingernails that needed trimming, and a full head of black hair. I, in typical fashion, restrained my delight, but Vilma and the staff at New York Hospital went wild over our beautiful baby girl. Six weeks after Leslyn's birth the New York training was complete, and we were off to Jamaica.

17. JAMAICAN PROSPERITY

Our first Jamaican address was a hotel, the Courtleigh Manor on Trafalgar Road in Kingston, where the staff welcomed us beautifully and seemed to serve us with genuine delight. I fondly remember the Bombay mango trees in the courtyard, the swimming pool at the outdoor bar and the fruit plates we got at breakfast. Most of all, I remember the wonderful feeling of the soft water that made such great suds in the shower.

We lived at the Courtleigh Manor for two weeks before moving to our first rented home at 7 Norbrook Drive in the Constant Spring/Manor Park area. The house was a three-bedroom bungalow with a nice front lawn, an extensive grassed backyard and a lit fountain. We got ourselves a dog and I was allowed a cat as well. I had had one in graduate school but had not been able to accommodate another one until now. This added to my happiness.

We settled in pretty quickly and soon went through two new English cars, a Singer Vogue and a Humber Hawk, before we settled for a Fiat 125 with stick shift, all within two weeks. We paid cash for the new Fiat from the dealer, 1,200 pounds, about US$ 2,800. I taught Vilma to drive stick in a few hours.

My first posting was at the Halfway Tree branch, a few miles from the bank's main location at King Street in downtown Kingston. The general manager, Bill Rhodes, had his office upstairs. A Chinese Jamaican, Noel Pinchong, was the manager in charge. I was the lending officer, along with Douglas Archibald, a bright young black Jamaican educated at New York University. He helped me a lot, but Noel tied me in knots. In New York, I was taught a great deal about lending, but hardly anything about operating procedures, and nothing at all about navigating through the labyrinth of inter-office politics. Noel Pinchong had grown up in the colonial system and was quite adept at steering perceived competitors onto the rocks. I, in my naivete, was consumed with demonstrating my MBA analytical techniques and my New York flair, not to mention my Canadian sartorial coolness, and mostly overlooked what I considered to be pettyfogging nonsense. The customers loved me, but I could not get anything done.

Two nice ladies in the branch took me in hand and guided me through the minefield. Mrs. Polly Murray, an experienced loan processor, and Mrs. Pam Bodden, a young teller, became my procedural guides. Polly Murray has gone on to the Promised Land, but Pam Bodden is still my friend. She visits us often in our Atlanta home as her business brings her our way. I am the proud godfather to one of Pam's sons and a treasured friend of her extended family.

Citibank had lured many bright, young male high school graduates away from the British and Canadian banks and into its clerical ranks. All of these men had the potential to be managers and longed to be, but none of them had the advanced education to assume the positions of leaders in the modern business environment. They were ambivalent about me. On the one hand, they did not take well to the fact that I was a Barbadian – as well as their boss – and on the other hand, I was an example of the rank that they could achieve with appropriate education. I took it upon myself to develop a course in credit analysis and credit-granting to train appropriate staff members for higher positions in the bank. My general manager and senior officer in the field liked the idea and arranged for the bank to pay for the textbook.

Within a month, six men and two women signed up for my course. I felt that there were a couple of young men who could have benefitted from taking the course but were too blinded to participate. I was later privileged to watch them wallow in frustration as they observed those course participants steadily climb up the officer ranks. I was most pleased to note that a couple of years after I left Citibank, one of the men who had taken my course was appointed general manager of the bank in Barbados. Several others among my protégés, male and female alike, later became managers and executives of other financial institutions in Jamaica.

The custom at Citibank at this time was for lending officers to sit on an open platform; many people came by to meet me. Some fathers brought their sons to talk with me about careers and universities. I particularly enjoyed the visits of the Reverend Ivan Francis, a Baptist minister, school principal and businessman, and the Reverend Mr. Walters, the leader of the Seventh Day Adventists in Jamaica at that time. The bank granted me a lending limit of $200,000.00, which was at that time the largest in any bank for a junior officer on the island. Of course, I had to get one other signing officer to sign a loan with me, but that was standard procedure even for a senior officer in the field.

Citibank brought progress to the banks in Jamaica by introducing the term-loan principle. We would make loans to anyone as long as they demonstrated the ability to retire the loan within a fixed period and met the other requirements of the established terms. Until then, Jamaica operated on the old overdraft system, which denied entry to new businesses, propped up inefficient ones, spawned nepotism, stifled entrepreneurial imagination, and prolonged a culture where a few chairmen could report to their boards of directors that their bank had just renewed their overdraft for the seventy-fifth year in a row.

Cash flow, and no longer not just a family name, became a business' compulsory calling card. This fact added to the challenges facing a lender, for in 1969 there were no fully established credit bureaus in Jamaica, making it virtually impossible to get an objective report on the creditworthiness of a potential borrower. Collateral, covenants, strict payouts, market need for the product, and the fit of the product into the new production matrix were also paramount. We structured loans to be repaid out of cash flow with a mortgage debenture as security. This opened up the market to new entrepreneurs who had creative ideas for making money.

I determined the conditions of the loan agreements at my desk. I set all the covenants, determined the timing of report submissions, and made a packet that could be defended before a fellow officer before it went off to our solicitors who drew up security documents and crafted a mortgage debenture. The team of credit analysts that I undertook to train would become very important in my work throughput because financial statements submitted by borrowers had to be transposed to the bank's format. The increased cash flow that the solicitors began to generate no doubt attracted the attention of the barristers – who hardly ever did this kind of lowly work – and perhaps helped to accelerate fusion in the Jamaican legal profession.

Fitting nicely into this scenario was a young businessman named Basil Buck, an assistant accountant at Caribbean Cement Company when he started a credit bureau in 1968. He became one of my very first customers. I believe that he later sold his company to a much larger credit bureau service, becoming an early stockbroker on the fledgling Jamaica Stock Exchange.

My earliest clients were Tomas Désulmé of Thermoplastics Jamaica, Barclay Ewart of Tanners Jamaica and Jamaica Sulphuric Acid; Billy Young Chin of Jamaica Carpet Layers and Jamaica Carpet Mills, as well as Ossie Simpson of Tropical Plaza Meats and Jamaica Meat Packers. Unsurprisingly once my general manager saw how I was handling myself, he transferred his most challenging client, Dr. Jimmy Burrows, to me.

Burrows sharpened up my skills in a very short time. He was trying to build a private hospital uptown and had great difficulty financing the project, primarily because local banks at the time would not facilitate him. Citibank took him on to help them establish a presence in the market, and the wily doctor had his hospital halfway finished and functioning on a Citibank overdraft. My challenge was to get Burrows to give the bank a mortgage incorporating all the terms of our five-year term loans, and Burrows' objective was to get his hospital finished and maintain control over it without being hamstrung by the bank's provisions.

As it turned out, he was the smart pro and I was the neophyte. My learning curve was steep and fast-moving, resulting in a larger-than-anticipated loan by the bank, a much longer than usual payout period, a project of questionable viability but one of great national need.

***

I continued an exercise routine in Jamaica that I had been introduced to when I was eighteen years old in Nassau. I awoke early every working day and went for a morning run. This is not difficult in the tropics, for the sun rises very early, and gets bright so quickly that it is difficult for one to stay in bed. Additionally, there is always a rooster somewhere inviting you to join him in welcoming the new day. I could run around Norbrook in about forty minutes and by 7:00 a.m. I would have showered, had breakfast and been off to the office. By 8:30 a.m., I completed all my paperwork and dedicated the rest of my day to people. Before lunch, I saw customers, and after lunch, I went to call on potential business, mostly via cold calls, which I regarded as fun, in part because nobody ever refused my visit or threw me out. This success spoiled me for later life, but it helped to expand an unshakable confidence.

It was during my business calls that I came face to face with the socioeconomic structure of Jamaica and its unique nature. As in the general population, so in the business community, I encountered every race, shape, gender and color. I called on merchants, manufacturers, importers and a few exporters, businesspeople of African descent, English, Scottish, East Indian, Pakistani, Arab, Jewish, American, Syrian, Lebanese as well as folks from other Caribbean islands. There was no disharmony among the business people, because they all had a common goal, but there was tremendous conflict among the blacks in the poorer urban areas, where there was a vicious form of tribalism – supposedly fired by political leaders – which demonstrated itself in the ghastliest fashion.

My call program was very successful and brought several new customers into the bank. It was here at the Halfway Tree Branch that I honed my skill at constructing term loans, for soon I was keeping two secretarial assistants busy typing and formalizing my loan presentations. There were no boilerplates available at that time.

After a year at Halfway Tree, I became a senior lending officer and was transferred to the main branch of the bank in downtown Kingston. Many of my customers, both corporate and individual, transferred their accounts to my new branch. At King Street, I became acquainted with the principals of the Duke Street law firms, the solicitors, and many of the young businessmen who were taking over from the British and Canadian interests.

I met and dealt with Carlton Alexander, the chairman of Grace Kennedy, Jamaica's leading corporation; Danny Williams, president of Life of Jamaica; Karl Hendrickson, chairman of the Hendrickson Group, a leading conglomerate known mostly for its bakery products; Pat Chen See, a leading hardware merchant; Henry Fullerton, a chartered accountant and business consultant; Maurice Berry, deputy governor of the Bank of Jamaica; Pat and Peter Rousseau of Key Homes and Dennis Lalor of Insurance Company of the West Indies and one of the most successful men on the Island. It was there at Kingston Branch that I became associated with Oliver Jones, then general manager of Manufacturers Life Insurance Company of Canada. I later became one of the founding directors of Island Life Insurance Company along with Oliver as chairman, when we took over Manufacturers Life's business in Jamaica.

Allan Byles of Small Cars Ltd. was one of my early clients and I worked out a bonded warehouse facility for him with Jamaican Customs and Volkswagen of Mexico so that he could have a ready inventory of cars on hand without control over them. Peter Rousseau and his brother Patrick brought Gordon "Butch" Stewart to meet me one day and suggested that I help him. Butch was banking with Barclays at that time and had a very small overdraft. I believe he had a shipment of appliances on the wharf and not enough money to clear the goods. I loaned him fifteen hundred pounds, and within a month Butch paid off that first loan and was on his way up. I was able to see him grow from small appliances to refrigerators and window air conditioners, to installation of central air in buildings, and his first forays into the tourist industry while I worked in Jamaica. I remember being told by a former minister of finance who later was employed by Butch, that he was a true patriot who made all his overseas business activities known to the government authorities in Jamaica, at a time when many people were pulling their cash out of the country, and that Butch was destined to do well.

One day Jim Lim and O.K. Melhado, young directors of Desnoes & Geddes, makers of the renowned Red Stripe beer, brought Michael Manley to the bank to meet me. Michael was then the leader of the opposition People's National Party (PNP) in the Jamaican parliament. I had met Michael's father, Norman, some twelve years earlier in Nassau and was happy to make the man's acquaintance. It's so interesting that both men were leaders of the opposition in parliament when I first met them. Lim and Melhado were not on a casual mission. They explained that they wanted me to take Manley on as a client and free him from the mundane concerns of keeping his financial affairs in order. I bristled a bit, for I did not see myself as having the time for such detailed work, but then I had the staff to help.

Recognizing what this could mean positively for the bank and for me personally should Michael Manley become prime minister of Jamaica, I readily agreed to become his personal banker. My general manager was extremely pleased that we finally landed that personal account, and he had wanted me to handle his affairs long before, but couldn't get it done. We now had Eddie Seaga, the finance minister in the Jamaica Labor Party (JLP) government of the day, as our general manager's customer, and I had Manley as mine. We were destined to be in good shape, no matter who formed the next government.

I consider 1970 a watershed year for me. In August when Vilma delivered a son, we moved to a beautiful house in Gordon Town at the foot of the Blue Mountains, and I became acquainted with three young men who brought me into close contact with Jamaica's aspirations. The first of these was Conran Pyne, a bright young insurance agent. He had earned a bachelor's degree in economics from the University of the West Indies and a master's in business from the University of Toronto before working with Dennis Lalor in the general insurance business. Connie came from a family of high academic achievers, and he was adept at bringing bright young men together.

On Friday evenings after work, the fellows met at Connie's house in Barbican Village for food, drink and conversation. Connie invited me to join this ad hoc group, and I became a regular. It was here that I met George Beckford, a bright young lecturer in economics at UWI; Moxy Morrison, a leading architect out of Howard University; Mansfield Brown, a local businessman, Archie Hudson-Phillips, a practicing physician, Trinidadian, and brother of Karl Hudson Phillips, attorney general of Trinidad and contender for national leadership, and Neville Murray, along with dozens of other aspiring young social thinkers.

Murray was the most passionate of us all, maybe because he was the only member of the group who had supported the Hugh Shearer government of the time. Neville later went on to elective office in Seaga's government which succeeded the eventual Manley administration (1972-1980). It was in one of these Friday night gatherings that I met the Honorable Mia Motley's father, who turned out be a university mate of some of our regulars. I took the opportunity to tell Mr. Motley how all the high school boys in Bridgetown during the 1940s and early 1950s regarded his father Earnest Motley as a model, and some of us saved our pennies in Motley's Penny Savings Bank on Swan Street. All of us boys took our first girlfriends to Civic Day in Queens Park, an event sponsored by the elder Motley.

The other two young men were Eric Bell and Horace Clarke. Both were members of the PNP. Eric was a Duke Street solicitor and mayor of Kingston at a very early age. He and I found common ground and liked each other's philosophical positions from the first day we held discussions. Eric was never a bank client of mine, and he showed no particular interest in commerce or amassing wealth. Manley was a man of similar bent; as a matter of fact, it was generally believed by many Jamaicans that the Manleys were not generally driven by the wealth motive.

Michael never asked for a loan or an overdraft. His salary was forwarded to his account, and the bank forwarded payments to those that we contracted to pay out of his account. Eric frequently visited me at my office in the bank, just for conversation. We had discussions on education policy, urban development, central banking, development banking, and Caribbean unity. I was like a sounding board for him, and later when Eric became Minister of Finance, our discussions continued, this time over lunch in the private dining room at his ministry office.

Horace Clarke was not my friend initially, but he was a client and friend of my colleague Douglas Archibald. It was Douglas who introduced me to Horace. On the few occasions that Horace and I met, we talked about government policy. At this time, the JLP was in government, but it was generally believed that the government would change in the upcoming elections and that Michael Manley would become the next prime minister. Horace and I talked mostly about land use, public utilities, (he was then an executive at the telephone company), minerals policy, and rural development. In perspective, it is clear that these young turks were sharpening their tools for the collegial battles they expected while vying for positions in a future Manley government. I was fortunate to be brought by fate into a position to be a foil for their ideas, and hopefully to offer them new perspectives.

My ideas on public policy in a developing country had come under an interesting variety of influences over the years. I had been an observer of colonialism before adult suffrage in both Barbados and the Bahamas, had studied Canadian government and Canada's challenges as a neighbor of the United States. I was now engaged in weekly dialogue with the Jamaican intelligentsia (mostly supporters of the People's National Party), and equally significantly, I was spending a lot of time with Tomas Désulmé, an older Haitian politician, government minister and successful businessman, who had chosen Jamaica as his exile home. Arguably, I was bringing something of value to the table.

Tom Désulmé was like a father to me. Born in 1913, the same year as my father, he had come out of the Haitian political cauldron. He watched his proud country deteriorate through successive incompetent presidential administrations, including the U.S. interregnum, and was able to grow out of humble beginnings to be elected four times as a senator, serving first under President Estimé. Tom was the archetypical Latin kingmaker, finally losing the game to "Papa Doc" Duvalier, the simple country doctor whom Tom's power group thought they could control. Tom was able to escape Duvalier's purges and find final refuge in Jamaica.

I met Tom Désulmé on my first day at Citibank's Halfway Tree branch and was given the Thermo Plastics account almost immediately. Citibank helped Tom to build one of the largest industrial manufacturing companies in Jamaica and by definition in the West Indies. He persuaded me that if I spent the time to teach him the subtleties of business practices in the British and Canadian systems, he would undertake to show me how to operate as an independent businessman, and how to handle the politics of the third world. This was heady stuff; I had not thought up to that time of building anything permanent in Jamaica – or anywhere else for that matter. I was just a young man enjoying my corporate success without really thinking of how it could be leveraged into something much larger.

At the end of 1972, following four years with Citibank, I resigned and joined Thermo Plastics as executive vice president and member of the board of directors. My education in the subtleties and enormity of business challenges was now truly underway. Tom's primary conviction at this time was that the Jamaican dollar was grossly overvalued at \$J1.00 to \$US1.20, that this was an unsustainable position, that we should borrow as much as we could and build as fast as we could, both corporately and privately. In this way, we would be servicing our debt with less valuable dollars as the value of our assets increased in line with the devaluations that were to come. With this strategy in mind, I led the charge to develop multi-million-dollar loans from the Development Bank and Citibank to build and equip a state-of-the-art plastics manufacturing enterprise at Twickenham Park in Spanish Town.

I now entered an entirely new phase in my development. Working with a very competent architect, I assumed the role of an internal project manager. I now had to protect the bankers' money in addition to ensuring that we paid only for work completed, and keeping the project moving along so that we could come in on time. Some costs are impossible to factor, like protection against shutdowns and theft. During this period, I started building my own estate by extending my interest in livestock farming and the tourist industry. I borrowed heavily to build a chicken farm and hog farm in Spanish Town, as well as to build a villa in the tourist area at Runaway Bay for rental. This was all in line with our strategy of building before the collapse in currency value arrived.

For almost seventeen years, every weekend that we were both in Jamaica, Tom and I met to chat about a multiplicity of topics. On those occasions when we stayed on the south coast, he paid the chauffeur double-time and came to my farm outside Spanish Town on Saturday afternoons at 2:00 and left at 6:00. Tom and I would have tea on my verandah overlooking the St. Catherine plains and we would talk business strategy plus local and worldwide political outcomes for four hours. Occasionally, my wife Vilma would join us, but not for long.

Tom and I were like each other's students. On the weekends that we were on the north coast at Runaway Bay, I would swim and walk the beach with our children and their friends in between drinking scotch whiskey and talking with Tom. Our personal and corporate interests were now focused on import substitution and the earning of foreign exchange, Thermo Plastics with its production of PVC pipe and fittings, Tom with his many rental villas for tourists, me with my livestock farm producing meat to reduce imports and my villa for rental to tourists.

★★★

"Grey Stones", our new home up in Gordon Town, was the most interestingly constructed house one could imagine. I later incorporated many of the features I found in this house into the homes that I later built, especially our family home on the farm near Spanish Town. Grey Stones was designed and built by an architect to accommodate the interests of his actress wife. It was built largely out of materials brought up from the Hope River which ran along its lower property border, field stones from the surrounding hillsides and left-over or used materials brought from building sites that the original owner supervised.

The home was built on four levels, with a basement at the bottom, and was cut into the hillside. It was a split-level that you entered at the top, into the kitchen and dining room floor, up to the bedrooms, or down from either end into the living room and study, then outside to the lawn and pool, or down to the basement. From the front lawn one could walk through the white picket fence, and down the mountainside to the river. The bedroom floor floated over the living room, with the joists supported on the inside by suspension wire rope. One could also exit the living room through a side door onto a grape-lined, pergola-covered patio and into a rock garden. The house even had a working fireplace. It can get cold in the higher elevations in Jamaica, and for the first time, Vilma had a sewing room overlooking the kitchen.

About a year after the PNP took over the government of Jamaica in 1972, the Cabinet decided to turn several government-owned entities into statutory corporations run by independent boards of directors accountable to the ministers responsible. The two international airports were taken out of the Civil Aviation Department and placed under a new statutory board, the Airports Authority. My friend, now the Honorable Eric Bell, was the minister responsible, and he appointed me to the very first board. Within a year, the first chairman emigrated. When Mr. Woodstock, the Civil Service's representative on the board announced that the minister wanted me to take over the chair, it was a huge surprise. Several members were far more experienced than I was, and who were far more vociferous, but I gingerly took the chair as bidden.

Island Life Insurance Company was the next board I was invited to join. I was one of the original investors who joined Oliver Jones, then general manager of Manufacturers Life Insurance in Jamaica, in establishing a company to buy Manufacturers' Jamaican interests, and I was pleased to be a part of the early wave of locals replacing the old established foreign interests. My friend Connie Pyne also called me to his General Insurance Company's board around this time, so I was learning new fields. Vilma and I concluded that if I were heading into private directorships, we would be best served by developing our independent sources of income, and this led us into more serious commitments to the livestock industry. We had what was essentially a hobby farm on the outskirts of Spanish Town, and while we made our home on it, we began to learn the livestock business in earnest. With Tom Désulmé's and Ossie Simpson's stimulation, we borrowed as much and as fast as we could, and over thirteen years, we developed a very viable broiler chicken farm along with a beef feedlot and two pig farms comprising a total of two hundred breeding sows. I believe that we were the second-largest pig farmers on the island, and our goat and sheep herds in the hills around Halse Hall in Clarendon Parish ran into the hundreds.

Our veterinarian found me to be a willing student, and soon I was able to deliver calves when cows were having difficulties, and baby piglets when a sow was struggling. I also castrated male piglets (I even got fast enough to do one per minute), clamped lambs and bull calves, and had studied the visiting blacksmith's shoeing techniques so closely that I felt ready to shoe the children's horses but didn't have the time for such an undertaking. It was not lost on me that I had seen my father carry out most of the husbandry practices in our little village in Barbados, that I now carried out on a much larger scale on our farm. In short order, I became the chairman of the Jamaica Pig Farmers Association, a director of the Jamaica Livestock Association, and a director of the Agricultural Development Corporation, a government statutory corporation.

At this period of the mid-1970s, I was going through perhaps the most highly exciting and developmental part of my experiences. I still had my Conran Pyne urban brain trust meeting every Friday night, I was now a member of the Masonic Lodge (English Constitution) and I was involved in my rural agricultural activities as a hands-on farmer.

My Phoenix Lodge was one of the oldest in Jamaica, and I believe it was first established shortly after the English took the island away from Spain. This was right after the Oliver Cromwell interregnum and during that period when the bad boys of the Caribbean Sea, including Black Beard the pirate, would convene at Port Royal, Jamaica, to divide their spoils, settle scores, and party hardy. Over the years, Phoenix had become a Lodge of mostly businessmen. I came under the influence of several ancient extant Past Masters, some of them born as early as the last two decades of the nineteenth century, black colonials, I called them, who came to lodge in their well-cut ancient tuxedos. I particularly remember one delightful brother, burnt shining brown by the ages, race indistinguishable but unmistakably Jamaican, who wore his monocle to lodge with an English flair that would make any old duke sit up and take notice. He knew his scotch whiskey too, single malt preferred.

I enjoyed a slightly different kind of experience with my agricultural colleagues. On the one hand, I was closely involved with the traditional farmer on basic day-to-day concerns. On the other hand, I had a group of agricultural professionals of my age who met informally to discuss broader agricultural policy and trends. This group comprised of Aston Wood, PhD., animal nutrition; Ian Whittaker, PhD., agronomy; Lloyd Wiggan, PhD., genetics; Keith, Roach PhD., cattle husbandry; Ossie Thomas, PhD., chicken culture; Jack Muchette, MSc., small-stock specialist; Don Juan Bunting and Shirley Brown, leading dairy farmers.

As often as we were able to get together on a Saturday at around eleven in the morning, we would meet in Old Harbor at "The Hot Spot", Aunty Mum's kitchen on the beach, for a fish feed. Following Jamaican tradition, we met under the mango tree in the backyard. There was no menu because the regulars didn't need one. We started with fish tea (a broth made from trash fish) and a little white rum on the side with one or two of us opting for Red Stripe beer or a weaker Appleton red rum. As the conversation warmed up, Aunty Mum would lay out steamed snapper and bammy. This was followed by escoveitch kingfish and hard-dough bread. All this fare was being cooked on a coal pot in front of us as we squinted our eyes against the smoke and spices. The fish feed typically continued with grilled lobster when available, and ended with foil-wrapped roast turbot. We usually left Aunty Mum's yard about 1:30 p.m., filled up, fired up, and liquored up. It is remarkable how men in the West Indies learn early how to hold their liquor. It was out of this group of Wood, Weekes, Whittaker and Wiggan that our agricultural consulting group was formalized, with Aston Wood as principal. We called it AgroCon, after an idea from Joscelyn Grant, a resident master and agricultural engineer at the Jamaica School of Agriculture.

Our third and last child, Melanie came along in November 1972, and I started to take more notice of my growing family. It was still the custom in the Caribbean for men to leave much of the child-rearing in the exclusive hands of spouses, and worst, in the hands of servants for those who could afford it. I was as guilty as my colleagues in this respect, but I tried to make my time spent with the children as constructive as possible, exploring every corner of Jamaica with much of the time spent in Runaway Bay on the north coast. Our custom was to load up our Volkswagen Combi van with our kids and their friends on Saturday mornings and set out for the weekend on the north coast. On most occasions, Vilma would set out before me, and I would join the group on Saturday evenings.

Sunday on the north coast found us swimming and exploring the beaches and the surrounding St. Ann villages. We took every imaginable route from Spanish Town to Runaway Bay. Sometimes, we went up to Newcastle, through Hard War Gap, and down to Buff Bay, before heading west through St. Mary and down the road into Runaway Bay. My favorite route was to take the southern coastal plains through Old Harbor and May Pen up to Mandeville, then over to Christiana and Spalding, through Cave Valley and Borough Bridge, into Alexandria and Browns Town, before dropping down into Discovery Bay and Runaway Bay. On occasion, we would explore the parish of Portland. After overnighting at Frenchman's Cove, we would swim at Blue Hole, eat jerk pork at the original beach sites, head through Port Antonio, the lush Portland capital, raft on the Martha Brae river and then head west to Runaway Bay. When our villa was rented, we would stay at one of Tom Désulmé's.

Every summer, relatives and friends in the USA, Nassau and Barbados would send their children to visit with us on our farm. I enjoyed taking them on hikes and adventure tours through our rugged countryside, over and under barbed wire fences, through briars and pastures, mango walks and orange groves, taught many of them to swim, and sat most of them on their first horse. It was great therapy for me to be with the youngsters, and to become a part of their memory banks. My family and I used to enjoy changing into our swim gear behind the bushes at Ocho Rios in the early days, but not nearly as much as nude swims out by the lighthouse at Negril Beach before the onrush of tourists.

Our trips to Negril were truly exciting affairs. My favorite vehicle for those trips was our 1972 Fiat 125 stick shift. The route of choice was Spanish Town to Mandeville, over to Christiana, and then down the hills through Trelawny into Falmouth. The terraced hills were a delight, contrasted against the commercial coastal route along the north coast through Montego Bay into beautiful Lucea, and on to the innocent Negril, before the days of the orgies.

The trip home from Negril saw a different kind of beauty through Sav-la-Mar into Black River for peppered shrimp and bammy, then turning the Fiat loose through Spur Tree Hill as we made all five gears scream on our way up to Mandeville, then cruising quietly down into May Pen and Old Harbor and back to our Spanish Town retreat. Our children still talk about those days when we gather together now, but the grandchildren don't seem very interested in our reminiscences.

With our home and farm fully established by the end of 1975, I resigned as an operating officer at Thermo Plastics, remained as a director, and became a fully independent businessman. I felt fine, with no doubts or misgivings about my ability to succeed on my own. I was now a director of nine companies, a founding member of the Spanish Town Kiwanis Club, and a hands-on livestock farmer. There was no time for misgivings, but there was certainly time for self-assessment.

It was Carmen, the village teacher, who triggered my concerns about the purpose of my life. My little community of Belle View, six miles into the hills beyond Spanish Town, was a poor community of mostly chicken farms owned by better-off families. One of my neighbors up the road was a committed elderly lady named May Hart, the kind of person who had a heart of gold and an undying will to serve. Mrs. Hart and her husband, a retired Methodist minister, had built a small church across from their home to spread the Gospel to the villagers, and after her husband passed away, she started a kindergarten in a shed at the back of her modest home. When our last daughter Melanie was about four, we started taking her to join the other children up at Mrs. Hart's. After a while, I became intrigued by our child's excitement about going up to Mrs. Hart's school every morning, and soon I started walking her up there.

I was struck by the skill of Carmen, a young lady of about eighteen with no teacher training, being able to keep about a dozen four- and five-year-olds quiet and attentive. Carmen had made all her own teaching aids and drawings, models and decorative items, and had turned a galvanized steel-covered shed into an interesting learning center. She had collected *objets d'art* from sundry places and furnished their little den. Carmen was a natural teacher, and I would help her in any way I could.

I invited her to stop by our home and have a chat with me about her thoughts and aspirations, and I learned that she had not finished high school and had no viable plans for progressing towards her goal of being a primary school teacher. I decided that I would get her started by giving her private lessons. I loved to teach and had been doing so since I was twelve years old when I was called on to help my elementary school as a pupil-teacher. I had also taught high school for over a year before setting out to experience the world. Plus, I trained credit analysts at Citibank when I first got to Jamaica. Of course I was a teacher.

We obtained the necessary textbooks, and every day after lunch Carmen came to my study and we covered the necessary ground for her to be able to pass the high school graduate exams. This was a watershed time for me, and it was out of this experience that I decided to use the proceeds from my farm to build a trade training shop on my property to teach skills to the village teens. Unfortunately, I never got to carry out this mission, but I am happy to state that a few years ago my wife met Miss Carmen on a visit to Jamaica and saw that she was the Principal of a leading primary school on the island. Carmen sent me a photograph of herself and it occupies a proud spot on my desk. It's uncanny how lives can be connected without the participants being aware of the effects. The chairperson of the board at Carmen's school was my wife's best friend from childhood, and none of the three parties knew the degree to which they were all connected.

My willingness to help underprivileged children had been apparent a few years earlier. During my first year in Jamaica, I had become friendly with Bruce Murray, Principal of the Stony Hill Approved

School, a training center for wayward boys. Bruce's wife Polly was one of the women who had guided me through the local bank culture when I first got to the island. Bruce told me that one of his wards showed unusual promise, and enquired whether I would be willing to take him into my home and teach him the responsibilities of manhood. How could I say no? Not only was my ego well stroked by Bruce's enquiry, but I genuinely felt that I could help a youngster. I brought this fifteen-year-old into our home in Gordon Town, and mostly by osmosis showed him the responsibilities of manhood. I do not recall ever having sat down and given a talk or lecture to Garnet. He learned by observation and by being kept constructively busy. Garnet completed his primary school education with us and went on to be a security guard.

I developed a very positive relationship with workers from the parish of St. Elizabeth. They all seemed to be honest hard workers. Vilma trained the cousin of one of our farmworkers to be our cook, and Donna became very competent. I brought her son Hector in from St. Elizabeth to our home on the farm in Spanish Town, sent him to school, and when he was sufficiently competent, got him a job at Thermo Plastics in the city. The brightest of my charges, though, was a young man named Winston Salmon. He was a student at the José Marti Cuban school in Spanish Town. Fidel Castro had built several agricultural schools around Jamaica, and many youngsters found a place to prepare themselves for positive contributions to society in them. A part of my community contribution was to supervise the construction of some commercial chicken houses at the José Marti School near Spanish Town. Winston started to hang around me, and Mr. Joseph Earl, the Principal, noted the budding relationship and asked me if I could take him into my home and teach him to be a responsible citizen. Earl explained that Winston came from a very large ambitious family, that he was the last of very successful siblings, but his father had died, and he needed parental guidance.

We took Winston in. Our home was large, with a finished but unoccupied basement, and we lived on a commercial farm. There presented much to occupy young Salmon, the agricultural student. Winston fit in beautifully, and he learned about several areas of livestock husbandry with the opportunity to see in practice most of the principles that he was already studying at school. Winston helped me establish a rose garden for my wife and to propagate a species of Persian limes that I had brought to Jamaica from Nassau. The poor lad suffered painfully with sickle cell anemia, and it pained us greatly to observe what he had to undergo when he had an attack. His was a well-researched case, however, and the public hospital and the university did everything they could to help him. Winston got married in our home to a lovely village girl. Now a grandfather and a successful man in Boston, he drove down to our home in Atlanta a few years ago and brought his new wife to meet us.

"Griner", the last young man we had a chance to influence in our home in Jamaica, was perhaps the most interesting case. One day I came home and found this young urchin sitting in the kitchen talking to my wife and our cook. We had dogs, but I didn't fear for his safety because even though our ridgebacks and Dobermans weren't pets, I knew that all sorts came to our door and that the animals were locked away in the daytime.

I learned that Griner, whose real name turned out to be Desmond, had come into the yard and asked to be taken in by us because he had no family, had heard that we were good people, and he would help around the yard if we would take him in and give him a chance. We had lots of room in the basement and a spare room off the garage, access to more food than we could ever use, a big yard and garden, cars to clean, and spill-over work on the farm, plus plenty of constructive activity to attract a young man, so we took Desmond in. He made more progress than any of my other young charges did. It was several years later that we found out that Desmond was distantly related to my wife. He knew of the relationship all along, but never declared it.

When we left Jamaica in 1985 to emigrate to the United States, Desmond looked after our property until it was sold. Several years later, I was working in my garden in Stone Mountain, Georgia, when this boat of a Cadillac with Ontario license plates drove into our yard. Out popped Desmond. He had emigrated to Canada and was doing well for himself. He always knew where we were and decided to surprise us with a visit on his way from Toronto to Tampa. Desmond spent the night with us, and he and our children had a marvelous time recounting their early experiences on the farm in Spanish Town.

It became clearer to Vilma and me that we could do truly valuable work in our community by developing training programs for young people, so Vilma would teach job and homemaking skills to young women. I started to construct a chill room on the farm. We managed to teach meat cutting skills to only two young men before circumstances changed and moved so fast that we never got back to completing the program. I have remained disappointed, for we could have done so much more for the underprivileged in our rural community.

By 1980, Vilma and I had built up a highly productive livestock farming enterprise on two farms in the parishes of St. Catherine and Clarendon. Our feed bill was high, but our sales were good, and we had an excellent line of credit with our bank, plus everything in place for our future sustenance and the protection and education of our children – or so we thought. We were producing and selling nearly five thousand eggs a day, up to sixty hogs a week, fifty fattened steers a year, and a throughput of 96,000 broiler chickens in the same period. We had a staff of twelve people and maintained three children in private schools. Life was so good that we never even kept track of the subscription from our sheep and goat herd. Vilma and I were involved in building our community, she with the friends of the Spanish Town Hospital, and I with the town's Kiwanis Club, of which I was a founding member.

Then, just like that, the government changed, taking many of my official connections and economic protections with it.

18. THINGS FALL APART, THEN TOGETHER

The 1980 Elections in Jamaica were brutally contested. The People's National Party government of Prime Minister Michael Manley was pitted against the Jamaica Labor Party under the leadership of Edward Seaga, who was generally supported by the United States. Michael Manley was a strong supporter of Fidel Castro, Muammar Gaddafi, Venezuelan socialist aspirations, and African independence movements in general. Manley felt that his was a sovereign nation like the USA and that he had every right to associate with whomever his country chose and to speak out on their behalf. His excellent skills of oratory were stoked by leaders on a larger playing field than his, and the United States was bent on making Jamaica pay for the impudence of their prime minister.

The US State Department posted travel advisories about visiting Jamaica and threw its support behind the Jamaica Labor Party. Earnings of hard currency from the tourist industry started to dwindle, with concurrent pressure on those who depended on tourist dollars. My family had to dispose of our tourism investment including the villa because it was eating up our earnings in the livestock industry. The JLP won the elections in a landslide.

Immediately afterward, the US Government offered Jamaica a thirty million-dollar, thirty-year loan at a concessionary interest rate to buy stipulated foods. In literally a matter of days, the market became flooded with cheap meat products such as pigtails, cheap pork cuts, salt beef, chicken necks and backs, chicken feet, and every animal fifth quarter imaginable. All of us, as farmers who had built our enterprises on import replacement strategies, were under immediate pressure. To make matters worse, the new government lowered import restrictions in general, and companies like Thermo Plastics which had taken on heavy debt obligations to support import substitution found themselves in increasing difficulty to meet those obligations.

The Jamaican public began a retreat from trying to satisfy its food consumption to what we produced locally and surrendered to its penchant for figurative corn flakes, scotch whiskey and Bally shoes. Much of the work that all of my predecessors had done before and since Independence, and with which I allied myself since 1970, was now greatly set back. I could not sell my farm production fast enough, and I started feeding most of my egg production to my hogs, while the merchants resumed their ascendancy. Foreign exchange controls were gradually relaxed, the black market in US dollars gradually became rampant, and the Jamaican dollar began a steady downward spiral to find its market level while the country took on increased foreign debt to be serviced out of decreased foreign exchange flows.

It did not take my bank very long to cancel my overdraft privilege. It became impossible to feed my laying hens and my hogs with the same brand, quality and quantity of feed as I had been using, and in a few days our egg production dropped from over eighty percent to less than fifty. This killed our egg business. And so, we asked ourselves, what does one do with 6,000 unproductive laying hens? A laying hen is a different bird from a broiler, which is a large bird usually over four pounds at eight weeks, specially bred and fed to be eaten by humans. The Leghorn laying bird, on the other hand, may weigh no more than sixteen to twenty-four ounces and is bred to be a laying machine. She will start to lay at eighteen weeks of age, and under proper management can give profitable performance for up to eighteen months. Farmers would replace entire flocks when their cycle ended, but this was a planned exercise. Starter pullets had to be planned for months in advance, production cycles had to be set up to maintain the market for eggs, and arrangements had to be made in advance with sausage makers and pet food manufacturers who bought the spent birds. One also had to have the birds processed. No farmer can maintain an unproductive laying flock.

The challenges on our hog farms were equally pressing. At that time, we had 200 breeding sows and ten boars over two farms, and our fattening pens were full of animals from one day old to market age of about 150 days. With hardly any cash flow, I had to quit buying commercial feed. I started sending my truck to the banana shipment ports the day after the banana boats sailed for England and bought truckloads of rejected fruit to feed my hogs. Naturally, weight gain decreased immediately, and in most cases ceased. Milk supply from nursing sows fell sharply and diarrhea broke out in the farrowing pens.

I stopped breeding my sows and slaughtered my boars. In conjunction with the Government Experimental Station at Bodles I had imported Landrace and Duroc boars from Arkansas in the USA, and now ran one of the more advanced sire programs on the Island. The local bacon and ham producers had sought my output when their finished products were in demand. Now I was slaughtering my market prime animals and putting the carcasses into cold storage at a penny a pound per day. I began to build up cold storage charges of $45 per month per carcass. If this continued, my friend and lodge brother who owned the cold storage facility would soon end up owning my farms. At forty-five years of age, I was walking and talking to myself, having built a multi-million-dollar operation but could not buy a pack of cigarettes. I was a director and in a few cases chairman of large public businesses, but now I faced ruin in my own business.

I clearly recall watching the pomp and splendor displayed at the wedding of Prince Charles and Princess Diana as I lay despondent in bed in 1981, and compared it to the joy expressed by my countryfolk at the announcement of Prince Charles' birth in 1948. The latter occasion had also been a low point in my life, for I was fully ready for entrance into high school, and my father would not pay the tuition costs in spite of pleading form me and my mother. Why would they be high points for him and low points for me? I would change that. I would not give life an easy victory over me.

My wife and I started a meat-cutting operation and sold our own production of pork cuts, lamb and chickens to Kingston supermarkets, restaurants, and anyone who would buy. We also arranged to sell the surplus production of other pig farmers who had also been forced to hold their production in cold storage.

As we rebuilt our operations, theft of our livestock became more rampant. Praedial larceny had always been a problem in Jamaica, and the theft of my feed and small stock plagued us constantly, but from 1981 onward, the problem escalated to the point where the culprits started slaughtering my sheep and goats on the property itself. I dared not go down on the farm at night to investigate any noise or alarm because I could not match the manpower (or gun power) of the bandits. Those guys had heavy weapons and all I had was a Remington five-shot semi-automatic and a .38 Police Special revolver, with no backup to expect. I didn't even think of calling the police. On the one hand, we had no phone, and secondly, one had to defend his property because the state seemed to have tacitly given up its responsibility of protecting people and their property. Things got quite frightening when a burglar broke in on our neighbor Mrs. Hart (she of the community spirit and caring nature), beat her up and knocked out one of her eyes. Police took days to respond to her complaint. Around this time also, a gunman robbed and murdered Mr. Alexander, our village's small shopkeeper. As far as we could tell, the police did nothing about it.

For several years, Vilma had been pleading with me to wind down our interest in Jamaica and emigrate to the USA where our children would have wider opportunities and we could live in less fear. I had always resisted, for selfishly, I did not want to take on the challenge of being a black man in America. Recent incidents, including one where a young urchin ripped my wife's gold chain from her neck at a traffic light in Kingston, really focused my attention. We asked Vilma's sister Maxine (Joy), a nurse in New Jersey, to sponsor us as immigrants to the United States. Fortunately, our eldest child Leslyn was born in the USA, and we got green cards quite quickly. Even then, I still was not ready or willing to leave. I loved Jamaica, and I had not fully given up on her.

I was suddenly confronted with three new and exciting challenges. First, Thermo Plastics, where I was a director, was placed into receivership; second, Jamaica Citrus Growers Ltd. sent a headhunter to recruit me as its managing director, and third, I became a founding member of a Scottish Free Mason's Lodge, St. Jago de la Vega, in Spanish Town. I'll take them in order.

Tom Désulmé should not have been surprised when the bankers forced Thermo Plastics into receivership. By way of information, receivership under the British system is similar to Chapter 11 bankruptcy in the USA. It's a legal process where a company's creditors obtain authority to participate fully in the management and control of a debtor's business until the debtor can demonstrate to the courts that it can service its debt obligations in the agreed manner. Receivership is not necessarily a bad thing. It can be a way to keep one's creditors at bay while an overstretched company is given time to efficiently organize its turn-around programs, and also to keep strong-headed owners under restraint.

Thermo Plastics had not been servicing its loans as agreed; inventory levels were far too high, sales were too low, receivables collections were slowing and the company had too many unproductive machines. Furthermore, Tom mostly acted alone, a fact aided and abetted by his effective ninety-five percent ownership of the company. He felt that as a third world manufacturer, he was constrained by different factors than one would face in a developed country, and so he had to keep his warehouse full of finished products, maintain more machines on hand than were immediately needed, have extra amounts of raw materials in the bins, and prop up his clients by granting them very liberal payment terms. To be fair to Tom, he understood better than any of us the results emanating from uncertainty in the timing and supply of foreign exchange.

Tom also had to nurture his non-governmental buyers of pipe and fittings, for they comprised the backbone of his market. Thermo Plastics was geared to produce PVC pipe and fittings to replace the asbestos pipe that still carried most of the potable water to homes and businesses on the island. A local well-loved homeboy owned the asbestos pipe factory and controlled the sale of water pipe to government in spite of the well-established fact that asbestos products were bad for people's health. Thermo Plastics simply could not fully make the case for acquiring such large portions of the Water Commission's pipe business.

Tom came to me, the youngest man on the Thermo Plastics board, and asked me to design the strategy for cooperation with the receivers, to turn the company around, bring it out of receivership, and keep it out of the hands of corporate hustlers. There was one man in particular whom the receivers had appointed as one of their directors and whom we knew had always harbored personal designs on ownership of the company. My underlying tactical plan was to observe his intent and prepare countermoves.

Tom accepted my suggestion that we choose as our nominees to the new board, people of unimpeachable character as well as business and professional acumen, names that could color any argument in our favor. I suggested the Honorable Robert Lightbourne, OJ, former head of the Jamaica Industrial Development Corporation, former member of the defunct West Indies Federal Parliament, a successful manufacturer of supplies for the British forces in England during World War II, and former Minister of Trade and Industry in the previous Jamaica Labor Party government; Mr. David Muirhead, QC, one of the most distinguished barristers practicing at that time, later Jamaica's ambassador to the Court of St. James in England; Mr. George Fattah, a streetwise Duke Street solicitor and a minority shareholder in the company, and Mr. Henry Fullerton, CA, an experienced auditor. These men, Tom and I, were all accepted by the receivers as board members, along with the receivers' appointees. The receivers placed Price Waterhouse, I believe, in charge of operations, represented by one of their partners, a chartered accountant from India.

To be in a private meeting with men like Tom Désulmé and Bob Lightbourne was like being in a graduate seminar at a top-notch university. Tom was always the chairman but it was I who orchestrated the agenda. Here were two men of uncommon experience. Tom had been a successful businessman in his native Haiti, who became a political kingmaker and four-time elected senator in Haiti, later building one of the most exciting industries in a country where the language was foreign to him. Bob, of princely colonial birth, became an industrialist in the mother country, England, during World War II, and a leader in the failed attempt to keep together the Federation of the West Indies as a member of the Federal Parliament in Trinidad. He was the architect of Jamaica's industrial development, a former minister of trade and industry, composer of the music for the Jamaica national anthem, and a man once seriously considered for the office of prime minister. I was forty-four at the time; both men were sixty-seven. I listened and observed, as Paul must have done at the feet of Gamaliel.

I am moved to share a story that Tom Désulmé told me about Bob Lightbourne, which was never refuted by Bob. The moral of the story is directional for young leaders – at least I took it that way. When Sir Donald Sangster, then prime minister of Jamaica, died in office, Lady Bustamante, the wife of former prime minister, Sir Alexander Bustamante, summoned Lightbourne to their residence to allow him to form a government. Constitutionally, this was and is the role of the Governor-General, the monarch's representative under the Westminster model of government. No one would have been bold enough to challenge Lady Bustamante if they had gotten away with such a maneuver. I presume that a way would have been found to get the Governor-General on board, but instead of heading to "Lady B" post haste, Bob Lightbourne wasted time calling his cabinet colleagues to determine who would be willing to serve under his leadership. During this interval, Governor-General Sir Clifford Campbell summoned Hugh Shearer, and the rest is history.

Within about two years, Thermo Plastics Ltd. reached a level of comfortable viability with its creditors, and the company was allowed out of receivership. My efforts to persuade Tom to take the company public were never given recognition. Even though I remained a director up to the time I left Jamaica in 1985, my major concentration centered on the turning-around of Jamaica Citrus Growers Ltd., an old but important company steeped in the fabric of Jamaican culture and agricultural development. I understand that after Tom's death, family disputes and intransigence caused them to lose Thermo Plastics and unknown other assets. I was disappointed that no one in the family ever sought my help, especially since I had been a mentor to the strong-headed male heirs at different times, and they knew how close I had been to their father.

After much persuasion from recruiter Dr. Franklin Johnston, my friend and colleague, I agreed to accept a three-year contract as managing director of Jamaica Citrus Growers in Bog Walk, St. Catherine. The company was the wholly-owned subsidiary of Jamaica Citrus Growers Association, a cooperative, established before World War II by local citrus farmers. Inept management over the years had steered the company into a position of near-bankruptcy, to the point where the company would be forced to cease operations if it did not immediately find a leader acceptable to all stakeholders. My advisors in corporate Jamaica suggested that I not accept the offer from Jamaica Citrus Growers to join the company. One older gentleman, now of blessed memory, reminded me that the company was started to promote the interests of the directors of the parent company, and I was bound to run into difficulty with them, as had all previous general managers or managing directors. The contract provisions were very generous, and the challenge was inviting, for I was beginning to gain something of a reputation as a turn-around director.

In June 1982, I joined Jamaica Citrus Growers as managing director. I had previously seen the financial statements, and I knew that the company was in bad shape, but I hadn't fully studied the plant. When I got there, there was no managerial leadership at any level, so I called on the assistant plant engineer, an older veteran, Mr. Genus, to walk the plant and talk with me. I found that the roadway throughout the plant was in total disrepair; the bins that stored the citrus on delivery were mostly broken and unsafe; one of the two boilers that generated steam to power the plant was out of order and had been inoperative for a couple of years; the compressor inside the factory that acted as the first line chiller of its citrus concentrate was out of order, and the three compressors cooling the three main cold rooms were all kaput.

Orange and grapefruit concentrate production was the major business and the company had to place its production in public cold stores, building up huge external cold storage charges. The floors in the maintenance shop were cracked or broken; there was only one forklift, a relic of World War II vintage, one tractor-head, an old English Leyland with over one million miles on the odometer, and an engine that had been rebuilt three times over. There were no up-to-date vans to deliver our juices and drinks around the island, office facilities needed complete repairs, and there was no managerial staff in either factory or offices. Besides, there was this haunting fear among the directors that they were close to losing the factory to the Sharpe family, owners of a competing citrus processing plant in Clarendon.

Within a few days, I had drawn up a reconstruction plan, got a meeting with the minister of agriculture, arranged for a comfort letter to the bank and received an increase in accommodation totaling several million dollars. I believe that the Jamaican dollar was J$ 1.00 to US$ 0.75 at that time.

When the citrus farmers heard what we were doing at their factory, they started to send us more fruit, and within two months we had rebuilt the storage bins, restored our pavements, installed a new compressor on the factory floor, installed new compressors and new doors on the cold rooms, repaired our maintenance shop, and increased the price paid to farmers for citrus. Recommissioning the boilers took several weeks, but we got it done under the supervision of Genus, that remarkable home-grown engineer. I put a man in the field to instruct farmers in tree culture and restoration, and by the end of my second year, we were selling orange and grapefruit concentrate in Barbados, Trinidad, London, and in Orlando, Florida. We were able to recapture our fresh-fruit export markets to those places as well, and I became known as "Speedy Gonzales". Fears of a takeover by the Sharpe family of Clarendon and Manchester became much less intense.

In the winter of 1982-1983, I met a likable elderly white man at a dairy show in Chicago. I believe I was the only noticeable black man there, and he eventually engaged me in conversation. When he learned that one of my company's products was a heavily orange juice-based drink, he offered to introduce me to the real opportunity for making money in the refreshment drink business. "In the heat and on the move, folks want a drink that is cold, flavorful, sweet, and affordable. You can meet all of those requirements by using only a fraction of the orange juice that you're using now," he told me.

Before I left Chicago that week in 1982, I contacted manufacturers of an orange drink mixture, arranged for the supply of drink containers, color scheme and the name of product. Within weeks, we had a new drink on the market. It had a strong fruity aroma with high orange flavor. As a cold, sweet drink it was very reasonable in price, very economically produced, and beat the heck out of our more nutritious orange juice product. Every dollar earned made the company more and more viable and increased the speed out of near-bankruptcy – and towards collision with the trades union.

I had taken part in a fight with Mr. Morrison, the union leader, on a previous occasion. That was during my days as executive vice president of Thermo Plastics. I had only been an advisor to the president of the company at that time, but this time it was solely my fight. I was not happy that the union went on strike. I had taken great pains to build a relationship with Mr. Foga, the shop steward, and had kept the lines of communication open to Morrison. They hit us with their best shot, a strike in the middle of the orange season. Farmers had expanded their production, harvesting was fully underway, we had contracts to fill in the Caribbean and London, and there was a citrus tree disease in Florida, luckily bringing us sales in McAllen, Texas and Orlando, Florida. At the end of the first week of the strike, the non-union workers were prevented from entering the plant by those on the picket lines, and fights broke out. This allowed us to shut the plant down and significantly weaken the union's case for claiming a lockout. We would now see who could stand the pain longest.

The threat of personal violence against me became so strong that I had to travel with a bodyguard at all times and to maintain guards at our home in Spanish Town. Additionally, I wore an ankle-holstered .38 Police Special and kept my Remington 500 semi-automatic rifle on the floor of the car in front of me. Mr. Knight, my bodyguard, became very close and dear to my family, to the point where he was the only person who was welcome into my inner sanctum at home no matter my state of dress or toilette. He was a young soldier when I hired him; my young children did not appreciate Knight's strictness, but I welcomed it as he became my companion and trusted guard. I was saddened to learn a few years after we left Jamaica that he became very depressed and committed suicide.

I do not fully remember how the strike ended. Not with a bang, but with a whimper, I'm sure. Normalcy resumed after the support lines of all parties got stretched and detached and trusted parties of interest came to our rescue and untangled us. Work resumed as if nothing had happened. I came out of it wiser and more resolute.

★★★

One night I had the strangest and most realistic dream. I distinctly heard people on my street calling to me, pressing me to come out and join them because they had caught the vagabond who was terrorizing the village, and who had robbed my neighbor Mrs. Hart, the good widow, and knocked out one of her eyes. I dreamt that I went out to them and was swept up the street to a clearing where I was witness to an execution. There he was, this poor fellow being beaten by the village toughs. Helplessly, I watched as they bludgeoned him to death.

I woke up in a cold sweat. Only weeks before had a lone gunman robbed and murdered Mr. Alexander, the small shopkeeper on the corner of the village main, and the thieves were stealing and slaughtering my goats with increasing boldness. Taking my dream as a sign of things to come I concluded that I truly had to take my family out of our beloved Jamaica. Vilma would handle all the paperwork and preparations while I looked after the clean-up of our debts and business affairs. I secretly kept hoping that I would not have to leave, that there would be some enlightened intervention that would make it possible for me to place my family in the safety of the USA, while I remained in Jamaica and enjoyed my established lifestyle, like so many of my colleagues were doing.

I had had the honor of traveling to Europe four times as a chairman, director, or managing director of corporate entities. On a trip to London to arrange the sale of fresh fruit – mostly oranges and ortaniques through our representatives in Piccadilly – I took a proverbial bath. I had been given the impression that our agent in London was a commission agent and prices quoted were prices paid by the wholesaler. It turned out that our agent was usurping our ownership, and the net price that we were getting had nothing to do with what the wholesalers were paying. I quickly learned the value of research and intelligence. Fortunately, our lawyers in Kingston had included a clause in the sales contract making all arrangements ratifiable by our board of directors. The British taught me that smart negotiators deal with you at your level of knowledge, so be well informed before entering negotiations.

On other trips to Europe, I was a member of a team that was well briefed. The first team represented the Port Authority of Jamaica, of which I was a director, and we were successful in gaining significant help from the government of Norway. Prime Minister Manley of Jamaica and Odvar Nordli, prime minister of Norway had an excellent relationship, and the Norwegians agreed to help us with the training of harbor pilots, with new pilot vessels to speed up entry and exit from Jamaican harbors and to build a school for the education of harbor pilots. This trip also took us to Stavanger to observe fish-canning operations, and also to the Jutland Peninsula in Denmark to look at fish meal plants. At the time the Port Authority of Jamaica was about to start a fish processing operation at Newport East, so we needed to become aware of the environmental implications. I remember our nostrils were invaded by a foul stench half an hour before we reached the town of Skagen in northern Denmark, where the entire city was built around fish meal plants. Fish meal is a very important ingredient in creating the proper balance in livestock feeds. There was no way that we could consider introducing that odor to Kingston or to any part of Jamaica for that matter. We did not stay long in Skagen. There was much more pleasant activity in Tivoli Gardens, and in observing the live female offerings at a city bar.

Visiting Norway with a team representing the Caribbean Cement Company, of which I was the chairman of the board, we took the chance to enjoy the beautiful fjords and parks around Oslo, to eat reindeer burgers, cloudberries and compare Norwegian lagers with our own Red Stripe beer. Norway was a large manufacturer of cement and was very helpful to us in the development and implementation of our plans to change the expensive crude oil base of our energy source to natural gas. We knew what was needed, but we had to go where the funding was to be advised. We got the loans and advances we sought, and a couple of Norwegian engineers got the pleasure of working in a tropical paradise for a year.

Living outside the developed world can truly blunt one's mind to developments in advanced societies. I also observed in Norway that within seconds after we made a change in the text of our agreement, a secretary would return with a new page incorporating the changes. It took a little while for me to recognize that I was witnessing the modern computer age unfolding. Additionally, while visiting a machine shop at a local factory, I saw lathes running with no operator, shaping tools to make molds and dyes that would make marketable products, only later to meet the technician sitting in front of a computer monitor in his office observing the performance of preset computer-operated machine tools on the shop floor. In London, Oslo and Lausanne I noticed new car models that had not yet reached my third world.

There was also the enjoyment of walking around Lake Geneva with Joy, an old family friend, from Switzerland into France and lunching on a loaf of bread, sharp cheddar cheese, and red wine at a replica of a country shop one might find in any Caribbean island. I also enjoyed the conviviality of tasting the new wines with farmers at a Caveau in Geneva and being mistaken for the son of Patrice Lumumba. That young man had been visiting Switzerland at the same time, and no protestations on my part could dissuade the locals from their belief that I was a luminary in their midst. My Jamaican hosts advised me to let the locals enjoy themselves and tell lies to their grandchildren.

Two nights later, after a lovely dinner in London, I responded to a knock on my hotel room door, only to be asked by a young Englishwoman of the night if I wanted a bit of fun. She must have had to pay several guineas to the front desk operator to be allowed into that quality establishment. I was also panhandled by a slightly worn black princess outside a bar in London, who on noticing my shock, bluntly asked me if I had never met a fallen sister. Indeed, I had not, nor had I yet enjoyed the highlight of my travels to Europe, which was to fly on the Concorde from London to New York, all seats first class, in three hours flat – only to spend three hours clearing immigration and customs at Kennedy Airport and getting to my hotel in Manhattan.

I think that I first encountered the motto "Be Prepared" when I was a Boy Scout back in the mid-1940s. I was probably a freemason, English constitution for about seven years and had risen to the position of Warden when I helped to found a Scottish Freemasons lodge in my city of Spanish Town. I was coasting along in the lower hierarchy as Outer Guard of the new Lodge in the third year when I was elevated by the leaders to be the new Master of the lodge, and thus proceeded to the chair ritualistically having been at one time occupied by none other than King Solomon. My English brothers were not pleased that I chose to go first to the chair in a Scottish Lodge rather than wait several more years to be elevated in my English Constitution lodge. I make the point because such things take on great importance in highly structured societies where the subtleties of the pecking order are more noticeable in the breach than in the observance.

If you have ever closely observed the coronation of a bishop in churches that adhere to the Catholic tradition, you would recognize the ritual employed in installing a Master of a masonic lodge. Masons' performance is grander and filled with more lofty speeches and charges, but the ceremonies come from the same ancient sources and are both meant to impress the followers and create a sense of mystery and transported mysticism. There seems to be a spot in the human psyche where all of us find it thrilling to be enshrouded for a limited period in an otherwise illogical transportation. I must confess that I love ritual, and never feel that I have worshipped if I attend church in a plain and unadorned setting. I crave the roaring, sonorous organ, the stained-glass windows, the flowers and colors of the seasons, the chants – and incense of course – with disciplined Thurifers if possible. Our son who never goes to church, informed me after attending a funeral ceremony at a Coptic church, that he felt transported by the ritual, the dirges, and the richly embroidered robes and chasubles of the clergy, leaving me to wonder how the unlettered masses of earlier times managed to cope with such strong opiates.

While the formal and limited exclusivity of my installation as master in the upper floor was thrilling and profound and bore a religious tinge, the banquet downstairs afterward was tudoresque in its exorbitance. I comforted myself by pretending that it made up for the small and unpretentious wedding to which Vilma and I treated ourselves almost twenty years before. There were so many cakes that there had to be a special table for them. There was so much food that there was excess for institutions in the town. All the Jamaican specialties were served, including ackee and saltfish, roast suckling pig and curried goat from my farm, plus rice and peas, bammy, escoveitch fish and mannish water, of course. The brethren came from every town, village and hamlet in Jamaica, from Port Antonio to Lucea, and from St. Ann's Bay to Mandeville. That evening, we drank a lot of scotch, which for some inexplicable reason, was the libation of choice among Jamaican masons, with single malt preferred for the more discerning. It's remarkable how none of us ever got locked up for driving under the influence or faced property damage suits. But then, many of us had designated drivers or chauffeurs for that very possibility.

Before the end of my three-year contract with Jamaica Citrus, the company was on a profitable footing, and I started preparing a prospectus to take it public. This was the second time in my career that I engaged in such an exercise. Twenty years earlier, I developed the prospectus which introduced the short-term paper of British Columbia Central Credit Union to the short-term money market in Vancouver, Canada. The current exercise was more comprehensive, even though the stage was smaller, for I was charged with preparing a document which would not only satisfy the Jamaica Stock Exchange that the company met their criteria for listing and the government regulatory authority that the public interest was not being betrayed, but above all the prospectus had to be a strong enough marketing tool to persuade the public to buy the company's stock.

After completing my work on the prospectus, I turned the booklet over to the company's auditors for them to add the audited statements before the project was passed on to the lawyers for final vetting. That was my final project with the company, as I left Jamaica two months later to join my family in America. A few years later, I learned that the Jamaica Citrus Growers had taken over their feared nemesis, the Sharpe family-owned Citrus Company of Jamaica in Clarendon.

When the separation with my family finally did come, I was not as strong as those colleagues who placed their families in the USA and continued to live in Jamaica. I was immensely pained to leave Jamaica, but I could not face life without the daily sustenance of my wife and children.

19. AFTER FIVE ACTS, A SIXTH

Our home in Atlanta is only two and a half hours drive from Ashville, North Carolina, the hometown of the writer Thomas Wolfe. My wife Vilma and I have been to this mountain resort a few times. Apart from being a great place to recharge one's batteries away from the hustle and bustle of Atlanta, Ashville boasts the Vanderbilt house, the largest private home in the United States, which at its construction was the most advanced in the country. The landscape architecture is spectacular, and the wines produced from their vineyards are as good as any produced anywhere.

A few years ago, there was a great Thomas Wolfe revival and I joined book lovers in exploring his writings and life. On reading Wolfe's You Can't Go Home Again, it struck me that I too could never recapture the feeling of "home", not for the same reasons as Thomas Wolfe perhaps, but with the same conclusion. Encouraged by my daughter Leslyn who shares an alma mater with Wolfe (Washington and Lee University in Virginia) I agreed to take a closer look at Ashville on our next visit there.

All life is driven by a dynamic that seemingly cannot be stopped. This is so for places as well as for individuals. The Ashville of Thomas Wolfe's youth was gone. His boyhood home was still there, of course, but it had gone through several iterations and was now restored as a tourism marketing tool inspired by the town's famous son. The town was no longer a place where rich folks came to be cured of tuberculosis and other health problems. Now, they wandered through the trinket and gift shops. All the familiar landmarks of Wolfe's youth were gone. Wolfe too had found himself changed. He had been caught up in the dynamism of life and was no longer an organic part of the community.

My Cane Garden changed too. The ancestral home no longer stands. Lack of occupancy and the ravages of time and weather have led to its destruction, and the old lands have not been tilled or cultivated for over two generations, lost to the bush and the monkeys. The elementary school has been torn down and built in a different district; the church and vicarage have been torn down, the tradesmen have died out, and the soil has shifted due to natural landslides and erosion. Even the village boundaries have been gerrymandered into two different parishes, to the point where Cane Garden isn't really in St. Andrew anymore, anyway. I literally can't go home again, either.

I too have changed – constructively I think, for I seem to have met a new challenge with succeeding regularity every five years, with the result that I can hardly recognize my old home village. And no one there would recognize me.

***

My wife and I bought our Stone Mountain, Georgia home during the spring of 1985, assuming the previous owner's VA mortgage at a time when the country had not yet gotten over the high-interest market that had gripped it in the 1970s. The house was six years old and had seen only one owner to date. A four-bedroom traditional starter home, it sits on a half-acre heavily wooded lot, four miles from Stone Mountain Park. We thought that we would live there for six years at most so that all three of our children could finish high school at the same excellent local Redan High.

After thirty-four years and three grandchildren who are now on their last stages of college, entering college or graduate school, we are still in the house, mostly by ourselves, raking mounds of leaves every fall, mowing grass, renewing gardens and cutting down weak trees. Our home has been our refuge and sustenance in times of storm and need. We have refinanced it, changed mortgage companies, lowered interest rates, taken equity loans to help start new businesses, run home-operated businesses out of it, painted it three times, installed a new roof twice, replaced water heaters four times, changed the floors, bathrooms, drapes and sofas, storm doors, garage doors, installed new air conditioning compressors twice, put in one new furnace, replaced kitchen cupboards, countertops, stove, dishwasher, microwaves twice and planted two new mailboxes. Somehow, our home manages to exude old back-home village ease.

Every visitor makes the same comment, "Oh, Mrs. Weekes, your home is so 'lived in'." Friends and visitors become relaxed very easily and usually are in no hurry to leave. Some of the children too have come back for periods when fortune has not favored them. Our subdivision is quite large, about four thousand people in single-family, mostly contemporary homes. I know every nook and cranny, every hill and hollow and all the old residents, for I have been walking through my village three times a week for more than thirty years.

In 2010, I entered the Department of Graduate Studies at Clayton State University to prepare for the master's in health administration degree. I was in my seventy-fifth year and healthcare was the big topic at that time. The Affordable Care Act, "Obamacare" for short, was passed in 2010 and everyone seemed to have an opinion about it, but very few seemed to appreciate the national implications of healthcare policies, including me. I set out to be better informed on the topic. I did not learn until the day I went to pay my fees that as a senior aged more than sixty-two, my studies would be tuition-free. I decided that I would show my appreciation by fully applying myself, and for the entire two-year span of the course, I maintained straight A's except for one B+, which caused my graduating average to slip from a perfect 4.0 to a 3.87.

The daily commute from Stone Mountain down to Morrow, Georgia was a very pleasant half-hour. Pretty much all of my fellow students were between twenty-five and thirty years of age, and the head of the department was born around the time I had first entered graduate school back in British Columbia so many years before. The professors would sometimes ask me to confirm the dates of references they drew. Very often, I was old enough to have been actively engaged when the events occurred. I never disappointed any of them.

The nature of healthcare, its cost, complexities, and implications for the nation continue to be points of national discussion and concern, and I will not dare to join that debate here. But consider for a moment that the topic consumes the largest portion of the national budget, larger than defense, that the consumer, for the most part, is not the demander of the service, does not know what he wants or needs, and is not the person whose choices can affect the cost of the service. The supplier of the service determines what the demand will be, and may in many cases set the cost, except for constraints that occur when supplier and payer are the same, or when the payer is powerful enough to argue with the supplier over the setting of costs.

To leave the public naked before such counter-intuitive forces in a free society is one of the consuming considerations of government, no matter its philosophical complexion. I am a much better-informed citizen for having taken the MHA Degree, and I am a more satisfyingly productive one for having learned how to use the computer, as I continue to please my technical teacher, my eldest daughter Leslyn, with my improving skills at the instrument.

★★★

Now past eighty, I still rise every morning by six o'clock, bring my room to military inspection standards, do my calisthenics and make breakfast for myself, as well as for anyone sufficiently motivated to join me. After showering and dressing, I repair to my study to write and read until any outside appointments intervene. I fit in walking or treadmill work on days allotted for such activity.

For further intellectual stimulation, I have introduced my dear wife Vilma to the challenge of learning to trade foreign exchange, futures and options, and we are having fun on simulation platforms so far. Vilma is fine, but I have to unlearn my bent toward fundamental analysis and follow the technical program. Every so often a light comes on and shows me that the technical programs have pre-thought my analysis and I would have spared myself a lot of time had I been smart enough to adhere to the program.

I wish that our grandchildren could free up a little more time in their calendars and include us more often, but I guess we have enough on our plates, what with church, choir and all. The grandson is a high school mathematics teacher, and our second grandchild is finishing the twelfth grade in high school and doing college courses at the same time; our youngest grandchild is a freshman electrical engineering student at Penn State University. The latter two are young women.

I am now ready for new endeavors, and I believe that I have immediate access to a vehicle ideally built for the enterprise on which I intend to set out.

As a Rotarian, the motto of 'Service Above Self' impels me towards my objective for future contributions to society. Rotary encourages its member clubs and individual members to work, together or singly, in identifying and developing needy services around the world. For approved projects, Rotary Foundation and/or Rotary International will help the participating clubs fund the project. The whole world has needy areas, and participating clubs can be drawn from all over. I do not fully know the process, but many members of my home club do. There is the need for assistance with nation-building, whether it is in education, health, sanitation, water resource development, women's and children's health, micro-financing, crop development, food storage, or things not yet identified by me, but which will reveal themselves after study. Others will guide me through the process.

I honestly have not done much in Rotary. I am ready, as it were, to come out of the pews and go to work. I owe the world my input and will hear the call. My Stone Mountain Rotary Club seems to have sensed my uneasiness, for after seeming not to notice me hiding in the shadows for the last ten years, the leadership has made me secretary now, and president-nominee for 2021 to 2022. The Lord will have mercy on the geriatric willing.

There are truly no regrets about the course that my life has taken. I believe that it is evident that I have been carried along by circumstance, rather than creating them. I happen to have been ready and prepared to make use of challenges and opportunities as they came. Two very close West African friends often remind me that their countries have suffered immensely because too many well-prepared and decent nationals refused to enter politics, thereby leaving the space in the arena to be occupied by scoundrels.

So sometimes I feel that I should have defied my wife and mother and entered elective politics. I believe I would have had a better shot at political success back in Canada during my British Columbia years. But then, I would have denied my family our superlative sojourn in Jamaica, where I experienced the joy of knowing the liberation of manhood, the unbridled freedom of participation without thinking of race, place or expectation of myself or others, and the greatest challenge of all, making myself and my family viable in the USA. What was it that the Melodians sang?

By the rivers of Babylon
There we sat down
And there we wept
When we remembered Zion
When the wicked carried us away in captivity
Required from us a song
Now how shall we sing the Lord's song
In a strange land?

For the time being, I shall continue dancing, for I shall as long as I hear the drums. I shall continue walking, as long as I can awaken and move. I'll continue singing in church, in my quarters at home, and wherever I am asked. I shall sing even when I cannot hear external noises, for I shall hear the melodies and rhythms in my head.

www.ingramcontent.com/pod-product-compliance
Lightning Source LLC
Chambersburg PA
CBHW021942290426
44108CB00012B/934